THOMAS GRAY

A Biography

BY THE SAME AUTHOR

HORACE WALPOLE
NORFOLK PORTRAITS
A NORFOLK GALLERY
COUNTRY NEIGHBOURHOOD

Published by Faber and Faber

THOMAS GRAY
From a painting by Benjamin Wilson, in the possession of
Sir John Murray, K.C.V.O., D.S.O.

R.W. KETTON-CREMER, 1906-

THOMAS GRAY

A BIOGRAPHY

CAMBRIDGE

AT THE UNIVERSITY PRESS

1955

PUBLISHED BY
THE SYNDICS OF THE CAMBRIDGE UNIVERSITY PRESS

London Office: Bentley House, N.W.1
American Branch: New York

Agents for Canada, India, and Pakistan: Macmillan

Printed in Great Britain at the University Press, Cambridge
(Brooke Crutchley, University Printer)

To the memory of
LEONARD WHIBLEY

CONTENTS

PREFACE

I

In the summer of 1935 I published, in Messrs Duckworth's series of *Great Lives*, a short biography of Thomas Gray. Soon afterwards I received a letter from Leonard Whibley, who was just completing the edition of Gray's *Correspondence* on which he had been working for many years, at first in collaboration with Dr Paget Toynbee and single-handed after Dr Toynbee's death. His letter, so searching in its criticisms and so kindly in its commendations, led to a friendship which lasted until his death, and to which I shall always look back with gratitude.

Later in the same year he published the three volumes of his *Correspondence of Thomas Gray*. He had hoped, when this great work of scholarship was at last completed, to crown his labours by writing a biography of Gray. He did in fact prepare an outline of Gray's life in narrative form as far as the year 1760; but most of this was still in draft at the time of his death in November 1941. He wrote to me, a few months before he died, suggesting with his accustomed kindness that I should write the biography which he now felt himself unable to undertake; and at the same time he expressed to certain friends his wish that in the event of his death I should have access to the notes and manuscripts which he intended to bequeath to Pembroke College, Cambridge. I was unable to give him any promise at the time, and we did not have an opportunity to meet and discuss the project. But in due course, with the sanction and encouragement of the Master and Fellows of Pembroke College, I determined to do my best to carry out his wishes.

I cannot over-estimate the debt which I owe to Whibley's own work on Gray. His edition of the *Correspondence* is a splendid achievement, a model of accuracy in text and footnotes alike. Most valuable of all are the appendices, twenty-six in number, in which he discussed various problems of Gray's life and writings. I have drawn on these appendices perhaps even more generously than on his footnotes to the letters themselves. The notes and papers which he bequeathed to Pembroke College consist mainly of the materials used in this edition; but they contain a certain amount of *addenda* and *corrigenda*, and also include the extremely helpful biographical outline to which I have already referred. I have likewise made use of his interleaved and annotated copy of Gosse's *Life of Gray*, the pages of which are black with his remorseless corrections.

Although I wish to associate the name of Leonard Whibley as intimately as possible with this biography, I am solely responsible for its arrangement and its content. In statements of fact I have tried, perhaps in vain, to comply with the standards of that most accurate of scholars. In matters of opinion I do not think, from my recollections of the talks which we had long ago about Gray, that there is much with which he would have strongly disagreed. But it is with a sense of great humility that I inscribe my book to his memory.

II

I am deeply grateful to the Master and Fellows of Pembroke College for allowing me to use the Gray Manuscripts in their possession, and the books and papers bequeathed to them by Leonard Whibley. In particular I would thank the Master, Mr S. C. Roberts, for his constant interest, encouragement and advice. His knowledge of Gray, of the eighteenth century, and of the past history of Cambridge has been most generously placed at my disposal, and the entire text of my book has undergone his wise and careful scrutiny. My thanks are due also to Mr Matthew Hodgart, the Librarian of the College, and to Mr Bryan King, who occupies the rooms formerly tenanted by Gray. I will not single out other names from a society whose members have shown me such unfailing kindness and hospitality over a number of years.

At Peterhouse, Gray's earlier college, I am similarly grateful to the late Master, Mr P. C. Vellacott, and to Professor Michael Postan for their friendly help.

In matters connected with Eton, I have had the benefit of the advice of the Headmaster, Mr Robert Birley, the Librarian, Mr T. Lyon, and Mr Richard Martineau.

At Windsor I have received the kindly assistance of Sir Owen Morshead. At Stoke Poges the Rector, the Rev. D. H. Bryant-Bevan, and the present owners of the Manor House, Mr and Mrs H. Frye, have been most patient and helpful.

For the benefit of their conversation and writings on various aspects of Gray, I stand much indebted to Lord David Cecil and Professor Geoffrey Tillotson. I acknowledge a similar debt to the correspondence of Mr C. F. Bell, and to his essay *Thomas Gray and the Fine Arts*. The Warden of All Souls, Mr John Sparrow, has adorned my book with his translations of the passages which I have quoted from Gray's Latin poetry; and Monsignor Ronald Knox has allowed me to use his beautiful rendering of *O lachrymarum fons*.

For permission to inspect and in some instances to quote from manuscripts in their possession, my thanks are due to Sir John Murray (who has also allowed me to reproduce his portrait of Gray by Benjamin Wilson), Mr W. S. Lewis, and Mr Roger Senhouse. I am allowed to reproduce other portraits through the kindness of Viscount Harcourt, Lord Walpole, Dr Brian Rhodes, M. Wolfgang de Reding-Biberegg, the National Portrait Gallery and the Fitzwilliam Museum.

For help on particular points I would like to thank Mr J. W. Goodison of the Fitzwilliam Museum, and Dr George L. Lam of Yale University.

Until her death Mrs Leonard Whibley maintained her kindly interest in the progress of my work, and this has been continued by her niece Miss Pauline de Almay.

Preface

Finally, I would like to associate this book with the memory of my friend Hugh Gatty, Fellow and Librarian of St John's College. It was always his wish that I should undertake it; and its earlier stages had already begun to benefit from his fine scholarship, and his great knowledge and love of Cambridge, before his untimely death.

R. W. K.-C.

FELBRIGG HALL
NORWICH

December 1954

LIST OF PLATES

[See Appendix B, "A Note on the Illustrations", pp. 274–5.]

Plates I, IV, V, VI, VII, VIII are reproduced from *The Correspondence
of Thomas Gray*, edited by Toynbee and Whibley, by permission of the
Delegates of the Clarendon Press, Oxford

CHAPTER I

CHILDHOOD AND ETON
1716-1734

I

IN the first years of the eighteenth century two sisters, Mary and Dorothy Antrobus, set up a shop in the city of London. It was variously described as a millinery business[1] and 'a kind of India warehouse',[2] and the sisters conducted it with tolerable success. About 1709 their partnership was interrupted by the marriage of Dorothy to a London scrivener and exchange broker named Philip Gray. An arrangement was made by which Mary carried on the business with such assistance as Dorothy, in her married state, could give her; and it was transferred to a shop forming part of a house in Cornhill which belonged to Philip Gray.[3] He and his wife, and presumably Mary Antrobus as well, lived in the rest of the house. There were twelve children of the marriage, all of whom died in their infancy except the fifth, who was born on 26 December 1716, and was given the name of Thomas.

The Gray and Antrobus families, and their connections by marriage, shared much the same background of commerce and the professions. They were prosperous in a modest way, but never achieved any distinction or success. Philip Gray was the third and youngest son of a wine-merchant connected with the East India Company. One of his brothers had died at Madras in the Company's service; the other was a London merchant; there were four sisters. Mrs Gray's father, like her husband, was a scrivener, and her mother was the daughter of yet another scrivener. She had two brothers, Robert and William Antrobus. Robert spent his entire life as an assistant master at Eton; William was also a master there for many years, and then migrated to a Northamptonshire rectory. Her eldest sister Anne married an attorney named Jonathan Rogers; her second sister Jane married William Oliffe, vaguely described as a gentleman of Norfolk.[4]

The married life of Philip and Dorothy Gray was a miserable affair, ruined almost from the outset by the husband's peculiarities of temper. He was tortured by a corroding jealousy. He was jealous of his wife's kind-hearted brothers and sisters, and of Mary Antrobus in particular; he was even jealous of the shop, although he expected Mrs Gray to provide herself with clothes and other necessaries, and to pay for their son's education, out of its profits. At the best of times he was surly and morose; and at intervals his gloom gave place to moods of uncontrollable fury, when he would attack his wife 'in the most inhuman manner, by beating, kicking, punching, and with the most vile and abusive language'. Scenes of this description were still taking place, with ever-increasing violence, twenty-five years after their marriage. Mrs Gray, a woman of great courage and devotion, endured it all stoically for the sake of her son.[5]

Such was the background of Thomas Gray's earliest years. (In this uneasy household he grew into a sensitive and intelligent little boy, frightened of his father, adored by his mother, petted by childless aunts. A precocious only child, without cousins or close playmates of his own age, he became the centre of much elderly attention, but was obliged to rely for companionship upon himself and his books. His health, moreover, was feeble.) There is a story that his little brothers and sisters had died of suffocation, owing to too great a fullness of blood, and that he 'would certainly have been cut off as early, had not his mother, with a courage remarkable for one of her sex, and withal so very tender a parent, ventured to open a vein with her own hand, which instantly removed the paroxysm'.[6] Whatever the truth of this account may be, he was the only survivor of twelve children, the solitary living shoot from a weakening stock.

(His uncles, the masters at Eton, saw their nephew growing lonely and self-absorbed in the dispiriting atmosphere of his home. They determined to get him away into country air and into the society of other boys of his own age, and offered to arrange for his admission to Eton. His mother agreed, like the sensible woman she was. (His father refused to contribute anything towards his expenses at school; but funds were forthcoming from the profits of the shop, and his uncles also gave some assistance. In 1725, before he was nine years old, Thomas Gray entered Eton as an Oppidan, and was placed low down in the Second Form.)

II

It must have been an alarming experience for so timid and retiring a child, even with the reassuring presence of his uncles in the background, to be taken straight from home and plunged into the bewildering confusion of a great public school. Although Gray was an Oppidan, and did not have to endure the 'drubbing and tyranny' which he afterwards described as the accustomed portion of the Collegers,[7] life at Eton in the eighteenth century was far from being a cloistered affair. But his years there were unquestionably the happiest that he was ever to know; and so he always regarded them.

His uncle William Antrobus became Rector of Everdon in Northamptonshire in 1726, and presumably left Eton at that time; but his uncle Robert remained, and carefully watched over the little boy as he progressed slowly up the school. He took great pains to instruct his nephew in botany, an interest which remained with him throughout life; and in particular he directed his attention to the properties of herbs and simples.[8] It was his wish that Gray should take up the profession of medicine, and in his will he bequeathed 'to my nephew Thomas Gray all such books as relate to the study of physick, provided he be educated in that profession'. But Robert Antrobus died at the beginning of 1730; and Gray's study of physic never

1-2

developed beyond a life-long and sometimes rather excessive preoccupation with the care of his own health.

His appearance in mourning for his uncle Robert fixed a curiously vivid impression in the mind of Jacob Bryant, a boy who had come to Eton the previous half. 'I remember he made an elegant little figure in his sable dress, for he had a very good complexion, and fine hair, and appeared to much advantage among the boys who were near him in the school, and who were much more rough and rude.' Bryant was more than eighty years old when he wrote down the reminiscences which include this passage, and his memory sometimes played him false; but if his little vignette of the demure child in his mourning clothes was accurately drawn, it is our earliest picture of Gray.[9]

He had reached the Upper School in 1729; and, much though he must have grieved at his kindly uncle's death, he had already learnt to look after himself and to pursue his own independent line. His passion for books, his eager acquisition of all sorts of knowledge, developed very early. He began to feel the first stirrings of his own creative powers. When he was asked, at the height of his fame, 'if he recollected when he first perceived in himself any symptoms of poetry, he answered that he believed it was when at Eton he began to take pleasure in reading Virgil for his own amusement, and not in school-hours, or as a task'. Although he never figured as one of the leading scholars at Eton, his exercises in Latin verse were thought to be very good, and Jacob Bryant could quote a passage from one of them seventy years later.[10]

His poetry was to be deeply influenced by his love and understanding of English history; and this may likewise be traced back to his Eton days. Windsor Castle, with its wealth of associations and legends, dominated all the smiling landscape. The Castle was seldom visited by King George the Second; but its chapels and halls, its galleries and wards and terraces were in consequence all the more accessible to a studious little boy from Eton. And at Eton itself the memory of a very different monarch haunted him. A few years before, the fine bronze statue of King Henry the Sixth had been placed in the centre of School Yard; and every day, as he passed to Chapel and to the long hours of work in Lower and then in Upper School, the story of the Founder was brought home to him in all its sadness. 'The murther'd Saint', 'the meek Usurper', 'her Henry's holy Shade'—time and again that devout and gentle presence was to figure in his poems.

When he was thirteen or fourteen, he became one of a small group of friends who had drifted together in the general turmoil of the school. Superficially they were very much of the same type—delicate in health, disinclined to take part in games or adventure, poetical and romantic in temperament, a trifle conceited, rather old for their years: the sort of little clique that has existed in every school in every century. They called themselves the Quadruple Alliance.

The leader of the group was a year or so younger than the others, a precocious and talented child called Horace Walpole. He was the youngest son of Sir Robert Walpole, the First Minister, born in the eighteenth year of his marriage to a wife to whom he was persistently unfaithful, and who had begun to return his indifference. Horace Walpole, like Gray, was adored and indulged by his mother; but the disagreements between Sir Robert and his wife were conducted with decorum, and Horace never knew parental conflicts of the type which saddened the childhood of his friend. He was a pale and fragile little boy, vivacious, self-possessed, somewhat conscious of his position as the son of the great Minister, but associating quite happily with companions whose background was very different from his own.

Richard West was a boy of Gray's own age, tall and slender, thin-faced and pale-complexioned, so shy and retiring that only a few perceptive friends realised his promise as a scholar and poet.[11] Within that small circle his reputation was high, and it was thought likely that he would eventually outshine his comrades of the Quadruple Alliance. Stories were told of his power of versifying in his sleep, and of how, plunged deep in studious abstraction, he would snuff a friend's candle when he meant to snuff his own.[12] He was the only son of a distinguished lawyer, who for a few years was Lord Chancellor of Ireland, and his mother was a daughter of Bishop Burnet. Their marriage was not a happy one; and although West's father died when the boy was only ten years old, his character was affected by the disturbed background of his early life as Gray's had been by very similar conditions.

The fourth member of the Alliance was Thomas Ashton, the son of a schoolmaster at Lancaster. He afterwards developed into a very unattractive figure, and his general unpopularity in later years makes it impossible to obtain a fair impression of him at this early age. It is sufficient to say that as a boy he displayed qualities which won him a place in a singularly fastidious group, and that he continued on equal terms with its members long after their schooldays were over.

The intimacy of the Quadruple Alliance was enhanced by the fanciful and high-sounding names which its members bestowed upon themselves. Gray was known as Orosmades, a variant of Oromasdes, the chief Zoroastrian divinity; Walpole was Celadon, the name of many a shepherd swain in poetry and romance; Favonius, the gentle and kindly west wind, and the occasional variant of Zephyrille were obvious titles for West; and Ashton became Almanzor, a character in Dryden's *Conquest of Granada*. They also coined similar names—Tydeus, Plato, Prato, Puffendorf—for other friends; for the Alliance was in no way exclusive, and Walpole particularly had several close friends outside the little circle. In fact it was to one of these, George Montagu, that Walpole addressed from Cambridge the description of his Eton days which so frankly sums up the attitude of his set to the ordinary life of the school:

Dear George, were not the playing fields at Eton food for all manner of flights? No old maid's gown, though it had been tormented into all the fashions from King James to King George, ever under-

went so many transformations, as those poor plains have in my idea.
At first I was contented with tending a visionary flock, and sighing
some pastoral name to the echo of the cascade under the bridge:
how happy should I have been to have had a kingdom, only for the
pleasure of being driven from it, and living disguised in an humble
vale. As I got farther into Virgil and *Clelia*, I found myself transported from Arcadia, to the garden of Italy, and saw Windsor
Castle in no other view than the *capitoli immobile saxum*....I can't
say I am sorry I was never quite a schoolboy; an expedition against
bargemen, or a match at cricket may be very pretty things to
recollect; but thank my stars, I can remember things that are very
near as pretty. The beginning of my Roman history was spent in the
Asylum, or conversing in Egeria's hallowed grove; not in thumping
and pummelling King Amulius's herdsmen.[13]

That was the atmosphere of the Quadruple Alliance—the
classical allusions and gentle pastoral dreams, the self-
sufficiency, the shrinking from contact with the herd.

III

In the lustre of these new-found friendships the distresses of
Gray's home life faded into insignificance. Nothing is now
known about the way in which his holidays were passed, and
the relations of the growing boy with his father are equally
obscure. The house in Cornhill may not have been so quarrel-
some and disturbed a place as is generally supposed. Mrs Gray's
acccount of her troubles, as detailed in a case submitted for
counsel's opinion a few years later, was certainly most lament-
able;[14] but the *ménage* somehow held together for a length
of time which seems hardly conceivable without long stretches
of comparative peace. It is likely that both parents were
gratified by the unusual promise of their only child; and this
impression is strengthened by the painting, now in the Fitzwilliam Museum at Cambridge, which shows him at the age
of fourteen or fifteen. We shall never know whether his father
or his mother commissioned it; but it is the portrait of a boy of
whom his family were very proud. Although it has always

been attributed to Jonathan Richardson, doubts have long been felt as to whether he ever painted quite so badly; and the authorities seem hitherto to have ignored a passage in Jacob Bryant's reminiscences of Gray, where it is ascribed with much greater probability to Arthur Pond.[15] The boy is seated, holding a book, beside a table on which are volumes labelled 'Temple' and 'Locke', and a pen and standish. These indications of studious tastes are offset by the richness of his dress— embroidered blue coat lined with peach-coloured silk, black velvet breeches, white stockings, red leather slippers. The head is more competently painted than the rest of the picture: the expression of a lively, self-possessed, precocious boy is skilfully caught; and although it is on the whole a mediocre piece of work, the gay colouring and superficial likeness may have given much satisfaction to an unexacting household in Cornhill.

This portrait alone throws some light on Gray's home background at this time. For all his family affections, his heart was at Eton; and there his happiness, during these later years, was absolute. The companionship of his friends, the beauty and tradition of his surroundings, the constant exploration of new territories in poetry and history and classical literature— everything was harmonious and delightful. He was experiencing, as never again, that cloudless serenity of mind which he was one day to describe in an unforgettable phrase—'the sunshine of the breast'. When he came to write the *Ode on a Distant Prospect of Eton College*, it was through no haze of retrospective sentiment that he viewed those idyllic years. Even while they were passing, he seems to have known instinctively that they were the golden period of his life; and afterwards their mere recollection could refresh and console him.

> Ah happy hills, ah pleasing shade,
> Ah fields belov'd in vain,
> Where once my careless childhood stray'd,
> A stranger yet to pain!

THOMAS GRAY

From a painting attributed to Jonathan Richardson the Elder, but possibly by
Arthur Pond, in the Fitzwilliam Museum, Cambridge

I feel the gales, that from ye blow,
A momentary bliss bestow,
As waving fresh their gladsome wing,
My weary soul they seem to sooth,
And, redolent of joy and youth,
To breathe a second spring.

The idyll was broken all too soon. The musings under the
noble trees, the saunterings beside the Thames, the Virgilian
quotations, the private jokes, the daily companionship of the
Quadruple Alliance came to an end. Before its members lay
the world of men and affairs; and all but Walpole were faced
with struggles, with duties, with the distasteful necessity of
adopting a profession. Gray and Ashton went to Cambridge in
1734, and Walpole followed a few months later; while West, so
gentle and retiring, so dependent on his friends, was separated
from them all and made his way reluctantly to Oxford.
Nothing was left of Eton but a long after-glow of remembered
happiness, which found expression in Gray's ode, in Walpole's
letters, in the sad little poem which West composed as he
wandered in solitude through the Walks at Magdalen:

The thought, which still my breast invades,
Nigh yonder springs, nigh yonder shades,
Still, as I pass, the memory brings
    Of sweeter shades and springs.

Lost and inwrapt in thought profound,
Absent I tread Etonian ground;
Then starting from the dear mistake,
    As disenchanted, wake...

Oh! how I long again with those,
Whom first my boyish heart had chose,
Together through the friendly shade
    To stray, as once I stray'd!

Their presence would the scene endear,
Like paradise would all appear,
More sweet around the flowers would blow,
    More soft the waters flow.[16]

CHAPTER II

CAMBRIDGE
1734–1739

I

G R A Y was nearly eighteen when he first went up to Cambridge
and was entered at Peterhouse. For the past nine years, almost
as far back as he could remember, he had been at Eton. He had
passed there, in the happiest circumstances, the whole eventful
span of life from early childhood to approaching manhood; and
the transition from those accustomed scenes to the unfamiliar
world of Cambridge was sufficiently disconcerting. The beauty
of Eton, the river, the meadows, the ancient trees were exchanged for an unattractive provincial town set in dull fen-
land country. The vitality of a great school, the gaiety and
companionship of his friends, gave place to the glum and
hierarchical society of a stagnant little college.

Cambridge in the eighteenth century had not achieved the
visual beauty which is so impressive today. The loneliest fresh-
man now must find consolation in that serene harmony of trees,
water, lawns and flowers, the result of the care and thought of
many generations. In Gray's time the colleges were bordered
only by a weed-choked stream flowing sluggishly through
tousled meadows. And in most of the colleges, for all their
architectural and antiquarian charms, life flowed as sluggishly
as the Cam. The whole university contained little more than
four hundred undergraduates; and the number of Fellows,
resident and non-resident, was almost exactly the same. The
only colleges with any considerable number of students were
Trinity and St John's. In the other colleges, a large and well-
remunerated body of Fellows—tutors, deans, lecturers, bursars
—held sway over ten or twenty undergraduates. There were

only about a dozen undergraduates in residence at Peterhouse when Gray first entered the college.[1]

Peterhouse was chosen for him because his uncle Robert Antrobus had been a Fellow of the college. He was admitted there as a pensioner on 4 July 1734, under a condition that he should later approve himself to the examiners. There was also the prospect of a scholarship as soon as this condition was satisfied, since more scholarships were available at Peterhouse than there were students to hold them. Gray came into residence on 9 October, and a week later was duly elected to a Bible Clerkship, on Bishop Cosin's foundation, of £10 a year. He described the ceremony of admission to his scholarship in a letter to Walpole. 'First they led me into the hall, and there I swore Allegiance to the King; then I went to a room, where I took 50000 Latin Oaths, such as, to wear a Square Cap, to make six verses upon the Epistle or Gospel every Sunday morning, to chant very loud in Chapel, to wear a clean Surplice, etc.'[2] He was, in fact, required to wear a square cap and a long-sleeved gown; not to sport long locks or to indulge in hair-powder; to study music under the college organist, so as to take an active part in the Chapel services; and to produce to the Master, at the dinner hour on Sundays and feast-days, a copy of Greek or Latin verses on a subject taken from the Epistle or Gospel for the day.[3] It may be doubtful to what extent, under the casual discipline of Peterhouse, some of these provisions were actually enforced. Eight months later he exchanged his Bible clerkship for a Hale scholarship, of which the emolument was slightly greater but was still extremely modest. Its requirements as to dress and conduct were much the same.

Ashton was already at King's, having preceded Gray to Cambridge by a few weeks; but Walpole was not to join them until the following term, and for his benefit Gray described his new experiences in a series of lively letters. The earliest of these, written three weeks after his arrival, shows that he had already formed very definite opinions about Cambridge and its inhabitants.

It is a great old Town, shaped like a Spider, with a nasty lump in the middle of it, and half a dozen scambling long legs: it has fourteen Parishes, twelve Colledges, and four Halls...there are five ranks in the University, subordinate to the Vice Chancellor, who is chose annually: these are Masters, Fellows, Fellow-Commoners, Pensioners and Sizers; the Masters of Colledges are twelve grey-hair'd Gentlefolks, who are all mad with Pride; the Fellows are sleepy, drunken, dull, illiterate Things; the Fellow-Commoners are imitatours of the Fellows, or else Beaux, or else nothing: the Pensioners grave, formal Sots, who would be thought old; or else drink Ale, and sing Songs against the Excise. The Sizers are Graziers' Eldest Sons, who come to get good learning, that they may all be Archbishops of Canterbury.[4]

In the same vein, a little later, was his tart dismissal of Peter-house as 'a thing like two Presbyterian Meeting-houses with the backside of a little Church between them'.[5] His own rooms were on the north side of the First Court—at that time the only court—of the college, and probably consisted of a single large chamber with a minute study partitioned out of it.[6]

The air of gaiety and sophistication, which Gray strives to impart to such passages as these, hardly disguises the loneliness of his first months at Cambridge. He saw a good deal of Ashton; together they could talk of Eton days, and revive the jokes and slang of the Quadruple Alliance; but Ashton was no substitute for Walpole or for West. And in general Gray found his new associates uncongenial, and their social gatherings intolerable.

Do but imagine me [he wrote to Walpole after some sort of party at a tavern] pent up in a room hired for the purpose, and none of the largest, from seven a-clock at night, till four in the morning! 'midst hogsheads of Liquor and quantities of Tobacco, surrounded by thirty of these creatures, infinitely below the meanest People you could even form an Idea of; toasting bawdy healths and deafened with their unmeaning Roar.[7]

His means also, during his earlier years as an undergraduate, were very limited. Some of his college bills have survived, and show that in his first year the whole charge for his 'sizings'—the extra or alternative dishes which might be ordered in Hall to supplement the ordinary 'commons'— amounted to only a few shillings.[8] Moreover, the situation between his parents was particularly trying at this time. Philip Gray consistently refused to pay anything towards his son's expenses at Cambridge; his violence of temper, and his ill-treatment of his wife, were approaching a climax; and Mrs Gray in desperation was nerving herself to seek a remedy at law.

During this gloomy winter, Gray had one unfailing solace: the prospect of Walpole's arrival early in the new year. The tedious round of Cambridge life would soon be illumined by the gaiety and high spirits of his friend. In the meantime he did his best to recapture the atmosphere of their Eton days in a stream of vivacious and eccentric letters. Every week Orosmades would write to Celadon; or he would assume some still more fantastic character, and address Walpole in verse as the ghost of John Dennis, or in rich oriental imagery borrowed from *The Turkish Spy*, or in graveyard metaphors as a corpse in 'Saint Peter's Charnel-house'.[9] Walpole probably replied in similar terms. His only surviving letter to Gray during these years is just as fanciful, an elaborate parody of the style in which Addison described his travels in Italy.[10] Gray did not go home at Christmas, and so lost the opportunity of seeing Walpole and accompanying him to operas and plays; possibly the family dissensions made it advisable for him to stay away from the house in Cornhill. His only diversion, in a place where 'everything is so tediously regular, so samish, that I expire for want of a little variety',[11] was this daydream correspondence with Walpole, with all its gay absurdities and boyish endearments and foolish far-fetched jokes.

Walpole's arrival at Cambridge was several times postponed, and he did not finally make his appearance at King's until the middle of March. The joy of 'a long ungainly mortal of King's College', as Gray described Ashton, and 'a little, waddling Fresh-man of Peterhouse', as he described himself,[12] was unrestrained. They were reunited under social conditions somewhat different from the democracy of a great school; Walpole was a fellow-commoner, Gray and Ashton were scholars, and the distinction between them was not merely one of academic dress or different tables in hall. But Walpole did not allow the conventions of Cambridge to interfere with his Eton friendships. Gray and Ashton, and another Etonian whom they all knew as 'Plato' and who has never been satisfactorily identified, remained his closest associates; and only the absence of West prevented a complete revival of their old fellowship. After a few months at Cambridge, Walpole wrote to West:

> Orosmades and Almanzor are just the same; that is, I am almost the only person they are acquainted with, and consequently the only person acquainted with their excellencies. Plato improves every day; so does my friendship with him. These three divide my whole time—though I believe you will guess there is no Quadruple Alliance: that was a happiness which I only enjoyed when you was at Eton.[13]

As far as Gray was concerned it was happiness enough to have Walpole close at hand, that lively presence magically dispelling the boredom and depression which had clouded his spirits for so many months past.

II

As might have been expected, West at Oxford was feeling isolated and forlorn. He had gone to Christ Church early in the summer of 1735; and throughout his years there the burden of the poem written in Magdalen Walks occurs perpetually in his letters to his three friends at Cambridge. He missed them all intensely, and found little to console him for the loss of their company. His descriptions of his Oxford life, and notably a set of verses in the manner of Pope, bear a strong resemblance to Gray's early impressions of his own university:

Meantime how heavily my days now roll!
The morning lecture! and the evening bowl!
The cobweb-school! the tutor's flimzy tale!
The feast of folly! and the flow of ale![14]

Occasionally his letters become plaintive in tone. Had all his friends entirely forgotten him? Why did they write so seldom? Why had Gray, in particular, only written once in all the months since he first went to Oxford? To the latter charge Gray replied:

I do not wonder in the least at your frequent blaming my indolence, it ought rather to be called ingratitude, and I am obliged to your goodness for softening so harsh an appellation. When you have seen one of my days, you have seen a whole year of my life; they go round and round like the blind horse in the mill, only he has the satisfaction of fancying he makes a progress, and gets some ground; my eyes are open enough to see the same dull prospect, and to know that having made four-and-twenty steps more, I shall be just where I was. . . . However, as the most undeserving people in the world must sure have the vanity to wish somebody had a regard for them, so I need not wonder at my own, in being pleased that you care about me. You need not doubt, therefore, of having a first row in the front box of my little heart, and I believe you are not in danger of being crouded there.[15]

The answer to West's accusation of neglect was reassuring enough; but the general tone of the letter lacks some of the warmth and intimacy with which Gray would have addressed Walpole in similar circumstances. There can be no doubt that at this time Walpole was the ascendant star of Gray's firmament, and that West was a little eclipsed. His two closest friends personified two opposing ways of life and thought, between which Gray's inclinations were much divided. Walpole moved in the world with the effortless assurance that befitted a son of the great Minister. He stood for influence and social position, wealth and elegance and fashion. Gray was keenly susceptible to these advantages; and the fact that he was excluded from them, by nature and by circumstance alike, did not lessen their attractions for him. On the other side stood West, the gentle scholar, the shy recluse, fostering in retirement his little flame of poetry. Temperamentally he was the more akin to Gray; and his chosen way of life was ultimately adopted by Gray, and pursued to the end. But for two or three years to come Walpole's spell remained the stronger.

There was, of course, no conscious rivalry between West and Walpole for Gray's allegiance. Their letters show that the Quadruple Alliance was standing firm, all four of its members still linked together in equal friendship. A surprising number of these letters have survived. Walpole paid small regard to his obligations of residence at Cambridge; Gray also was absent sometimes for considerable periods; and West wrote constantly from Oxford asking for news of them all. Thus a criss-cross of correspondence developed between Celadon and Favonius, Orosmades and Almanzor, and was in intermittent progress throughout their university years. They retained their schoolboy names so far into manhood that Walpole, the last survivor of them all, would snip away with his scissors the prefixes and signatures of Gray's earliest letters, as he read and docketed these records of their happy and foolish youth. Fortunately he seldom went further. He told his executor that he 'was so partial to those early blossoms of his friend's wit, genius and humour, that he could not determine to destroy them'.[16] So they remain—a strange miscellany, sometimes silly and childish, sometimes brilliant and touching and prematurely wise—for the irritation and delight of posterity.

III

Gray did not leave Cambridge at all for nearly ten months after his first arrival there; but at the end of July 1735 he returned home, and was away until late in October. He was in London again at the turn of the year. A letter to Walpole of that date speaks cheerfully of operas and plays; but his father's brutality to his mother had now reached an intolerable pitch, and she was preparing a case to be submitted to counsel for an opinion as to the possibilities of a judicial separation. The 'eminent civilian' whose advice she sought was Dr John Audley, who had been a contemporary of her brother Robert Antrobus at Peterhouse many years before; and his opinion was delivered from Doctors' Commons on 9 February 1736.[17]

It was a sad story that Mrs Gray had unfolded to Dr Audley. She and her sister Mary had carried on their business successfully for close on thirty years. She had been no charge to her husband; on the contrary, she had paid him £40 a year for the rent of the shop which formed part of their dwelling-house. Furthermore, throughout their married life she had 'not only found herself in all manner of apparel, but also for all her children, to the number of twelve, and most of the furniture of his house; and...almost providing every thing for her son, whilst at Eton school, and now he is at Peter-House at Cambridge'. Yet her husband's cruelties to her, the beating, the punching, the foul language, had grown steadily worse, so that 'she hath been in the utmost fear and danger of her life, and hath been obliged this last year to quit her bed, and lie with her sister'. All this ill-treatment 'she was resolved, if possible, to bear; not to leave her shop of trade for the sake of her son, to be able to assist in the maintenance of him at the University, since his father won't'.

Physical violence the brave woman was ready to endure; but Philip Gray, in his half-demented jealousy, had devised another means of carrying out his threat that 'he will pursue her with all the vengeance possible, and will ruin himself to undo her, and his only son'. He had given notice to Mary Antrobus that she must leave his shop at Midsummer next. If she was obliged to set up her business elsewhere, Mrs Gray would have to go with her, since the shop was her only means of supporting herself and completing the education of her son. And with that possibility in view, she now asked Dr Audley whether her husband could compel her to return to him, or otherwise molest her and interfere with the business.

Dr Audley's opinion, though expressed with kindness and sympathy, was not very comforting. If Mrs Gray left her husband's house he could compel her, by process in the Ecclesiastical Court, to return home and cohabit with him. If she was able to prove in that court that her husband's cruelties were such as to endanger her life or safety, the judge might order a separation; but it was all very doubtful.'This is a most unhappy case, and such a one, as I think, if possible, should be referred to, and made up by some common friend; sentences of separation, by reason of cruelty only, being very rarely obtained.' And more to the same effect.

In the end, as Dr Audley had advised, some sort of reconciliation took place. There were no legal proceedings; Philip Gray did not compel his sister-in-law to quit the shop; he may even have grown alarmed at the possible developments of the situation which he had created. After so much commotion, the affairs of his household seem to have settled down again on a happier basis than for many years past. He may have been additionally sobered by another family event which took place just at this time. His unmarried sister Sarah died on 12 February, and was found to have left her entire property not to him but to his son Thomas, who proved the will a few days later. The amount of his inheritance is not known, but it included 'all my messuages, tenements and houses upon London Bridge or elsewhere', in addition to ready money and personal effects.[18] The houses were probably sold, since no more is heard of them, and the proceeds otherwise invested. Henceforward Gray had an income of his own. It was not considerable, but it made him less dependent on his father's caprices and his mother's exertions in the shop. Life became easier for him both at home and at Cambridge. As a small indication of the improvement in his means, his 'sizings' in Hall, which had hitherto been so modest, exceeded the charge for his 'commons' in every quarter of 1736–7.[19] And it is possible to trace in his letters, from this time forward, a new note of confidence and self-assurance.[20]

Gray spent the summer vacation of this year with his mother's eldest sister and her husband Jonathan Rogers, a retired attorney of sporting tastes. They had settled at Burnham in the south of Buckinghamshire, in a small house known as Cant's Hill.[21] Gray must already have known something of the neighbourhood from his Eton days. His uncle, as he told Walpole, was 'a great hunter in imagination; his Dogs take up every chair in the house, so I'm forced to stand at this present writing, and tho' the Gout forbids him galloping after 'em in the field, yet he continues still to regale his Ears and Nose with their comfortable Noise and Stink; he holds me mighty cheap for walking, when I should ride, and reading, when I should hunt'.[22] He went on to describe to Walpole the beauties of the little forest known as Burnham Beeches, and how he indulged there in the only form of exercise he was ever known to take—those slow meditative walks, Virgil in hand, watching the birds and animals, and noting attentively every aspect of the face of nature. Gray was certainly never a horseman, and all his life he disliked the society of dogs. No doubt he deserved the scorn of his jovial uncle. But those observant saunterings about the countryside, so dull and spiritless in a young man who might have been riding to hounds, were to bear abundant fruit in the *Ode on the Spring* and the *Elegy* only a few years later.

Shortly before Gray returned to Cambridge in the autumn, there took place an amusing exchange of letters with his tutor, the Rev. George Birkett. A little conscious, perhaps, of the measure of independence which his aunt's legacy had secured for him, he addressed Mr Birkett in a somewhat offhand manner:

Sir,

As I shall stay only a fortnight longer in Town, I'll beg you to give yourself the trouble of writing out my Bills, and sending 'em, that I may put myself out of your Debt, as soon as I come down: if

Piazza should come to You, you'll be so good as to satisfie him; I protest, I forget what I owe him, but he is honest enough to tell you right: my Father and Mother desire me to send their compliments, and I beg you'd believe me

Sir

your most obedient humble Servant
T. GRAY.

His tutor did not care for the jaunty tone in which these requests were made, and decided to administer a reproof. Unfortunately, he was drunk at the time; and two drafts of his reply, which still exist, are a mass of blots and scrawled corrections. The earlier draft was intended to bring 'pretty Mr Day'—presently altered to 'Gray'—to his senses; but it soon trails off into some fuddled nonsense about 'Tyrants or Rebulicans', and only recovers coherence with the sentence 'I wd doe any service for yr your Uncle Antrobus tho'. The later and soberer draft, a copy of which was presumably sent to Gray with his bills, was still somewhat curt in tone, but was signed forgivingly 'your very friend G.B.'

This trifling episode furnishes the only surviving evidence of Gray's relations with his tutors. Birkett seems to have been an amiable character—not all dons would have been so forbearing towards a conceited undergraduate—but he never made any impression on his brilliant pupil; and when Gray, in his first letter from Cambridge, spoke of the Fellows of colleges as 'sleepy, drunken, dull, illiterate Things', it seems probable that his own tutor's shortcomings played some part in this general condemnation.[23]

IV

Hitherto Gray had been reading for a degree. His obligatory studies had lain in fields particularly distasteful to him —logic, philosophy, mathematics. 'Must I plunge into metaphysics?' he asked West plaintively. 'Alas, I cannot see in the dark: nature has not furnished me with the optics of a cat. Must I pore upon mathematics? Alas, I cannot see in too much light; I am no eagle.'[24] On the other hand, there was no place in his Cambridge routine for classical studies. In addition to the Greek or Latin verses required from him on Sundays and feast-days by the terms of his scholarship, the college exacted further verses from its scholars on certain anniversaries; and copies of the Latin hexameters in which Gray celebrated Oak Apple Day and the Fifth of November are still in existence. But these mechanical exercises bore no relation to the wide classical reading in which he had delighted at Eton.

All this was suddenly changed in the autumn of 1736. Of the three learned professions, divinity, physic and law, it had now been decided that he should adopt the last. He had in fact been admitted at the Inner Temple about a year before. It was not necessary to hold a university degree in order to become a barrister; and Gray joyfully told his friends that he would no longer have to drudge for a degree after the end of the current term, and might even read a little philosophy now that there was no need for it.[25] The college treated him very well, even allowing him to retain his scholarship for as long as he continued in residence.[26] He was not in the least attracted by his proposed career, and may have had little intention of adopting it; but he gratefully accepted this release from studies which he disliked, and the prospect of unlimited reading in his own chosen fields.

No longer burdened with lectures and tutorials, and not very seriously concerned about his future prospects, he settled down for two more years at Cambridge. Although he could not suspect it at the time, these two years foreshadowed the existence which he was destined to lead for almost the whole of his life—Chapel each morning and evening; dinner and supper in Hall; solitary walks in the countryside; long hours of reading, with an occasional interlude at his harpsichord, in the quiet of his college rooms. He pressed on with his study of Italian, in which he and Walpole both took lessons from the Signor Piazza mentioned in his letter to Birkett. He widened his knowledge of English and French poetry, and amused himself with lighter works—memoirs, travels, novels and plays—in both languages; but he had not yet developed the interest in history which characterised his later years. His main devotion was still to Greece and Rome. The ancient world held an inexhaustible fascination for him, and he was constantly exploring fresh fields of classical learning—geography, antiquities, inscriptions.[27] He translated passages of Propertius and Statius into English verse, and sent them to West, who responded with renderings of Horace and Tibullus; and he began to be known in the university as a writer of Latin verses. In company with Walpole and Ashton he contributed to the *Gratulatio* with which Cambridge celebrated the marriage of the Prince of Wales in 1736; and next year he received the greater distinction of being asked to compose one of the sets of 'Tripos Verses', which were customarily printed and issued with the Tripos lists.[28] The theme chosen for his verses was *Luna est Habitabilis*; and he exercised his fancy very pleasantly in describing the landscape of the moon, and the activities and passions of its inhabitants.

Slowly and fastidiously, Gray began to make some other friends besides Walpole and Ashton. Foremost among them was a man of his own age, Thomas Wharton, a pensioner of Pembroke Hall. Wharton came from a long line of Durham physicians, and was himself studying medicine at Cambridge. He was a steady, sensible, kind-hearted young man, and was to prove himself, to the end of Gray's life, a most faithful and reliable friend. Another friendship was established about this time with the Rev. James Brown. A Londoner by birth, and with much the same commercial background as Gray, he was nine years his senior, and had lately become a Fellow of Pembroke. Small, precise, determined, always known to his friend by such affectionate diminutives as 'le petit bonhomme' and 'the little old Roman', he also was destined to figure pleasantly throughout Gray's life, and to perform the last offices at its close. Even at this early stage, Gray had begun to form the links with Pembroke which eventually led him to migrate across the street to that college, and he seems to have associated little with his own contemporaries at Peterhouse; but with one of them, John Clerke, who like Wharton was studying to become a physician, he kept in touch for many years. And he saw a good deal, both now and later, of an Eton friend of his and Walpole's, William Cole, an undergraduate first at Clare and then at King's, who had already developed those antiquarian tastes and Tory convictions which marked his course through life.

In his letters to West, but never in those to Walpole, there is occasional mention of depression and low spirits. He was subject to attacks of 'the hyp', that malady of the age. 'We must all submit to that wayward Queen', he assured West; 'I too in no small degree own her sway.'[29] And again: 'Low spirits are my true and faithful companions; they get up with me, go to bed with me, make journeys and returns as I do; nay, and pay visits, and will even affect to be jocose, and force a feeble laugh with me; but most commonly we sit alone together, and are the prettiest insipid company in the world.'[30] But his physical health at this time seems to have been satisfactory. He told Ashton that 'the goodness of my own Constitution, is in some Sense a Misfortune to me, as the health of everybody I love seems much more precarious than my own'.[31] The influence of 'the hyp' bore lightly on him, and he may even have exaggerated his low spirits for the sake of West, whose depression was darker and more constant. Tormented by a persistent cough and violent nervous headaches, and isolated by circumstance from his friends, West sought the comfort and reassurance of their letters with pathetic eagerness, and treasured the memory of his occasional meetings with them in London and elsewhere.

As the son of a distinguished lawyer, West had always been destined by his family for a legal career. Like Gray, he looked forward to such a fate with extreme distaste; but its inescapable shadow loomed over them both, and they decided to share rooms in the Temple, and alleviate 'the disgusting sober follies of the common law'[32] with playgoing and poetry. West went down from Oxford early in 1738, and Gray proposed to join him later in the year. He anticipated their incursion into the world of law in the opening lines of an excellent Latin ode which he sent in a letter to West in June:

> Barbaras aedes aditure mecum
> Quas Eris semper fovet inquieta,
> Lis ubi latè sonat, et togatum
>   Aestuat agmen!*

and described the life of rural leisure and calm reflection that would have suited them both so well in a less exacting world.[33] He closed this letter, entirely written in Latin, with a single stanza which is one of the loveliest things he was ever to achieve:

> O lachrymarum fons, tenero sacros
> Ducentium ortus ex animo; quater
>   Felix! in imo qui scatentem
>   Pectore te, pia Nympha, sensit.

It has been described by Mr John Sparrow as 'at once perfectly Horatian and wholly unlike Horace: so Horace would have said what Horace could never have felt'. I am privileged to be able to quote the exquisite translation by Monsignor Ronald Knox:

> O Spring of tears, that, from a heart by grace
> Made tender, their divine procession trace!
> Happy, who from his bosom drawing deep
> That influence, dear Angel, learns to weep.

Now that the time was approaching for Gray to leave Cambridge, he found, as he told Walpole, that 'I have a sort of reluctance to leave this place, unamiable as it may seem; 'tis true Cambridge is very ugly, she is very dirty, and very dull; but I'm like a cabbage, where I'm stuck, I love to grow; you should pull me up sooner, than any one, but I shall be

---

* 'Soon must we make our way, my friend, to those grim halls where Strife unresting makes her home, where wide resounds the din of legal battle from the surging ranks of the long robe.'

ne'er the better for transplanting.'[34] After following his own inclinations in reading and research for almost two years, the prospect of close study in an unfamiliar and uncongenial field was most depressing. But in September he uprooted himself and his belongings, and returned home to Cornhill.

For a part of the year, West had been living in the Temple and making reluctant acquaintance with the routine of the law courts; but in the autumn he moved to his mother's house at Epsom, and remained there for some months. Although Gray had been admitted at the Inner Temple three years before, there is no evidence that he resided in chambers or kept terms there after his departure from Cambridge, or indeed at any other time.[35] It seems that both friends decided to spend the winter with their respective families, and to embark upon their legal studies together early in the new year. But their plans were suddenly altered by Walpole, who was setting out next spring on a tour abroad, and who now invited Gray to accompany him. He offered to pay all his expenses throughout the tour, but otherwise they would travel on equal terms in every respect. Gray accepted the proposal with delight.

It may seem a little surprising that Gray's parents allowed their son to squander two valuable years in wandering about Europe, instead of settling down industriously to the career which his means and prospects required. But at first it was only intended that the travellers should spend some months in France, with possibly a visit to Geneva; their long sojourn in Italy was not a part of the original scheme. And, after all, Sir Robert Walpole was still the greatest power in the land, and might be expected to have an eye to the future prospects of his son's closest friend. Ashton, who had left Cambridge in 1737, was comfortably established through the Walpole influence as tutor to the young Earl of Plymouth;[36] and when he had taken orders, adequate preferment would be arranged for him. Mr and Mrs Gray must have felt that their son's interests were likewise in safe hands. This impression is reinforced by the fact that Walpole made a will, before they started on their tour, in which he left to Gray everything that he then possessed in the world.[37]

West remained in London, and it is not known whether Walpole suggested that he also might have travelled with them. If so, his uncertain health might well have prevented it; but a stronger obstacle must have been the insistence of his mother's advisers that he should pursue his father's career. A letter has survived, addressed to Mrs West by an unknown friend, deploring her son's addiction to 'Wit, Poetry, and those pursuits with which he has too long amused, or rather abused, his good parts'. The writer of the letter clearly held the poorest opinion of the Quadruple Alliance and all that it implied. 'God knows how zealous I am for his success in the world, and how grieved I am when I recollect, that he is now twenty-two and has not read one book, since he left Eton, for which he, or his family, will ever be the better as long as he lives.'[38] So West was obliged to settle down to his law studies, to spend an occasional reminiscent evening with Ashton, to think of his absent friends and assure them that 'if wishes could turn to realities, I would fling down my law books, and sup with you tonight'.[39]

V

Gray had probably seen more of West, at intervals during the past year, than he had done since they were at Eton together; and an increasing sympathy had developed between them. They were both genuine poets, struggling to achieve expression, subject to all the varying moods and influences of the creative temperament. They were both scholars of retiring disposition, victims of low spirits, awkward in social life, unfitted to jostle successfully in the robust and noisy world. Gray was still strongly attracted by Walpole's charm and gaiety, his unflagging energy and vivacity. 'Certain I am, there are many people in the world, who in their top spirits are no better éveillés, than you are at four in the morning, reclined upon your pillow.'[40] But it is clear that lately he had been subjecting himself, and in a lesser degree his friends, to a dispassionate, humorous and sometimes quite ruthless analysis; and such a scrutiny could not fail to reveal how much more he had in common with West than with Walpole.

He already realised and accepted the fact that he would always be a little apart in the world. Owing to the education which he had received and the friends whom he had chosen, he had outgrown any society that he could possibly have encountered at home. Yet he was temperamentally unsuited to Walpole's own world, an intimate society linked together by long-standing family and social connections, most formidable to a shy and clumsy young man of academic breeding and a commercial background. His instinctive good taste, his inborn love of elegance and refinement, attracted him to Walpole and all that Walpole represented; but he saw clearly enough that he would never make one of that circle, acquire its deceptively easy manners, or gain the approval of its lovely and intimidating women. To the end of his days he retained this wistful admiration for the graces of life, for people gifted with good looks, personal charm, self-confidence, the *bel air*. He recognised the superficial nature of all these qualities; he was growing to appreciate more and more the sterling worth of West, who lacked them, and to perceive the flaws in the character of Walpole, who was richly endowed with them; but they held a lifelong attraction for him. His good-tempered and unresentful sense of his own social inadequacies was summed up—a little cryptically perhaps, but the meaning is clear enough—in one of his letters to Walpole. After the shock of his mother's death in 1737, and his father's speedy remarriage to a long-established mistress, Walpole had sought the distraction of a mild love affair; upon which Gray wrote:

I don't wonder at the new study you have taken a liking to; first because it diverts your thoughts from disagreeable objects, next, because it particularly suits your Genius, and lastly, because I believe it the most excellent of all sciences, to which in proportion as the rest are subservient, so great a degree of estimation they

ought to gain: would you believe it, 'tis the very thing I would wish
to apply to, myself? ay! as simple as I stand here: but then the
Apparatus necessary to it costs so much; nay, part of it is wholly out
of one's power to procure; and then who should pare one, and
burnish one? for they would have more trouble and fuss with me,
than Cinderaxa's sisters had with their feet, to make 'em fit for the
little glass Slipper: oh yes! to be sure one must be lick'd; now to
lick oneself I take to be altogether impracticable, and to ask another
to lick one, would not be quite so civil; Bear I was born, and bear,
I believe, I'm like to remain: consequently a little ungainly in my
fondnesses, but I'll be bold to say, you shan't in a hurry meet with a
more loving poor animal, than

your faithful Creature,
BRUIN.[41]

Such passages as these, of clear-sighted self-analysis veiled
in a slightly rueful humour, are not infrequent in the letters
of Gray's early manhood; and they show that his character
was rapidly coming to maturity. He was, in fact, developing
an independence of judgement and a critical outspokenness
which Walpole was soon to find disconcerting. He continued
to be deeply attached to his friend; but the days of sentimental
hero-worship, of extravagant schoolboy affection, were gone
for ever. As he grew older he could not quite excuse the
youthful vanities and affectations which Walpole still retained.
Walpole must have sensed this change of attitude at the time,
and in retrospect he saw it still more clearly. Looking back,
after Gray's death, across the gulf of thirty years, he recalled
that 'we had not got to Calais before Gray was dissatisfied, for
I was a boy, and he, though infinitely more a man, was not
enough so to make allowances'.[42]

With this growing disharmony of character added to their
inequality of social position, the omens for the success of their
tour might not have seemed very propitious. Yet it is a mistake
to emphasise, at the start, those stresses and constraints which
grew up between them in the course of the next two years, or to
interpret literally Walpole's phrase about dissatisfaction at
Calais. Gray's contentment, when they left England in the

spring of 1739, was almost without a cloud. He was reprieved
from the long-dreaded bondage of chambers and law courts;
he was in the company of the friend to whom, for all his faults,
he was still devotedly attached; historic lands and cities, the
art and civilisation of all the centuries, awaited his exploration.
As for Walpole, he was determined to enjoy himself to the
utmost. The delights of the Grand Tour, the vistas of pleasure
which opened before a rich young man setting out on his
travels, had inspired Pope, just about this time, to some of his
most radiant lines; and no one can have set out more light-
heartedly than Walpole

> To where the Seine, obsequious as she runs,
> Pours at great Bourbon's feet her silken sons;
> Or Tyber, now no longer Roman, rolls,
> Vain of Italian Arts, Italian Souls:
> To happy Convents, bosom'd deep in vines,
> Where slumber Abbots, purple as their wines:
> To Isles of fragrance, lilly-silver'd vales,
> Diffusing languor in the panting gales:
> To lands of singing, or of dancing slaves,
> Love-whisp'ring woods, and lute-resounding waves.[43]

CHAPTER III

THE GRAND TOUR
1739-1741

I

WALPOLE and Gray left Dover at noon on 29 March 1739.
A brisk gale was blowing; and Gray, alone of the company, was
'extremely sick the whole time' until they landed at Calais, in
a snow-shower, after a crossing of five hours. They both
experienced that sensation of dreamlike strangeness which
haunts the traveller's first hours on foreign soil and is never
afterwards repeated. Gray told his mother that 'Calais is
an exceeding old, but very pretty town, and we hardly saw
any thing there that was not so new and so different from
England, that it surprized us agreeably'.[1] And Walpole,
after many months of varied travel, was also to confess that
Calais had surprised him more than anything he had since
seen.[2]

By the time they reached Paris their surprise at the novelty
of everything had waned, and their critical instincts had fully
revived. They had rolled in a comfortable postchaise through
Boulogne, dined at Montreuil 'on stinking mutton cutlets,
addle eggs and ditch water', found the inns 'not absolutely
intolerable', surveyed the Cathedral at Amiens, and admired
the royal monuments and the jewels and relics at St Denis.
When they arrived in Paris, late on a Saturday evening, they
were greeted by Walpole's cousins Lord Conway and Henry
Seymour Conway, and their friend Lord Holdernesse, who all
supped with them and stayed until two o'clock next morning.
It was a foretaste of the rather exacting round of social
activities into which they were immediately plunged.

Next day they dined with Lord Holdernesse, where the

party was entirely English, with the distinguished exception of the author of *Manon Lescaut*. The day after, they dined with the Ambassador, Lord Waldegrave. They went to ballets, operas, comedies; they received visits from a swarm of their compatriots; they spent hours every day in seeing churches and palaces and works of art. Henry Conway accompanied them everywhere, not having seen any of the sights before they arrived, 'for it is not the fashion here to have curiosity'. Gray equipped himself with clothes of high Parisian fashion—coat stiffened with buckram and gay with silk and fringe; waistcoat and breeches fashionably tight; long lace ruffles, an elegant muff; hair curled *en béquille*, and *à la négligée*, and tied with a big solitaire.[3] He was enjoying everything immensely—the absurdities of the opera, the delights of the ballet, the gay and varied crowds, the view along the *quais* from the Pont Neuf. 'I could entertain myself this month merely with the common streets and the people in them.' There is no reason to suggest that he was neglected because he stayed at home one evening to write to West while Walpole dined with Lord Conway, or to suspect a touch of social *malaise* when he mentioned in the letter that he had been invited too.[4]

Walpole was not quite so contented as Gray. His addiction to sight-seeing was less fervent, his interest in all varieties of social life a great deal stronger; and if Paris had nothing to offer beyond dinners and suppers in English company, he might as well have remained in London. Operas and comedies, and a glimpse of the Abbé Prévost, were all very well; but he wanted to see something of French society, and the *salons* of Paris did not open easily to young Englishmen who shunned high play and had an imperfect command of the language.[5] Two months exhausted the sights of Paris and its neighbourhood. Versailles was twice visited, its great front dismissed as 'a lumber of littleness', and due admiration bestowed upon the magnificent *coup d'œil* from the garden front; Gray was delighted with a rather hasty inspection of Trianon; and all three —Walpole, Gray and Conway—were pleased with a visit to

Chantilly.[6] Then Walpole determined, after changing his plans several times, that they should retire to some quiet provincial centre, and perfect their knowledge of the language by mixing with a less formidable and exclusive society than that of the capital. At the beginning of June, therefore, they moved to Rheims, taking Henry Conway with them. He was a cheerful and friendly young man, whom Gray had known at Eton and welcomed two years before when he paid a visit to Cambridge.[7] Walpole looked upon him more as a brother than a cousin, throughout his life.

Gray was reluctant to leave Paris, and complained a little in his letters to Ashton about Walpole's vagueness and indecision.[8] It is difficult to know how much importance to attach to such passages. The letters between all four members of the Quadruple Alliance, linked together as they had been in intimate friendship for so many years, are full of fine shades of meaning and private turns of phrase which they alone could interpret. No other reader can expect to break into that closed circle.

Our tête à tête conversations, that you enquire after, did consist less in words, than in looks and signs, and to give you a notion of them, I ought to send you our pictures; tho' we should find it difficult to set for 'em in such attitudes, as we very naturally fall into, when alone together. At present Mr Conway, who lives with us, joins to make them a little more verbose, and every thing is mighty well.[9]

What is the true meaning of this passage in a letter from Gray to Ashton? It might equally well be a sarcasm, or a grumble, or a light-hearted joke—Ashton would have known, but we are not so clear. It is certain, however, that Gray said something about Walpole, in one particular letter to West, which hurt Walpole's feelings when he came upon it in helping Mason to prepare Gray's biography many years later. 'You see', he told Mason, 'how easily I had disgusted him; but my faults were very trifling, and I can bear their being known, and forgive his displeasure. I still think I was as much to blame as he was; and as the passage proves what I have told you, let it stand, if you publish the whole letter.'[10]

Mason did not publish any part of the letter, and it no longer exists; but it probably contained nothing very scathing, and Gray's irritation seems to have quickly subsided. Lord Conway had lately spent some time at Rheims, and his brother and his friends were now made welcome at the assemblies and card parties of the leading inhabitants. It was a dull and formal little society; but on one occasion, at least, its younger members displayed an unpremeditated gaiety which delighted Walpole and inspired Gray with one of the happiest of all his impressions of travel.

The other evening we happened to be got together in a company of eighteen people, men and women of the best fashion here, at a garden in the town to walk; where one of the ladies bethought herself of asking, Why should not we sup here? Immediately the cloth was laid by the side of a fountain under the trees, and a very elegant supper served up; after which another said, Come, let us sing; and directly began herself: From singing we insensibly fell to dancing, and singing in a round; when somebody mentioned the violins, and immediately a company of them was ordered: Minuets were begun in the open air, and then came country-dances, which held till four o'clock next morning; at which hour the gayest lady there proposed, that such as were weary should get into their coaches, and the rest of them should dance before them with the music in the van; and in this manner we paraded through all the principal streets of the city, and waked every body in it.[11]

No, Gray was certainly not unhappy at Rheims. The shy young man from Cambridge and Cornhill could enter without embarrassment into such simple gaieties as these. Now that the first strains of foreign travel had been adjusted, he was able to settle down with Walpole contentedly enough for months to come. Many years afterwards, when describing for Walpole's benefit an old print of a family group, he wrote: 'The room is just such a one as we lived in at Rheims.'[12]

As the result of much conversation and some genuine hard work, their command of the language quickly improved during their stay at Rheims. 'You must not wonder', Walpole told West, 'if all my letters resemble dictionaries, with French on one side and English on t'other.'[13] They had intended to go on to Dijon at the end of July; but two friends and Eton contemporaries of Walpole's, George Selwyn and George Montagu, wrote proposing to join them at Rheims. In the end the whole party lingered there for a further month, rather to the annoyance of Gray, who was longing to travel in the south of France before the coming of autumn. Selwyn and Montagu, agreeable and mildly eccentric characters both, were to figure afterwards among Walpole's closest friends and most regular correspondents; but Gray never found them particularly congenial, and saw little of them in subsequent life. At the end of August they returned to England; and Walpole, Gray and Conway moved on to Dijon early in September.

They stayed only a few days at the pleasant city of Dijon, just long enough to make them regret that they had wasted so many weeks at Rheims, and then went on to Lyons, which they enjoyed much less. Conway had arranged to spend the winter at Geneva; and towards the end of September he and his friends set out once more, taking the longer road through Dauphiné and Savoy in order to visit the monastery of the Grande Chartreuse. They had known nothing hitherto of mountains or torrents, crags or forests; and as the road left the autumnal lowlands and bore them into the landscape of a different world, they were filled with astonishment and exultation. At Echelles they left the main road and climbed to the monastery on mules, along the narrow winding path between the overhanging rocks above and the stupendous precipice below. They spent two hours at the Grande Chartreuse, were shown round and kindly entertained by the two guest-masters, and urged to stay some days among the silent brethren; but in the evening they retraced their path to the village below, through the same fabulous landscape, now veiled in places by the fast-gathering clouds. It was an experience that moved them both profoundly, though in very different ways. To Walpole it seemed that they were moving through a magnificent picture, some incomparable canvas of Salvator Rosa.

But the road, West, the road! winding round a prodigious mountain, and surrounded with others, all shagged with hanging woods, obscured with pines or lost in clouds! Below, a torrent breaking through cliffs, and tumbling through fragments of rocks! Sheets of cascades forcing their silver speed down channelled precipices, and hasting into the roughened river at the bottom! Now and then an old foot-bridge, with a broken rail, a leaning cross, a cottage, or the ruin of an hermitage! This sounds too bombast and romantic to one that has not seen it, too cold for one that has. If I could send you my letter post between two lovely tempests that echoed each other's wrath, you might have some idea of this noble roaring scene, as you were reading it. We...rode back through this charming picture, wished for a painter, wished to be poets! Need I tell you we wished for you?[14]

To Gray that unforgettable ride was of far deeper significance. It stirred, as nothing had previously done, the poetry that slumbered within him, the poetry of which the quiet scholar and the elegant Latinist had as yet given no sign; so that Walpole could write that 'we wished to be poets' without a suspicion that the greatest poet of their generation had been jogging on mule-back at his side. It made the most profound and solemn appeal to his religious convictions. In a letter to West, written several weeks afterwards, he described the beauty and awe of the experience which was still vividly present in his mind:

I own I have not, as yet, anywhere met with those grand and simple works of Art, that are to amaze one, and whose sight one is to be the better for: But those of Nature have astonished me beyond expression. In our little journey up to the Grande Chartreuse, I do not remember to have gone ten paces without an exclamation, that there was no restraining: Not a precipice, not a torrent, not a cliff, but is pregnant with religion and poetry. There are certain scenes that would awe an atheist into belief, without the help of other argument.[15]

They spent a few days at Geneva, saw Conway settled there, and returned by a different route to Lyons. It had been their intention to pass the winter in the south of France; but Walpole now received a letter from Sir Robert, giving him leave to extend his travels into Italy. Gray was delighted at the unexpected news. 'You may imagine I am not sorry to have this opportunity of seeing the place in the world that best deserves it',[16] he told his father, whose permission for this prolongation of his absence he seems to have taken for granted. His long devotion to classical studies, his awakening interest in painting and sculpture, were now to be richly rewarded. Walpole was almost equally pleased; and it was in complete harmony, and with the fullest anticipations of enjoyment, that they set out from Lyons on the last day of October upon the second stage of their travels.

II

The journey from Lyons to Turin lasted eight days. Winter was fast approaching, and the weather had turned foggy and cold. The crossing of the Alps was full of dangers and excitements, and even Gray was forced to admit that Mont Cenis 'carries the permission mountains have of being frightful rather too far'. On the sixth day, as their chaise crawled slowly along a narrow road with a precipice yawning below, a wolf sprang out of the fir trees on the other side and carried off Walpole's little spaniel Tory, who was waddling placidly along beside the horses. At the foot of the Mont Cenis pass the chaise had to be dismantled, and loaded, with the rest of their baggage, on mules; while they themselves were 'swathed in beaver bonnets, beaver gloves, beaver stockings, muffs, and bear-skins', and carried in matted chairs attached to poles. At the highest point of the road across Mont Cenis their bearers indulged in a drunken fight, with the muffled travellers sitting helpless and exasperated in their chairs. At one moment Gray's party rushed him past Walpole's party 'on a crag, where there was scarce room for a cloven foot—the least slip had tumbled us into such a fog, and such an eternity, as we should never have found our way out of again'.[17] But eighteenth-century England was not to lose her poet and her historian down an Alpine chasm. Peace was restored, and they embarked on a descent of terrifying swiftness, out of the snow and cloud of the mountains into a new climate and a new language.

After ten days at Turin, which did not provide much entertainment, they went on to Genoa, and spent a week of delight exploring the city in the winter sunshine of the Mediterranean.

Only figure to yourself [wrote Gray] a vast semicircular bason, full of fine blue sea, and vessels of all sorts and sizes, some sailing out, some coming in, and others at anchor; and all round it palaces and churches peeping over one another's heads, gardens and marble terrases full of orange and cypress trees, fountains, and trellis-works covered with vines, which altogether compose the grandest of theatres....We find this place so very fine, that we are in fear of finding nothing finer.[18]

Then they set out again for Bologna, by way of Piacenza, Parma, Reggio and Modena. After several days of strenuous sight-seeing at Bologna they made an uneventful crossing of the Apennines, and reached Florence on 16 December. Here they settled down for the winter as the guests of Horace Mann, who was then acting as *chargé d'affaires* for Mr Fane, the absentee British Minister at the Court of Tuscany.

Horace Mann was distantly related to the Walpole family, and owed his position and his prospects to the good offices of Sir Robert. He was some fifteen years older than Walpole and Gray, a fastidious invalidish bachelor. His principal duties were to keep a watchful eye on the movements of the exiled Stuarts and their sympathisers in Italy, and to assist and entertain the English travellers who were constantly passing through Florence. He found the newcomers agreeably different from the ordinary run of the 'travelling boys', the shy or boisterous youths performing their Grand Tour in the charge of a pedantic tutor. They were all soon on terms of cordial friendship, so that even the diffident Gray pronounced him 'the best and most obliging person in the world'.

Next evening Mann introduced them at an assembly of the Prince de Craon, who acted as Regent for the Grand Duke.

The Prince was 'extremely civil to the name of Walpole', and the travellers found themselves made welcome everywhere in Florence. They spent their mornings exploring the streets, the churches, above all the paintings assembled in the Palazzo Pitti and the fabulous collection of sculpture in 'the famous Gallery', the Uffizi. Gray's previous experience of classical statuary and Italian painting can only have served as a meagre introduction to the profusion of masterpieces now ranged before him;* but now in Florence and later in Rome he spent day after day in studying every available collection, and writing down his impressions of each painting and each statue in his crowded notebooks.[19] He ignored, and continued to ignore throughout his travels in Italy, the primitives and the painters of the *quattrocento*. His notes on certain works of Raphael, Parmegiano, Giorgione, Veronese, Titian expressed a temperate admiration; but his warmest eulogies were reserved for the masters of the seventeenth century—Annibale Caracci, Dominichino, Guercino, Pietro da Cortona, Salvator Rosa, Carlo Maratti, and above all Guido Reni. At the Palazzo Borghese in Rome, after contemplating several pictures by Raphael, Titian and Andrea del Sarto, he could find 'in none of them all, that heavenly grace and beauty, that Guido gave, and that Carlo Maratti has so well imitated'.[20] His artistic standards were, in fact, those of the best contemporary critics —of the Président de Brosses, who was writing his *Lettres d'Italie* during these same years; and of the younger Jonathan Richardson, whose book of notes on Italian paintings and statues he carried with him, and whose footsteps he followed through many a gallery and church.† But if his judgements were conventional enough, he expressed them with the liveliness and unconventionality of a natural writer.

* At this time the principal assemblage of classical sculpture in England was the Arundelian collection at Oxford, where Gray had never been. The greatest collection of Italian painting was Sir Robert Walpole's at Houghton. Gray may have visited Houghton, but there is no record of his having done so.

† *An Account of the Statues, Bas-reliefs, Drawings and Pictures in Italy, France &c.* (1722). Edited from the younger Richardson's notes and letters by his father the painter, it was a favourite guide-book for several decades.

Walpole, however, did not much approve of all this note-taking. He also spent long hours in the Gallery, was at intervals a diligent sight-seer, and hazarded speculations upon some lines of Virgil in a letter to West. But the delights of fashionable life were becoming ever more alluring, and he began to grow a little weary of the splendours of the past.

I see several things that please me calmly [he told West] but *à force d'en avoir vû* I have left off screaming Lord! this, and Lord! that. To speak sincerely, Calais surprised me more than anything I have seen since. I recollect the joy I used to propose if I could but once see the Grand Duke's gallery; I walk into it now with as little emotion as I should into St. Paul's.[21]

He told his friends that he did not intend to send them detailed descriptions of everything he saw. 'Only think what a vile employment 'tis, making catalogues!'[22] But Gray was making catalogues day after day; and at times Walpole found himself growing impatient with so much bookishness and learning. Such moods did not last long, since Gray was still perfectly willing to enter into any fun that was going. When, for example, a Florentine *cavaliere* had a difference with an English painter, and appeared at Mann's dinner-table to inquire if the painter's birth was high enough to justify a challenge, 'Gray and I flew behind the curtain of the door', and later sallied out in a coach in the hope of witnessing the duel.[23] All the same Walpole sometimes wished—though at this stage the wish remained unspoken—that his companion was slightly less erudite and slightly more versed in the social graces.

Carnival began, and Walpole plunged into its gaieties. 'I have done nothing but slip out of my domino into bed, and out of bed into my domino. The end of the Carnival is frantic, bacchanalian; all the morn one makes parties to the shops and coffee-houses, and all the evening to the operas and balls. *Then I have danced, good Gods! how have I danced!*'[24] He enjoyed the life of Florence more and more; his letters are full of its delights. Gray's letters said nothing of Carnival, and little of the sober Lenten weeks which followed it. But in February the Pope, Clement XII, died, and towards the end of March the travellers left for Rome in order to witness the ceremonies and festivities which would mark the election of his successor.

From the moment when he first saw the dome of St Peter's shadowed on the distant horizon, Gray surrendered completely to the spell of Rome. 'As high as my expectation was raised, I confess, the magnificence of this city infinitely surpasses it. You cannot pass along a street but you have views of some palace, or church, or square, or fountain, the most picturesque and noble one can imagine.'[25] Fascinated, he watched the pageantry and splendour of the Easter ceremonies at St Peter's. Once again his notes began to accumulate, page after page of detailed and lively description of churches and palaces, pictures and statues and the relics of antiquity.[26] He explored with Walpole the classic ground of the Campagna, tracing at Tivoli and Albano, with plentiful quotations, the familiar scenes of his school-books. At a grand ball at the Villa Patrizi, 'where the world danced, and I sat in a corner regaling myself with iced fruits, and other pleasant rinfrescatives', he was able to contemplate 'the rueful length of person' of King James the Third, with his two sons and his dejected little court around him. And he tried to communicate to West, drearily occupied with his law-books in London, the beauty of the southern nights. 'There is a moon! there are stars for you! Do not you hear the fountain? Do not you smell the orange flowers?'[27]

Gray was, in fact, completely happy. Walpole was restless and bored. He found Roman society much less congenial than the society of Florence; he was vaguely dissatisfied with the pleasures of travel, telling West once more that 'curiosity and astonishment wear off'.[28] He and Gray addressed joint letters to West and Ashton, which were perfectly harmonious in tone; but again there is a suspicion that he was growing tired of Gray's classical enthusiasms, his fund of quotations and allusions. This attitude is revealed briefly but unmistakably in a letter to Ashton. 'By a considerable volume of charts and pyramids, which I saw at Florence, I thought it threatened a publication. His travels have really improved him; I wish they may do the same for anyone else.'[29] It is easy to recognise the supercilious tones, the impatience of the brilliant amateur watching the laborious scholar. In spite of occasional frictions of this kind, however, there was as yet no serious discord between Walpole and Gray. Prolonged travel can be an exacting test of any friendship; and this friendship was still bearing the strain quite creditably.

All this time the Conclave was dragging on, providing Rome with endless stories of the intrigues and the tribulations of the immured cardinals, but advancing no nearer to the choice of a Pope. Walpole decided in the middle of June to make a few days' excursion to Naples. Gray described their journey, and the sights of Naples and its neighbourhood, in the liveliest and most readable of all his journals of travel;[30] and repeated more briefly, in a letter to his mother, his impressions of that smiling countryside, those delectable shores and that swarming population.

The great old fig-trees, the oranges in full bloom, and myrtles in every hedge, make one of the delightfullest scenes you can conceive; besides that, the roads are wide, well-kept, and full of passengers, a sight I have not beheld this long time.... The common sort are a jolly lively kind of animals, more industrious than Italians usually are; they work till evening; then take their lute or guitar (for they all play) and walk about the city, or upon the sea-shore with it, to enjoy the fresco. One sees their little brown children jumping about stark-naked, and the bigger ones dancing with castanets, while others play on the cymbal to them....[31]

On their return they found the Conclave no nearer a decision; and Walpole, tired of Roman society and apprehensive of 'a horrid thing called the *mal'aria*', determined to spend the rest of the summer at Florence. Gray left with sadness, conscious that he was unlikely ever to return to Rome, unlikely ever to revisit those scenes with all their beauty and all their inexhaustible wealth of association. Nevertheless Florence had many compensations. They lived in Casa Ambrogi, a pleasant small house which lay between the Via de' Bardi and the Arno, so that from the northward windows it was possible to fish in the river below. Mann used it as a guest-house for his friends, and during these years seems to have lived there himself as much as at his official residence, Casa Manetti in the Via Santo Spirito.[32] He proved once again the most agreeable of hosts; the climate was perfect; the summer days and nights drifted by in happy idleness. Gray occasionally repined a little. Florence, he told West, was 'an excellent place to employ all one's animal sensations in, but utterly contrary to one's rational powers. I have struck a medal upon myself: the device is thus O, and the motto *Nihilissimo*, which I take in the most concise manner to contain a full account of my person, sentiments, occupations, and late glorious successes.' But on the whole he accepted contentedly enough the easy indolent way of life that suited Walpole so well. 'Here you shall get up at twelve o'clock, breakfast till three, dine till five, sleep till six, drink cooling liquors till eight, go to the bridge till ten, sup till two, and so sleep till twelve again.'[33]

Horace Mann had now succeeded the absent Mr Fane as British Minister at Florence, and was to remain undisturbed in that post until his death forty-six years later. His duties were mainly of a social nature, which exactly suited his inclinations, and his house was already a favourite meeting-place for English and Florentines. That intricate society of *cicisbeo* and *cicisbea*, with all the additional complications of its Tuscan and Lorraine rivalries, mingled in his rooms with young Englishmen and their tutors on their travels, with English families in search of health or amusement, with the expatriates, reputable and far otherwise, who for various reasons had made Italy their home. Florentine matrons were confronted with Lady Mary Wortley Montagu, a pathetic but still indomitable shadow of her former brilliance; or with Lady

Pomfret and Lady Walpole, a discreditable sister-in-law of Horace, both of whom had intellectual pretensions and 'incessantly debated a rhapsody of mystic nonsense'.[34] Walpole himself became the *cavaliere servente* of Elisabetta Capponi, Marchesa Grifoni, one of the most beautiful women in Florence.

Gray quietly watched the stream of life that flowed through the halls and salons of the *palazzi*, and along 'the charming bridge'—the Ponte di Santa Trinità—where everyone used to meet in the warm nights. He always enjoyed fine company in which he could play the part of an inconspicuous spectator, as at the ball in Rome, 'where the world danced, and I sat in a corner'. There was nothing of the recluse about him at this time; he was on excellent terms with Mann, and took his share in the day-to-day life of the house. He is mentioned by Walpole[35] as joining a party of young travellers, including Edward Coke, the son of the builder of Holkham, and Sir Francis Dashwood, the future leader of the revels at Medmenham, in drawing the *Sortes Virgilianae* for all their acquaintances.* And he and Walpole both found a most congenial friend in a contemporary of Mann's, John Chute, who was travelling with his young cousin, Francis Whithed, and came to spend a few months in Florence at this time. Chute was a curious figure—a Hampshire country gentleman who had spent much of his life wandering about Europe, a man of taste and learning, a skilful amateur architect, nervous, short-sighted, tormented with gout, affected and extravagant in manner. To casual observers he seemed the most tiresome kind of *inglese italianato*, and Mann once described in a letter to Walpole how a dinner-party of ordinary English travellers 'disliked his fan extremely'. But under all this nonsense lay a hard core of courage, ability and common sense; and although he only figured occasionally in Gray's later life, Walpole regarded him to the end of his days as his most reliable and trusted friend.

* The sentence drawn for Lady Mary Wortley Montagu, *Insanam vatem aspicies*, struck Walpole as being extraordinarily apposite.

III

The happy summer drew to its close. Far away in Vienna the Emperor Charles VI died in October; reluctantly the Tuscan subjects of his son-in-law put an end to their gaieties, and not even the winter carnival could be held. Life at Florence began to grow tedious; and the lack of diversion seems to have brought into the light of day the latent disagreements between Gray and Walpole. Minor irritations and causes for mutual criticism could be kept in the background whilst the tides of social life were flowing strongly; but now the little group at Casa Ambrogi became conscious of a growing antagonism between the two friends.

It is unlikely that any pair of travellers, however phlegmatic, could have weathered two years of an eighteenth-century Grand Tour in a state of unruffled amiability. Both Gray and Walpole were excitable, emotional, deeply sensitive young men; and considering the differences between them in tastes and interests, in rank and fortune, it is remarkable that they had continued so long in reasonable harmony. More than once we have noted Walpole's boredom with his companion's learned preoccupations, the note-taking, the poring over guide-books, the quotations, the constant presence of Livy and Silius Italicus in the chaise. These tendencies, which it was so easy for Walpole to dismiss as pedantry, had not grown less at Florence. Gray spent weeks in assembling and copying out a great collection of manuscript music, of which nine volumes still survive; and music, except as an adjunct to social life, was wholly outside Walpole's range. Gray had also embarked on an ambitious didactic poem in Latin hexameters upon the philosophy of Locke. With all its fine lines and stately phrases, *De Principiis Cogitandi* is a somewhat forbidding production to have absorbed the energies of a youthful poet in such a city as Florence.

Walpole may have complained with some justice of this strain of pedantry in Gray; but Gray had greater cause to

HORACE WALPOLE

From a pastel by Rosalba Carriera, in the possession of Lord Walpole

condemn Walpole, whose head was thoroughly turned by his success at Florence, on the grounds of selfishness and arrogance. In after years Walpole readily admitted his own shortcomings, and was willing to shoulder most of the blame for their disagreements. It is fitting at this stage to quote the explanation which he gave in a private letter to Mason after Gray's death:

> I am conscious, that in the beginning of the differences between Gray and me, the fault was mine. I was too young, too fond of my own diversions, nay, I do not doubt, too much intoxicated by indulgence, vanity, and the insolence of my situation, as a Prime Minister's son, not to have been inattentive and insensible to the feelings of one I thought below me; of one, I blush to say it, that I knew was obliged to me; of one whom presumption and folly perhaps made me deem not my superior *then* in parts, though I have since felt my infinite inferiority to him. I treated him insolently; he loved me, and I did not think he did. I reproached him with the difference between us, when he acted from conviction of knowing he was my superior. I often disregarded his wishes of seeing places, which I would not quit other amusements to visit, though I offered to send him to them without me. Forgive me, if I say that his temper was not conciliating; at the same time that I will confess to you that he acted a more friendly part, had I had the sense to take advantage of it—he freely told me of my faults. I declared I did not desire to hear them, nor would correct them. You will not wonder that with the dignity of his spirit, and the obstinate carelessness of mine, the breach must have grown wider, till we became incompatible.[36]

That is Walpole's version of the affair, told with candour and generosity many years later, and there is no reason to disbelieve it.* On several points it is supported by contemporary evidence. For example, his disregard of Gray's fondness for sight-seeing is shown in one of his own letters to West, in which he almost boasts of not having seen Leghorn, Pisa, Lucca, Pistoia or even the villas of the Grand Duke, although they had now spent six months at Florence.[37] There can be no doubt that Gray would have liked to visit these

---

* Walpole also wrote a short paragraph, in which he adopted much the same attitude, for Mason to include in the *Memoirs of Gray* on which he was then engaged.

places, yet would have felt humiliated at the very thought of being sent off to see them alone, with Walpole's equipage and servants and at his expense. And a more important point which Walpole also makes, the greater intellectual maturity of Gray at this time, is clearly evident from Gray's letters to West. These letters contain passages of penetrating self-analysis, and passages of ruthlessly sensible advice upon West's varied perplexities, which demonstrate that Gray had far outgrown his companion in mental stature. As he explained to Mason, Walpole could not then regard his school-fellow and travelling companion, with the middle-class background and the diffident retiring manners, as his superior in any possible respect. And he was disconcerted and indignant when Gray allowed his consciousness of superiority to appear, and roundly told the much-courted young man, the Prime Minister's son and the successful lover of the admired Grifona, that he was behaving like a spoilt child. 'He loved me, and I did not think he did.' Walpole could not divine that the old affection still lay behind those untimely remonstrances.

So matters went on until the spring, with Mann and Chute watching the increasing estrangement of their two friends and powerless to check it. It had long been Walpole's intention to leave Florence for Venice in April, and then to return by slow stages to England. Despite the unhappiness of the last months Gray had grown attached to Florence, and now he said farewell in some Latin verses to the Arno and the groves of Fiesole, the villas among their cypresses, the white houses scattered over the hillsides. A few days before they left, with his thoughts already turning to England and the friend whom he had not seen for so long, he sent West a remarkable summing-up of the alterations which he had perceived in his own character since they last talked together:

Methinks I ought to send you my picture (for I am no more what I was, some circumstances excepted, which I hope I need not particularize to you); you must add then, to your former idea, two years of age, reasonable quantity of dullness, a great deal of silence, and something that rather resembles, than is, thinking; a confused notion of many strange and fine things that have swum before my eyes for some time, a want of love for general society, indeed an inability to it. On the good side you may add a sensibility for what others feel, and indulgence for their faults or weaknesses, a love of truth, and detestation of everything else. Then you are to deduct a little impertinence, a little laughter, a great deal of pride, and some spirits. These are all the alterations I know of, you perhaps may find more. Think not that I have been obliged for this reformation of manners to reason or reflection, but to a severer schoolmistress, Experience. One has little merit in learning her lessons, for one cannot well help it; but they are more useful than others, and imprint themselves in the very heart.[38]

Walpole and Gray set out from Florence at the end of April. Chute and Whithed were with them, and a young man named Francesco Suarez, the son of a Florentine *grande dame* who figures much in Mann's letters. The party stopped for a few days at Bologna, and then went on to Reggio. There they found the great annual fair in full swing, with its attendant operas, balls and masquerades. In the midst of all these diversions something took place, towards the middle of May, which caused a violent quarrel between Gray and Walpole. They parted in anger and resentment. Gray went on to Venice in company with Chute and Whithed, and Walpole stayed behind at Reggio.

For some weeks their relations had been so strained that the final breach may have been brought about by some quite trivial occurrence. Although it is unlikely that the facts will ever be known, there is a persistent tradition that their quarrel at Reggio was in some way connected with a letter. The least probable version, and one which rests on very poor authority, accuses Walpole of opening one of Gray's letters because he suspected it to contain criticisms of himself.[39] Another explanation is that Gray had made some complaint in a letter to Ashton, who had promptly and characteristically divulged the fact to Walpole. This is perhaps supported by Gray's remark, when describing the part played by Ashton in the reconciliation four years later, that 'he I found was to be angry about the letter I had wrote him'.[40] And some letter of Gray's is likewise mentioned by Mann, who had been told by Walpole of what had happened and wrote to him in a rather agitated strain on 23 May:

From an horrid uneasiness I find, and in justice to Gray (from whom I have received no letter or wrote to, though I designed to have done it last Saturday but was prevented by my fever) I cannot help adding two or three lines to assure you that in the late affair except writing that letter he was not so much to blame as on the sight of it you might imagine. I take the greatest part of the fault on myself and I am convinced of his regard for you; nay I have been witness to his uneasiness and tears when he suspected you had less confidence in him than his inward and real friendship for you made him think he deserved. This I think myself bound in justice to tell you, as I believed him sincere. As to the oddness of his behaviour with C— and the particulars you mention and Bologna, they indeed surprised me much, and would almost induce me to give another turn to the whole.* Adieu, my dear Sir, I can say no more, but that I heartily wish you could forget all that has passed.[41]

It is clear that Mann, who had been told all the details of the quarrel, thought that a reconciliation was possible and did his best to bring it about. In his next letter, written a few days later, he made another appeal on Gray's behalf. 'It gives me too much uneasiness to think of the late affair and the despair G. is in, therefore I will not enter into any detail, I do beseech you only that you will reflect on what I wrote in my last and a former letter about it, I can only say that you have it in you to do a most generous action, to forget and forgive. I would ask it on my knees if I was with you.'[42] In the meantime Walpole, left alone at Reggio, had suddenly developed a violent attack of quinsy; and it was only the opportune arrival of Lord Lincoln and his tutor, the amiable man of letters Joseph Spence, that procured proper medical treatment and perhaps saved his life. On his recovery he followed Mann's advice and

---

* The sentence about C—was crossed out by Walpole, but is still legible. The reference may be either to Chute or to Francesco Suarez, who was nicknamed 'Cecco'. Both were at Reggio at the time of the quarrel.

made some overtures to Gray, who came back from Venice but angrily rejected his offers of reconciliation. The only mention of this interview occurs in yet another letter from Mann:

> I received yours of the 2nd [June] and to my greatest surprise read the account therein of the interview, which I fear has destroyed all the hopes of a reconciliation with which I flattered myself, for the reasons I mentioned at large in a former letter. I must own I wished it extremely and should have been happy to be the means of bringing it about. I was astonished to see the terms and the reproaches, and much more that he could withstand your entreaties to return with you to England. I am highly sensible my dear Sir this was done at my request and heartily thank you for this proof of your goodness. I cannot help repeating again how sorry I am it had no effect but I will not dwell on so disagreeable a subject or trouble you any more on this affair.[43]

After this stormy scene Gray returned to Venice. Walpole followed a few days later, and established himself in a house on the Grand Canal where Chute and Whithed were already living. Some writers have sugested that Gray also may have lodged in this house. Undoubtedly he was still on terms of undiminished friendship with the other two; yet it hardly seems possible that he would have risked the embarrassment of frequent meetings with Walpole after all that had passed between them. Since Walpole had been paying all the expenses of their tour, he was now almost penniless; he had even been obliged to borrow ten *zecchini*, presumably from Chute, for his journey back to Reggio for the interview at which he destroyed the last chances of reconciliation. Although he had at once written to his parents in England for credit, some time would have to elapse before this could be arranged; and Mann, at Walpole's request, arranged for him to draw for money on Mr Smith, the British consul at Venice.

> I wrote formerly to Gray [Mann told Walpole] to offer him what money he might want as you directed me and punctually followed your orders in not mentioning your name in it, so that I am persuaded he thinks it came from me. He has I hear taken up

4-0 *zecchini* of Mr Smith.... This affair you see is delicate as I am unwilling to let Gray think he is obliged to me, and yet I have wholly concealed it from him because you insisted upon it.[44]

Venice can have offered little enjoyment to Gray, as he waited anxiously for the remittances which would enable him to return to England. In happier circumstances he would have been delighted by its beauty and strangeness—the churches and palaces and paintings, the gaiety and pageantry, the thronged canals, the motley crowds on Piazza and Piazzetta, the associations which the republic preserved with the mysterious East. But now everything was overclouded; and neither he nor Walpole ever spoke or wrote again of their stay in Venice, which to many travellers was the most fascinating experience of the whole Grand Tour. Towards the middle of July his letters of credit arrived, and he set out for home, with a single *laquais du voyage* in place of Walpole's elaborate equipage of carriages and servants. He travelled at a leisurely pace, spending a few days in Padua, Verona and Milan, and by 15 August had reached Turin. Next day he began to cross the Alps, and made a detour in order to revisit the Grande Chartreuse.[45]

It was almost two years since the September day when he and Walpole had ridden through that stupendous landscape, 'pregnant with religion and poetry'. Once again, but now alone, he was among those torrents, those forests, those precipices. On this occasion he must have passed a day or two, and perhaps longer, as the guest of the monks, and during his stay he composed his famous *Alcaic Ode*. The poem was suggested by their ideals of retirement and religious contemplation, and he inscribed it in the album which they kept at the monastery; but he contrived to give it a deeply personal note. In eloquent and dignified Latin he invoked the ' severi Religio loci', the deity whose presence he could feel in those awesome surroundings as never among the gold, the marble, the candles and incense of St Peter's or St Mark's. And he offered his own petition for retirement, for silence, for peace of mind—if not in his perplexed and anxious youth, then at least in his later years:

> ...Salve vocanti ritè, fesso et
> Da placidam juveni quietem.
>
> Quod si invidendis sedibus, et frui
> Fortuna sacrâ lege silentii
> Vetat volentem, me resorbens
> In medios violenta fluctus,
>
> Saltem remoto des, Pater, angulo
> Horas senectae ducere liberas;
> Tutumque vulgari tumultu
> Surripias, hominumque curis.*

In this solemn mood Gray resumed his journey. He did not linger in Paris to recapture memories of the first care-free weeks of his travels. At the beginning of September he landed once more in England, and returned to his parents' house in Cornhill.

---

* 'Be gracious to him who calls thus solemnly upon Thee, and grant repose to soothe his young but weary head. And if fate yields not to my longing for that happy home, where silence rules by divine decree, sucking me rudely back into the mid-waves of the world, grant, Father, this at least—that when I am grown old I may in some secluded corner lead a life that is truly mine, and withdraw me safe away from the tumult of the crowd and the cares that vex mankind.'

Mr S. C. Roberts has pointed out (*Thomas Gray of Pembroke*, p. 10) the anticipations in this Ode of the 'madding crowd' and the 'sequester'd vale' of the *Elegy*. It is significant also that at a later time of trouble, after his stormy exit from Peterhouse, he found himself at Pembroke 'as quiet as in the Grande Chartreuse'.

CHAPTER IV

THE EARLY POEMS AND THE
DEATH OF WEST
1741-1742

I

GRAY had been away from England for almost two and a half years, and the process of readjustment was not easy for him. The situation at his home was more depressing than ever. His father was just as ill-tempered and just as secretive about his business affairs, and his health was now failing rapidly. The atmosphere of London, with its brusque manners and jostling crowds, contrasted strangely with the ease and leisure of life in Italy. The war against Spain, into which the nation had plunged so eagerly two years before, was going badly, and everyone seemed worried and disagreeable. It was, of course, delightful to see West at last, and talk of books and poetry, and pour into his sympathetic ear the exact circumstances of the quarrel with Walpole. But when a long and cordial letter arrived from Chute, who by now had returned to Florence, enclosing another letter from Mann, he was overwhelmed with longing to be once again with his friends in that pleasant house beside the Arno:

If this be London [he wrote in reply] Lord send me to Constantinople. Either I, or it are extremely odd. The Boys laugh at the depth of my Ruffles, the immensity of my Bagg, and the length of my Sword. I am as an alien in my native land, yea! I am as an Owl among the small birds. It rains, every body is discontented, and so am I. You can't imagine how mortifieing it is to fall into the hands of an English Barber.

Then, after much more in the same strain, the customary gay badinage of Casa Ambrogi, he continued with touching seriousness:

Now I have been at home, and seen how things go there, would I might be with you again, that the Remainder of my Dream might at least be agreeable. As it is, my prospect can not well be more unpleasing; but why do I trouble your Goodnature with such considerations? Be assured, that when I am happy (if that can ever be) your esteem will greatly add to that happiness, and when most the contrary, will always alleviate, what I suffer.[1]

These were sad words, echoing the sombre mood of the *Alcaic Ode*; but up to a point they were justified. His future prospects were depressing enough. He would soon complete his twenty-fifth year, and was as yet unqualified for a profession; nor did he feel the least inclination to follow any profession at all. He could no longer hope that the Walpole influence, still powerful in many quarters even though Sir Robert's long reign was drawing to its close, would now be exerted for his benefit. And when early in November his father died, worn out by repeated attacks of gout, the financial position of the family was found to be very insecure. Philip Gray, besides refusing to contribute to the support of his wife and son, had for some years habitually neglected his business; and he had lately thought fit to build a large and expensive country house at Wanstead in Essex. His family were told nothing about it, and were shocked to find that a large portion of his depleted savings had been sunk in this pointless enterprise.[2]

Gray remained in London throughout the winter, trying to disentangle his father's affairs, and seeing few people besides West and possibly Ashton. Walpole had returned to England a fortnight or so after Gray, and was living with his father in Downing Street; he had been elected a Member of Parliament during his absence abroad, and was now immersed in the long and fluctuating struggle which preceded Sir Robert's fall from power. No communication took place between him and Gray, although the amiable Henry Conway had written Gray a sympathetic letter and had perhaps tried to bring about a reconciliation between them. West's friendship with Walpole was still maintained; and Ashton, now in orders and beginning to be known as a promising young preacher, had become a member of the Prime Minister's household in Downing Street while he awaited the vacancy of a suitable Crown living. Either or both of them may have attempted to re-establish the Quadruple Alliance upon its former basis; if so, they met with no success.

It may have been during this winter also that Gray had a conversation with Pope. The fact that they met at all is known only from a passage in a letter written two years after Pope's death. 'It is not from what he told me about himself', said Gray, 'that I thought well of him, but from a Humanity and Goodness of Heart, ay, and Greatness of Mind, that runs thro his private Correspondence, not less apparent than are a thousand little Weaknesses and Vanities mixed with those good Qualities, for no body ever took him for a Philosopher'.[3] Nothing else has been recorded about their interview; but the two greatest poets of the eighteenth century had at least touched hands.

II

It was the companionship of West, however, that made those winter months most memorable for Gray. In earlier years he had been dazzled by Walpole's worldly charm; now, bitterly disillusioned, he was able to appreciate the true value of West's friendship. Theirs was a relationship, moreover, in which Gray was able to give more than he received. West was ill and unhappy, deeply conscious of his loneliness as he drifted through an unsympathetic world. He had poured out his troubles to Gray in many letters during the last few years, and Gray had replied with unfailing wisdom, kindness and perception.[4] Now they were together once more; and Gray, the stronger spirit, found himself deriving comfort and a kind of reassurance from the dependence of his weaker friend. *On a bien aise de se savoir aimé.* As they talked together in London, went to the opera and the play, discussed the problems that beset them, criticised one another's verses and translations, they were conscious of a sympathy and affection such as neither had previously experienced.

It was soon to be cut short. West's state of health was far worse than anyone realised; he was in fact in the final stages of consumption. The private unhappiness which haunted him remains something of a mystery. Gray said many years afterwards that the disease itself was brought about by 'the fatal discovery which he made of the treachery of a supposed friend, and the viciousness of a mother whom he tenderly loved; this man under the mask of friendship to him and his family intrigued with his mother; and robbed him of his peace of mind, his health and his life'.[5] The friend in question was presumably John Williams, the secretary of West's father, who eventually married Mrs West after the death of her son. Whatever the precise facts may have been, something undoubtedly happened which contributed to West's early death. Towards the end of the winter he became seriously ill, and presently went to stay in the Hertfordshire countryside, at a house called Popes near Hatfield, in the hope of recovering his health and spirits.

Gray remained in London, except for one or two visits to Stoke Poges in Buckinghamshire, where his uncle and aunt, Mr and Mrs Rogers, had moved from their former home close by at Burnham. A lively correspondence with West at once began. Both young men were perpetually reading, writing and translating, and the content of their letters was mainly literary. They discussed the latest publications, *Joseph Andrews* and the new book of the *Dunciad*; and Gray made his much-quoted confession, which West received with gentle ridicule, that 'as the paradisaical pleasures of the Mahometans consist in playing upon the flute and lying with Houris, be mine to read eternal new romances of Marivaux and Crébillon'.[6] Gray was now working upon *Agrippina*, a tragedy inspired by and closely modelled on Racine's *Britannicus*, which he had probably begun at Florence. He sent West a passage consisting of a single enormous speech by the heroine, and they plunged into an argument as to the style and language most suitable for the contemporary English stage. West composed some touching Latin verses about the cough which kept him from sleep all night, that *importunissima tussis*, 'shaking and tearing me for half an hour together', which not even his friend's presence, *tua vox dulcis nec vultus amatus*, would have been sufficient to allay.

Before long the spring was upon them. West welcomed its reluctant approach with a delightful poem:

> Dear Gray, that always in my heart
> Possessest far the better part,
> What mean these sudden blasts that rise
> And drive the Zephyrs from the skies?
> O join with mine thy tuneful lay,
> And invocate the tardy May.... [7]

Gray's reply to the letter which enclosed it, though gratefully appreciative of the poem itself, was tinged with melancholy. 'I converse, as usual, with none but the dead: they are my old friends, and almost make me long to be with them.' But West, who now had less than a month to live, would not put up with such gloom. 'I converse with them too,' he wrote, 'but I must condemn you for your longing to be with them. What, are there no joys among the living?...I will take my leave of you for the present with a *Vale et vive paullisper cum vivis*.'[8] With these words of encouragement and farewell the gentle Favonius ended the last letter to his friend that has survived.

Gray was not, as it happened, living entirely in the past at this time. As the month wore on, a glance through his open window was enough to interrupt his conversations with the dead. For three years he had not known the delights of an English spring; now he could enjoy something of them even in London, and each time he visited Stoke Poges they were around him in full luxuriance. He went down for a longer stay towards the end of the month, and there the beauty of that Buckinghamshire countryside moved him to write his first English poem. He described his meditations as he wandered through the meadows, or lay beside a stream and watched the brilliant new foliage of the oak-boughs above his head. His lines conjured up the heat and languor of midday, the cattle drowsing in the shade, the song of birds, the hum of bees, the drone of insects and the flickering dance of butterflies. And in the concluding stanza he struck a deeply personal note which West, and perhaps West alone at this time, was able to appreciate to the full. He called it *Noontide, an Ode*, and early in June sent it off to his friend in Hertfordshire. The days passed, and there was no reply. Presently the letter containing the poem came back unopened. A terrible suspicion began to dawn upon him, soon deepening almost into certainty. At last his worst fears were confirmed. He saw by chance some stanzas in a newspaper—'To the Memory of Richard West, Esq: who died at Popes in Hertfordshire, June 1, 1742, after a tedious and painful Indisposition, in the 26th Year of his Age.'

He thought the verses might be by Ashton, and wrote to him at once. He had been deeply hurt by the cold-heartedness of the people at whose house West had died, in giving him no explanation when they returned his letter; but he now reflected, in a sentence which may have touched Ashton's conscience also, that 'I am a fool indeed to be surpriz'd at meeting with Brutishness or want of Thought among Mankind'. Congratulations duly followed upon Ashton's recent appointment by the new Prime Minister, Henry Pelham, to the Crown living which he had awaited so long; and the general tone of the letter, though without the old intimacy of the Quadruple Alliance, was friendly enough.[9] Ashton no doubt told him in reply all that there was to know. *Noontide, an Ode*, was put quietly away among his papers, with the sad endorsement: 'At Stoke, the beginning of June 1742 to Fav[onius] not knowing he was then dead.'[10]

It was a cruel ending to the month which had begun so happily with the writing of that first enchanting poem, and the sense of loss was to remain with him throughout his life.[11] But before the close of June he found himself able to give some expression to his grief in lines which he intended as the preface to a fourth book of *De Principiis Cogitandi*, but which now stand alone as a most noble lament for his friend—the last and the greatest of all his Latin writings:[12]

> Hactenus haud segnis Naturae arcana retexi
> Musarum interpres, primusque Britanna per arva
> Romano liquidum deduxi flumine rivum.
> Cum Tu opere in medio, spes tanti et causa laboris,
> Linquis, et aeternam Fati te condis in umbram!
> Vidi egomet duro graviter concussa dolore
> Pectora, in alterius non unquam lenta dolorem;
> Et languere oculos vidi, et pallescere amantem
> Vultum, quo nunquam Pietas nisi rara, Fidesque,
> Altus amor Veri, et purum spirabat Honestum.
> Visa tamen tardi demùm inclementia morbi
> Cessare est, reducemque iterum roseo ore Salutem
> Speravi, atque unà tecum, dilecte Favoni!
> Credulus heu longos, ut quondàm, fallere soles;
> Heu spes nequicquam dulces, atque irrita vota!
> Heu maestos soles, sine te quos ducere flendo
> Per desiderium, et questus jam cogor inanes!
> At Tu, sancta anima, et nostri non indiga luctûs,
> Stellanti templo, sincerique aetheris igne,
> Unde orta es, fruere: atque o si secura, nec ultra
> Mortalis, notos olím miserata labores
> Respectes, tenuesque vacet cognoscere curas;
> Humanam si fortè altâ de sede procellam
> Contemplêre, metus, stimulosque cupidinis acres,
> Gaudiaque et gemitus, parvoque in corde tumultum
> Irarum ingentem, et saevos sub pectore fluctus;
> Respice et has lacrymas, memori quas ictus amore
> Fundo; quod possum, juxtà lugere sepulchrum
> Dum juvat, et mutae vana haec jactare favillae.*

---

* 'Thus far, nothing loth, the Muses' spokesman, I had unveiled Dame Nature's secrets, the first to draw that flowing stream from a Roman channel through my country's fields. Then, with my work half done, you—who inspired that mighty task and at whose feet I hoped to lay it when completed—you left me, vanished into fate's eternal shade. With these eyes I saw your breast cruelly convulsed by that harsh anguish—that breast that could never resist another's pain—that face where never breathed aught but a rare piety and trust and deep love of truth and honesty unblemished. At length it seemed that the raging of the slow disease was abating, and I hoped for the return once more of health with rosy cheek, and hoped—too quick believer!—that as of yore

III

Throughout the year 1742 Gray experienced a surge of creative activity which was never to be repeated. It was checked for a few weeks, except for the lines which have just been quoted, by the shock of West's death. Then in August it was renewed, and poem succeeded poem—the *Ode on a Distant Prospect of Eton College*, the *Hymn to Adversity*, the sonnet in memory of West, perhaps even the beginnings of the *Elegy*.

It all happened with extraordinary suddenness. Hitherto his more important poems, the poems most personal to himself, had been written—eloquently, movingly and with great technical accomplishment—without exception in Latin. His only attempts in English verse, apart from the fragment of *Agrippina*, had been a rendering of some stanzas of Tasso and a few translations from Propertius and Statius, almost all dating from his Cambridge days. West also wrote a good deal in Latin; but quite a number of his English poems and translations have survived, and his modest talent may have prepared the way for the genius of his friend. It has been suggested, for example, that Gray began his *Agrippina* in emulation of West's *Pausanias*, an uncompleted drama the first act of which had been sent out to him in Florence; and that he wrote his *Ode on the Spring*—as *Noontide, an Ode* was presently to be renamed—as a companion piece to West's invocation of 'the tardy May'. The same month saw his first poem in English and his last poem in Latin; and by the close of the year he had already achieved a substantial portion of his life's work as a poet.

I might cheat the lingering day with you as my companion, belov'd Favonius! Hopes sweet in vain, alas! and frustrate longings! Ah, the sad days that now perforce I endure bereft of you, in weeping, in longing, and in vain complaints.

You need no grief of ours, blest soul! Enjoy the starry temple where you now abide, and the pure elements from which you sprang. If in your blissful and immortal state you look pitying down upon the troubles that once were yours, and are free to know our trivial cares; if it chance that from your lofty seat you regard our fears and the sharp stings of desire, our joys and sorrows, the rage that swells our puny hearts, and the fierce waves that break within the breast— look then upon these tears of mine; while I indulge my grief (what can I more?) beside your tomb, and scatter these vain offerings on your unanswering ashes.'

There is little to be said about *Agrippina*. The drama was
soon laid aside, largely owing to the criticisms of West, and
never resumed. The opening scene, a protracted dialogue
between Agrippina and her confidante Aceronia,[13] and a fragment of the second scene alone survive. They contain some
vigorous lines, some occasional flashes of eloquence. But few
works in our literature are more dead, and less susceptible of
revival, than these elaborate dramas of the eighteenth century
—Johnson's *Irene*, and Thomson's *Sophonisba*, and Dodsley's
Cleone, and all the rest. We cannot now understand the appeal
which many of them exerted in their own day, the applause
they received and the tears they drew. Gray's *Agrippina* might
have proved a worthy addition to this sad sisterhood; but no
one can seriously regret that he put the unfinished manuscript
away in his desk, and turned to other things.

The *Ode on the Spring* opens with a rapturous evocation of
the sights and sounds of the English countryside, and closes
with two stanzas of sombre moralising. The change of mood
is induced by the poet's musings, as he reclines beside his
Buckinghamshire stream, upon the teeming insect life around
him—those myriads of bees and gnats and butterflies 'eager
to taste the honied spring', volatile and fragile, enjoying their
brief hour of sunshine and all so soon to perish. How similar,
he reflects, is the fate of humankind! There too the bees and
butterflies, 'the Busy and the Gay', meet the same inevitable
doom:

> Brush'd by the hand of rough Mischance,
> Or chill'd by age, their airy dance
> They leave, in dust to rest.

This parallel, as Gray afterwards explained, was suggested by
his unconscious recollection of some lines by the delightful poet
Matthew Green. In his poem upon the grotto which Queen
Caroline had built in the royal gardens at Richmond, Green
had moralised upon the insect world which buzzed and darted
around the threshold of the little building, and its resemblance
to the restless world of men:

> They Politicks, like ours, profess:
> The greater prey upon the less.
> Some strain on Foot huge Loads to bring,
> Some toil incessant on the Wing:
> Nor from their vigorous Schemes desist
> Till Death; and then are never mist.
> Some frolick, toil, marry, increase,
> Are sick and well, have War and Peace,
> And broke with Age in half a Day
> Yield to Successors, and away.[14]

Gray's debt to these engaging lines is obvious; but there was an original and unexpected turn of thought in the concluding stanza of his ode. The insects in their turn reply to the poet. They justify their joyful mating in the sunshine, the gathering of their stores of honey, the vivid iridescence of their wings. They are at least more fortunate than the lonely celibate moralist who has been reflecting upon their vain and brief existence, and who has himself neither mate, nor riches, nor brilliance of any kind:

> Methinks I hear in accents low
> The sportive kind reply:
> Poor moralist! and what art thou?
> A solitary fly!
> Thy Joys no glittering female meets,
> No hive hast thou of hoarded sweets,
> No painted plumage to display:
> On hasty wings thy youth is flown;
> Thy sun is set, thy spring is gone—
> We frolick, while 'tis May.

It is a most revealing stanza, in which Gray contrived to sum up in a few seemingly artless lines his loneliness, his obscurity, the desolating sense of time passing and nothing achieved which Milton had felt at twenty-three and he himself was feeling at twenty-five.

With West taken from him, there was now no one to whom Gray could show the poems which he continued to write during this summer; and the poems themselves are full of his sense of solitude and loss. He wandered through the lanes round Stoke as the long summer days went by, thinking incessantly of West and Walpole and those joyous years at Eton, so short a distance away across the fields. During his walks the buildings of Eton often came into view. From his favourite vantage-points he would contemplate the grey pinnacles of the chapel and the warm brick turrets of Lupton's Tower, with the river among its trees and the long battlemented outline of Windsor Castle rising high above all. And so, contrasting the well-remembered happiness of his school-days with the melancholy of his present life, he came to write his *Ode on a Distant Prospect of Eton College.*

Once again it is a deeply personal poem. In the five opening stanzas, all filled with gaiety and sunshine, he conjured up the carefree delights of youth, and his own memories of the time when he was 'a stranger yet to pain' and life held the promise of nothing but happiness:

> Gay hope is theirs by fancy fed,
> Less pleasing when possest;
> The tear forgot as soon as shed,
> The sunshine of the breast:
> Theirs buxom health of rosy hue,
> Wild wit, invention ever new,
> And lively cheer of vigour born;
> The thoughtless day, the easy night,
> The spirits pure, the slumbers light,
> That fly th' approach of morn.

But then a note of foreboding is sounded:

> Alas, regardless of their doom,
> The little victims play...

and the next four stanzas grimly foretell the doom, in its various and terrible forms, that awaited each one of those happy children when they grew to be men. Gray had been so wounded of late, by his estrangement from Walpole and by the death of West, that he was becoming afraid of what the future might yet have in store for him. These four stanzas are urgent with the sense of insecurity, the apprehensiveness, the fear of illness and pain which were to haunt him throughout his life. 'The fury Passions' still lay in ambush—Anger and Love, Jealousy and Envy. He was fresh from a bitter experience of

> Hard Unkindness' alter'd eye,
> That mocks the tear it forced to flow.

Disease in any of its hideous aspects, poverty, old age—these too might be his fate, as they might be the fate of any of those boys playing in the fields or diving from the river bank. And then, suddenly returning to his earlier mood, he crowned the poem with its last lovely stanza:

> To each his suffr'ings: all are men,
> Condemn'd alike to groan;
> The tender for another's pain,
> Th'unfeeling for his own.
> Yet ah! why should they know their fate?
> Since sorrow never comes too late,
> And happiness too swiftly flies.
> Thought would destroy their paradise.
> No more; where ignorance is bliss,
> 'Tis folly to be wise.

In the same month, and in the same mood, he wrote his *Hymn to Adversity*. In solemn tones he invoked that dread visitant, the chastener of Virtue, the scourge and terror of Vice. He pictured Folly and Noise, 'the summer Friend, the flatt'ring Foe', everything that is vain and worldly fleeing at her approach; while Wisdom and Melancholy attend her sober footsteps, and Charity and Justice and Pity. It is not granted to humankind to escape Adversity; all must submit to her discipline, all must endure their portion of pain and grief. But to many her harshness at least is tempered; and the concluding stanzas are a prayer that her hand might fall gently upon his own suppliant head—that the severest of her torments, 'Despair, and fell Disease, and ghastly Poverty', might be averted from him:

Thy form benign, oh Goddess, wear,
Thy milder influence impart,
Thy philosophic Train be there
To soften, not to wound my heart.
The gen'rous spark extinct revive,
Teach me to love and to forgive,
Exact my own defects to scan,
What others are, to feel, and know myself a Man.

The three principal poems of this summer, although one was written before West's death and the other two after it, are clearly linked in thought and mood. The same themes run through all—the flight of youth, the certainty of suffering and death, the inevitability of human fate. It is even possible that the same surge of creative impulse led him to begin the greatest of all his poems, the *Elegy written in a Country Churchyard*; but the evidence is uncertain,* and the *Elegy*, when brought to its completed form eight years later, had attained a serenity and resignation which were surely beyond his reach at this anguished time. One more poem, however, was certainly written in the August of 1742. In the *Eton Ode* and the *Hymn to Adversity*, Gray had been striving to relate his private sorrow to wider philosophic issues, to see it as a part of the universal lot of man. Suddenly, as so often happens after bereavement, the sense of utter loss returned, as stark and hopeless as on the day when he first learned of West's death. The defences of religion and philosophy crumbled away; and he poured out his grief, the grief which he could not share with any other person, in a heartbroken sonnet:

In vain to me the smiling mornings shine,
And redd'ning Phoebus lifts his golden fire:
The birds in vain their amorous descant join;
Or chearful fields resume their green attire:
These ears, alas! for other notes repine,
A different object do these eyes require.
My lonely anguish melts no heart but mine;
And in my breast the imperfect joys expire.
Yet Morning smiles the busy race to chear,

* See Appendix A, pp. 271–3.

And new-born pleasure brings to happier men:
The fields to all their wonted tribute bear:
To warm their little loves the birds complain:
I fruitless mourn to him, that cannot hear,
And weep the more, because I weep in vain.

Gray was presently to acknowledge, in the closing lines of the *Elegy*, that 'Melancholy marked him for her own' at the outset of his life; and these early poems are all affected in their varying degrees by that indefinable darkening of the spirit. Melancholy throws a passing cloud across the radiance of the *Ode on the Spring*, and a deeper and more permanent shadow upon the *Eton Ode*. The mood of the *Hymn to Adversity* is one of Stoic melancholy throughout. In the sonnet the Stoicism is absent, and grief has intensified almost to despair. 'My lonely anguish melts no heart but mine'—few sadder lines can ever have been written.

Melancholy, spleen, hypochondria, *angst*—there are many names for the condition of which Gray was a self-confessed victim. Even in his Cambridge days it had come and gone, darkened his life for weeks and then suddenly dispersed, so that he would at one time alarm West with accounts of his low spirits and at another dismiss his friend's similar moods as 'vapours and dismals'. He could on occasion discuss its symptoms with the detached interest of a spectator. In his last surviving letter to West he had given an especially full account of its effects:

Mine, you are to know, is a white Melancholy, or rather Leuco-choly for the most part; which though it seldom laughs or dances, nor ever amounts to what one calls Joy or Pleasure, yet is a good easy sort of a state, and *ça ne laisse que de s'amuser*. The only fault of it is insipidity; which is apt now and then to give a sort of Ennui, which makes one form certain little wishes that signify nothing. But there is another sort, black indeed, which I have now and then felt, that has somewhat in it like Tertullian's rule of faith, *Credo quia impossibile est*; for it believes, nay, is sure of every thing that is unlikely, so it be but frightful; and, on the other hand, excludes and shuts its eyes to the most possible hopes, and every thing that is pleasurable; from this the Lord deliver us! for none but he and sunshiny weather can do it.[15]

If Gray could write thus of his darker attacks of melancholy before West's death, their intensity after the loss of his friend may well be imagined. But even then there would come the longer periods when Leucocholy was the dominant mood. The only letter that has survived from those sad but intensely creative months was written to Chute and Mann in July; a long letter filled with casual gossip and happy memories of Florence, with no suggestion that he had lately suffered the most grievous sorrow of his life.[16] The sights and sounds of the countryside would always calm his spirits, benign and gentle weather dispel his deepest gloom; and we are perpetually reminded, in poems and letters and even the entries in his notebooks, of his love and longing for the sun. 'He is my old friend, and an excellent nurse, I assure you. Had it not been for him, life had often been to me intolerable.'[17]

Gray's melancholy was first and foremost a trouble of the spirit, and at this stage of his life it is impossible to tell if any physical ailment was contributing to it. He had been delicate in childhood; he was slow-moving and unathletic by nature; as a youth he had incurred the scorn of his uncle Rogers by his lack of any sporting inclinations, and in later years he admitted to William Cole that 'he was never 'cross a horse's back in his life'.[18] He was never free from apprehension about his health; the penultimate stanza of the *Eton Ode* suggests how his mind had dwelt upon the varied possibilities of illness even at this early age. But his travels seem to have had something of a toughening effect upon him; at any rate there is no record of actual ill-health for the next few years. As for the melancholy that was clouding his spirit, he was able to draw upon some reserve of strength and withstand its worst assaults, now and always. So the memorable summer of 1742 drew to its close; and his life entered upon another stage.

IV

When Philip Gray's business affairs were finally wound up, it was discovered that in the last few years he had contrived to muddle away the greater part of his own capital. A fair amount of real property remained, including the house and shop in Cornhill and his recent extravagant building venture at Wanstead; but the income of his widow and son would be a good deal less than they had probably anticipated. There was no question of penury or even of hardship. It is entirely misleading to say that Gray had 'finally learned that he was to all intents and purposes a pauper', and that in consequence his *Elegy* was to be 'a protest, a *cri de cœur*, not only against his own personal misfortunes but also at the social order that had made them possible'.[19] But the means of the little family were likely to be unexpectedly straitened. Mrs Gray and Mary Antrobus, moreover, were growing too old to carry on the shop, and looked forward to passing their remaining years in peaceful retirement in the country, preferably within reach of their other sister, Mrs Rogers. As it happened Jonathan Rogers died in the autumn of this year, and the three sisters then settled down together in the house at Stoke Poges.

These devoted ladies, to whom Gray owed his education and so much else in life, still hoped that a successful career at the bar awaited him; and he could not bear at this juncture to disappoint them. On the other hand, he regarded the study and practice of law with even greater aversion than in his youthful days. It is also unlikely that he could have afforded, without drawing on the resources of his mother and aunts, to live in any comfort in London while awaiting his call to the bar; and drudging at text-books in some bleak lodging or garret was hardly within his contemplation. At this period, however, practice in the Ecclesiastical and Admiralty Courts was open only to advocates who had graduated in civil law at Oxford or Cambridge; and this offered a welcome solution of Gray's difficulty. He decided to return to Cambridge, and read for the degree of Bachelor of Civil Law. In a letter to Chute he talked of establishing himself at Trinity Hall, which was especially renowned as a lawyers' college. He told his friend that 'my sole Reason (as you know) is to look as if—', and there he significantly broke off the sentence.[20] He was glad of a pretext which enabled him to satisfy his family and at the same time to make his home at Cambridge. He was really returning there because he would have access to its libraries and might even hope for a certain amount of congenial society, and because residence in a college offered a reasonable degree of comfort to a man of his limited means. In return for these benefits he was prepared to attend lectures and make a show of studying law.[21]

Academic life, however, held no particular attractions for him, and it was necessity, rather than inclination, that brought him back to Cambridge. He celebrated his return with a *Hymn to Ignorance*, whose first forty lines have survived to show how he regarded the place and the society in which he was to spend the rest of his days:

> Hail, Horrors, hail! ye ever gloomy bowers,
> Ye gothic fanes, and antiquated towers,
> Where rushy Camus' slowly-winding flood
> Perpetual draws his humid train of mud:
> Glad I revisit thy neglected reign,
> Oh take me to thy peaceful shade again.
>   But chiefly thee, whose influence breath'd from high
> Augments the native darkness of the sky;
> Ah Ignorance! soft salutary Power!
> Prostrate with filial reverence I adore.
> Thrice hath Hyperion roll'd his annual race,
> Since weeping I forsook thy fond embrace.
> Oh say, successful do'st thou still oppose
> Thy leaden Aegis 'gainst our antient foes?
> Still stretch, tenacious of thy right divine,
> The massy sceptre o'er thy slumb'ring line?
> And dews Lethean thro' the land dispense
> To steep in slumbers each benighted sense?
> If any spark of Wit's delusive ray
> Break out, and flash a momentary day,
> With damp, cold touch forbid it to aspire,
> And huddle up in fogs the dangerous fire....

In this mood of ironical resignation he returned, not to Trinity Hall but to his old college of Peterhouse, in the autumn of 1742.

CHAPTER V

RETURN TO CAMBRIDGE
1742-1749

I

As Gray had left Cambridge in 1738 without taking a degree, he was still technically an undergraduate; but a man of his age and attainments could hardly reside in a college except as a fellow-commoner. It was on this footing, therefore, that he now returned to Peterhouse. His new status exempted him from the discipline imposed upon the humbler undergraduates, and entitled him to dine at the Fellows' table and to associate with them in combination room and parlour. The student body of the college was very small. There were fewer than a dozen undergraduates, including two or three other fellow-commoners, young men of independent means. The Fellows were more numerous—there were fourteen on the foundation, and eight bye-fellows on the special foundations of certain benefactors. The Master was Dr John Whalley, who had been elected Regius Professor of Divinity in this year.[1] There was no one of any particular distinction in the college, and an air of comfortable somnolence prevailed under Dr Whalley's unexacting rule.

In this society Gray settled down to a life of study and contemplation. He attended the lectures of Dr Dickins, the Regius Professor of Civil Law, and a book of his lecture-notes still exists to show that he followed them with some diligence. A year later, in December 1743, he took his degree of Bachelor of Civil Law, and noted with amusement that 'I am got half-way to the Top of Jurisprudence'. But he did not attempt to get any further. He never took his Doctor's degree, which would have enabled him to practise in the Ecclesiastical and Admiralty Courts; and from this time he dropped any pretence of adopting a legal career, and indeed was inclined to boast of his ignorance of the law in all its forms.[2]

His chief and almost his only friend at Peterhouse was John Clerke, who had been his contemporary there during his earlier residence, and was now a Fellow of the college; he studied medicine, and afterwards left Cambridge and practised as a physician at Epsom. Apart from Clerke and a promising young scholar named Henry Tuthill, who took his degree in 1744, the members of his own college are scarcely mentioned in his letters and appear to have meant very little to him. His most intimate friends were all in the college just across the road, Fellows of Pembroke Hall—James Brown, whom he had known and liked so well in earlier days; William Trollope, an amiable but shadowy figure, something of an invalid and rather older than the rest of the circle, about whom it would be agreeable to know more; and above all Thomas Wharton. Despite his more intimate friendships with Walpole and West, Gray had never lost touch with this wholly admirable man. He had written a long and entertaining letter from Florence to 'My dear, dear Wharton—which is a dear more than I give any body else',[3] and on his return to Cambridge had found him friendly, kind and sensible as ever. He soon grew to rely upon him, to confide in him and to trust his judgement implicitly, and continued to do so throughout his life.

He did not mix a great deal in the wider life of the university. His letters refer constantly to the indolence, the lassitude, 'that ineffable Octogrammaton the Power of LAZINESS',[4] which hung over the place like a pall. He was deeply sensitive to this atmosphere; conscious of the vein of indolence in his own nature, he saw himself as a potential victim to it. The whole system encouraged sloth and self-indulgence in the weaker brethren—the negligible duties required of a Fellow; the celibacy imposed upon him until some long-awaited living fell vacant and enabled him to depart and, if he desired, to marry; the laden tables and well-stocked cellars, the sleepy afternoons of port and tobacco in the college parlours. He could not find much pleasure in such company; but he did not eschew it entirely, and was always interested in the doings of the academic world around him, its gossip and its scandal. As for more general society, it was severely limited in a community where only the heads of houses and the professors were permitted by statute to marry. Some years later, when Wharton had resigned his fellowship on his marriage and was considering settling at Cambridge as a physician, he told his friend that 'your Wife, rather than you, will feel the Want of Company of her own Sex; as the Women are few here, squeezy and formal, and little skill'd in amusing themselves or other People. All I can say is, she must try to make up for it among the Men, who are not over-agreeable neither.'[5]

He found an exception to this rule at the house of Dr Conyers Middleton, the University Librarian. A doughty fighter—he had been one of Bentley's most formidable opponents during his stormy reign at Trinity—and a highly unorthodox theologian, much of Middleton's life had been passed in various forms of controversy. Despite his advancing years he was one of the best-known and most active figures of the Cambridge scene; and his house at the end of King's Parade, now replaced by the Waterhouse building of Caius, was the resort of many of the younger men, who were made welcome there by his three successive wives. Walpole had been on friendly terms with him since his undergraduate days; William Cole, while deploring his doctrinal unsoundness, liked him greatly as a man; and Gray regarded his third wife in particular as 'really a pretty kind of Woman both in Figure and Manner', and his house as 'the only easy Place one could find to converse in at Cambridge'.[6]

About the time of Gray's return to Cambridge his uncle William Antrobus died at his parsonage in Northamptonshire. His widow, the daughter of a Cambridge merchant and alderman named Thomas Nutting, brought her young family, two daughters and a son, to live there with her father. Alderman Nutting had twice been Mayor of the town, and at one time his business affairs had prospered greatly, but a fondness for good living and gay company brought about his downfall. In 1745 he was obliged to supplement his reduced means by becoming the postmaster of Cambridge, an office which he later resigned in favour of his daughter Mrs Antrobus. Gray did all he could to help the rather pathetic little household, and they in return provided him with something of a family background. The girls, Dorothy and Mary—Molly, who was his particular favourite—made his shirts and hemmed his ruffles, advised him about the best material for his new curtains, and looked after his comfort in all sorts of useful ways.[7]

In the year of Gray's return to Cambridge the Fellows' Building at Peterhouse had been completed after the designs of the excellent amateur architect James Burrough, Fellow and afterwards Master of Caius.[8] In this building a set of rooms on the second floor, high above Trumpington Street, was allotted to Gray. The rooms were tall, light and admirably proportioned. From the northward windows he looked straight across to the long pinnacled roof-line of King's College chapel. Below lay the church and churchyard of Little St Mary's, and just across the road was the chapel of Pembroke with Wren's elegant little cupola. Through the windows on the south side he could see the length of Trumpington Street and far beyond into the countryside. There can have been few more pleasant sets of rooms in the whole of Cambridge. Gray's only objection to them, an objection which grew stronger with the years, was that their height above the ground would make them extremely dangerous if there should ever be an outbreak of fire.

II

Towards the end of 1745 a reconciliation took place between Gray and Walpole. Their estrangement had lasted for four and a half years, during which time they had never met or corresponded. Walpole's father had died earlier in the year, leaving his youngest son a house in Arlington Street and a comfortable income mainly derived from patent places under the Crown, which were secured to him for life. He attended the House of Commons regularly, seldom taking any part in debate, but recording in a wonderful series of letters to Horace Mann, and presently in a succession of more formal *Memoirs*, the political history of his time as it appeared to a watchful and privileged spectator. For the rest he was leading a gay and active social life, and still had time to spare for literature, *virtù* and a growing interest in English antiquities.

Walpole told Mason many years afterwards that the renewal of their friendship was brought about by 'a Lady who wished well to both parties'.[9] Until quite recently the identity of this lady was unknown. All sorts of guesses had been hazarded—the second Mrs Conyers Middleton was suggested, and alternatively a sister-in-law of John Chute, both of whom had some acquaintance with Walpole and Gray. But it has lately been discovered that Walpole noted in his own copy of Mason's *Memoirs of Gray*, now in the Houghton Library at Harvard College, that the lady who reconciled them was a Mrs Kerr. No one of that name appears otherwise in the lives of Walpole or of Gray, and at present she remains a complete mystery. But whoever she may have been, she persuaded Walpole to write in friendly terms to Gray, who came up from Cambridge to see him at the beginning of November. A series of interviews followed, which Gray presently described in an amusing letter to Wharton.[10] From this it appears that at first Walpole was inclined to treat the situation altogether too lightly; and it is easy to picture the stiffness and reticence with which Gray received his airy overtures:

I wrote a Note the Night I came, and immediately received a very civil Answer. I went the following Evening to see *the Party* (as Mrs Foible says) was something abash'd at his Confidence: he came to meet me, kiss'd me on both Sides with all the Ease of one, who receives an Acquaintance just come out of the Country, squatted me into a Fauteuil, begun to talk of the Town and this and that and t'other, and continued with little Interruption for three Hours, when I took my leave very indifferently pleased, but treated with wondrous Good-breeding.

Next evening Gray supped in Arlington Street, with Ashton making a third at the table.

Ashton was there, whose Formalities tickled me inwardly, for he I found was to be angry about the Letter I had wrote him. However in going home together our Hackney-Coach jumbled us into a Sort of Reconciliation: he hammer'd out somewhat like an Excuse; and I received it very readily, because I cared not two pence, whether it were true or not. So we grew the best Acquaintance imaginable, and I sat with him on Sunday some Hours alone, when he inform'd me of abundance of Anecdotes much to my Satisfaction, and in short open'd (I really believe) his Heart to me with that Sincerity, that I found I had still less Reason to have a good Opinion of him, than (if possible) I ever had before.

All this provides no real explanation of the part played by Ashton in the disagreement and quarrel between Walpole and Gray long ago in Italy. It is clear only that he had been guilty of some breach of confidence, and that Gray no longer cared sufficiently about him to be resentful or even surprised. All was well in the end. 'Next Morning I breakfasted alone with Mr W: when we had all the Eclaircissement I ever expected, and I left him far better satisfied, than I had been hitherto. When I return, I shall see him again. Such is the Epitome of my four Days.' Their friendship was soon reestablished. They corresponded in the old easy fashion after Gray had returned to Cambridge, about the character of Pope, and the campaign against the young Pretender, and a still more urgent campaign which was being fought over a fellowship election at Peterhouse. For some while Gray could not feel quite assured that this link with the happy past was completely restored. His obstinate pride still made him cautious, even a trifle lukewarm, when discussing the matter with others. 'All is mighty free, and even friendly, more than one could expect',[11] he told Wharton after he had seen a good deal of

Walpole in London during the following summer. And when Chute, who had witnessed their growing estrangement and knew the circumstances of the quarrel, returned at last from Italy that same autumn, he explained the situation to him in a tone so reserved as to be almost apologetic:

I find Mr Walpole then made some Mention of me to you. Yes, we are together again. It is about a year, I believe, since he wrote to me to offer it, and there has been (particularly of late) in Appearance the same Kindness and Confidence almost as of old. What were his Motives I can not yet guess: what were mine, you will imagine, and perhaps blame me. However as yet I neither repent, nor rejoice overmuch: but I am pleased.[12]

Before long Gray's reservations had vanished entirely. He could not doubt the reality of the kindness and confidence that Walpole offered. Once or twice in the years to come the contrast of their temperaments, Gray's reticence against Walpole's exuberance, was to produce a slight and momentary friction. But in all its essentials their friendship endured unbroken until the day of Gray's death.

Since his return to Cambridge, Gray had passed most of each summer and autumn at Stoke Poges, with occasional visits to London. In July 1746 he was in London for an especially crowded fortnight, spending his mornings with Walpole and his evenings at Vauxhall or Ranelagh, and attending the trial of the Scottish lords in Westminster Hall. In the previous November, while he and Walpole were restoring their broken friendship in the calm of Arlington Street, the young Pretender's forces had been marching deep into England and the Hanoverian monarchy was facing its gravest crisis. Now Kilmarnock, Balmerino and Cromartie were on trial for their lives; and the reconciled friends were both among the spectators, and were describing the scene in letters packed with vivid detail, Walpole to Mann and Gray to Wharton. There were also occasional meetings with Ashton, who was still an assiduous follower of the Pelham interest, though growing secretly resentful of their neglect to bestow any further preferment upon him. 'Mr Ashton I have had several Conversations with, and do really believe he shews himself to me such as he really is: I don't tell you, I like him ever the better for it; but that may be my Fault, not his.'[13]

From this time Ashton gradually faded out of Gray's life. There was no open quarrel, and fifteen years later Gray did not hesitate to consult him, as a Fellow of Eton, about sending one of Wharton's sons to the College; but they seldom if ever met again. Walpole himself severed all connection with Ashton in 1750, and forbade him to enter his house. Their disagreement arose over a pamphlet contributed by Ashton to a controversy between Conyers Middleton and the Bishop of London. Walpole told the story in an indignant letter to Mann:

> I believe you have often heard me mention a Mr Ashton, a clergyman, who, in one word, has great preferments, and owes everything upon earth to me. I have long had reason to complain of his behaviour; in short, my father is dead, and I can make no bishops. He has at last quite thrown off the mask, and in the most direct manner, against my will, has written against my friend Dr Middleton.[14]

The attack on Middleton was part of Ashton's campaign to recommend himself, as a highly orthodox divine, to the ecclesiastical authorities. His 'great preferments' were further enlarged in due course, and in late middle age he acquired the additional consolation of a very rich wife; but all his efforts failed to bring him any high office in the Church. His splendid portrait by Reynolds hangs in the hall of King's College, where the spectator may reflect that this masterful and pompous cleric once shared the youthful intimacies, the verses and jokes and sentimental musings, of the Quadruple Alliance.

After a little sightseeing tour to Hampton Court, Richmond and Greenwich, Gray returned to Stoke, where later in the summer Walpole became a neighbour, having taken a house close by at Windsor. They used to meet at least once a week, and it was probably on one of these occasions that Gray first showed Walpole his *Eton Ode*. Walpole recognised at once—

and he must have the credit of being the first person to do so—
the genius of his friend. He was urgent that the poem should
be published, but for several months Gray resisted his persuasions. In the meantime the diffident poet sent him a copy of
the *Ode on the Spring*—'all it pretends to with you is, that it
is mine, and that you never saw it before, and that it is not so
long as t'other'[15]—and may also have shown him the opening
lines of the *Elegy*. For during this summer and autumn of
1746 Gray was struggling at intervals with an uncompleted
poem. 'The Muse, I doubt, is gone, and has left me in far
worse Company: if she returns, you will hear of her', he told
Wharton in August; and in September he wrote that the study
of Aristotle 'and a few autumnal verses are my Entertainments
during the Fall of the Leaf'.[16] It has been suggested that these
autumnal verses may have been the first stanzas of the *Elegy*.
And if we prefer to believe that the *Elegy* was begun in the
summer of 1742, this would still be the earliest occasion on
which Gray could have confided to Walpole any portion of
the incomparable poem which he later described as 'a thing,
whose beginning you have seen long ago.'[17]

The arrival in October of Chute and Whithed was a most
agreeable surprise. He knew nothing of their return until
they were actually in England, and affected to be a little hurt
at only hearing the news indirectly from Walpole. But a letter
from Chute at once placated him; and next month he went to
London and spent a happy fortnight 'flaunting about at publick
Places of all kinds with my two Italianized Friends'. Chute,
while professing to be 'lazy and listless and gouty and old and
vex'd and perplex'd', was in fact as lively, witty and affected
as ever. Whithed had blossomed into 'a fine young Personage
in a Coat all over Spangles', and was preparing to enter into
possession of his family estate and to marry a suitable heiress
as soon as possible. Theirs was the sort of company that Gray
most enjoyed—for a fortnight or perhaps even a month, after
which the claims of study and retirement could no longer be
denied. It may have been during this visit to London, and

through the introduction of these two friends, that Gray first made the acquaintance of Lady Brown, the wife of a former British Resident at Venice. She was a well-known hostess whose *salons*, held in defiance of English convention on Sunday evenings, were the especial resort of those who had been to Italy—'the great mark', in Walpole's words, 'of all travelling and travelled calves'. Gray never seems to have known her well, but it will be seen later that he kept in touch with her at least for some years.[18] At the close of this particular stay in London he returned to Cambridge and his books less willingly than usual, as he admitted in a letter to Wharton:

> The world itself has some Attraction in it to a Solitary of six Years standing; and agreeable well-meaning People of Sense (thank Heaven there are so few of them) are my peculiar Magnet. It is no Wonder then, if I felt some Reluctance at parting with them so soon; or that my Spirits, when I return'd back to my Cell, should sink for a time, not indeed to Storm and Tempest, but a good deal below Changeable.[19]

Walpole was full of literary projects at this time, in all of which Gray took a friendly interest, calling them his godchildren and asking especially about the progress of the *Memoirs*. They also discussed the publication of a volume containing Gray's poems and the remains, both English and Latin, of West. They anticipated the criticism that most of West's work was too immature for publication, but both were anxious that the memory of their friend should not fade unrecognised into oblivion. 'I should not care', wrote Gray, 'how unwise the ordinary Sort of Readers might think my Affection for him provided those few, that ever loved any Body, or judged of any thing rightly, might from such little Remains be moved to consider, what he might have been; and to wish, that Heaven had granted him a longer Life, and a Mind more at Ease.'[20] In view of Gray's minute output of English verse, it must be assumed that his translations and Latin poems would also have been included in the book. The scheme came to nothing, probably because Dodsley was at this time about to issue his *Collection of Poems*, in which the work of such obscure young poets could be more appropriately introduced. The first three volumes of this celebrated miscellany appeared next year, and Gray, Walpole and West were all represented in them.

About this time there was a minor tragedy in Walpole's household. He owned two beautiful cats, Zara and Selima, whom Gray had lately come to know well on his visits to the house. Selima was lying one day outstretched upon the rim of of a large tub of blue and white china which contained goldfish; she tried to catch the gleaming shapes as they darted to and fro, slipped, fell into the water and was drowned. Her master described her fate in a letter to Gray, who was moved to commemorate it in verse. The *Ode on the Death of a Favourite Cat, Drowned in a Tub of Gold Fishes* is one of those casual poems, written by grave authors on private occasions, which have caught the popular fancy and achieved an unexpected immortality. Graceful, touching, its rueful truisms delicately edged with wit, it reflects a mood which seldom appears in Gray's poetry, though often enough in his letters.

Gray's interest in current literature was unflagging, and the criticisms in his letters of the latest books are full of perception and wit. New figures began to appear upon the literary scene, and new poets in particular.

Have you seen the Works of two young Authors, a Mr Warton and a Mr Collins, both writers of Odes? It is odd enough, but each is the half of a considerable Man, and one the Counter-Part of the other. The first has but little Invention, very poetical choice of Expression, and a good Ear. The second, a fine Fancy, model'd upon the Antique, a bad Ear, great Variety of Words and Images with no Choice at all. They both deserve to last some Years, but will not.[21]

William Collins was to stand higher than this in the eyes of posterity, far above Joseph Warton and in rivalry with Gray himself. For the present Gray had few thoughts of competing in print with these new writers of odes. He did, however, allow Dodsley, at Walpole's persuasion and with Walpole acting as his intermediary, to publish the *Eton Ode* at the end of May 1747. It appeared as a sixpenny folio pamphlet, and seems to have aroused little interest anywhere.

At the beginning of 1748, however, some of his work was presented to a wider public in Dodsley's *Collection of Poems*. These three volumes formed a most valuable anthology of contemporary verse, designed, in the words of the editor, 'to preserve to the public those poetical performances, which seemed to merit a longer remembrance than what would probably be secured to them by the manner wherein they were originally published'. There was a certain amount of work by authors already well known—Thomas Tickell, who had died in 1740, and Lady Mary Wortley Montagu, whose *Town Eclogues* were now reprinted more than thirty years after their first appearance. Dodsley also reprinted the few pieces which the delightful Matthew Green had given to the world before his early death. But the great feature of the miscellany was the number of poems by younger writers, which had appeared as pamphlets or in little books likely to be soon forgotten, and which were now brought to the public notice again in a most effective way—such masterpieces as Johnson's *London* and Collins's *Ode to Evening*, Dyer's *Grongar Hill*, Gray's own *Eton Ode*. And there were many poems also which had never found their way into print at all. Gray's own contributions—the *Eton Ode*, the *Ode on the Spring*, and the *Ode on the Death of a Favourite Cat*—figured in the second volume, appearing modestly as 'By Mr —'. This polite anonymity was rather the rule than the exception, and was observed also in the case of Walpole's three contributions in the third volume; but the poem which immediately followed those of Gray, *A Monody on the Death of Queen Caroline*, was announced as 'By Richard West, Esq: Son to the Chancellor of Ireland, and Grandson to Bishop Burnet'.

Walpole himself had caused Dodsley to insert these details; and Gray, in a long letter discussing the *Collection*, remarked that 'I was glad to see you distinguished who poor West was, before his charming Ode'. The whole of this letter reveals Gray as a most perceptive critic of contemporary writing. He

fails to mention the three beautiful poems by Collins, and is
perhaps a little over-kind to Walpole's own contributions; but
his remarks on Green, Johnson, Dyer and others are singularly
just and true, and his gay dismissal of the mediocrities—
'Messieurs! this is not the thing! write prose, write sermons,
write nothing at all...'—is equally well deserved. He also
drew Walpole's attention to 'an ode...by Mr Mason, a new
acquaintance of mine, whose *Musaeus* too seems to carry with it
the promise at least of something good to come'.[22]

III

This new acquaintance, William Mason, was destined to
play an important part throughout Gray's life, and to be
chosen by him as his biographer and literary executor. He was
seven years younger than Gray, the son of a clergyman at Hull,
and was a member of St John's College. In 1747 the publication
of his poem *Musaeus*, a monody on the death of Pope, had
attracted some attention—more so indeed than Gray's *Eton
Ode*, which appeared almost at the same time. Gray liked
some of his poetry, and was amused by his youthful eagerness
to succeed in the world, his curious blend of ambition and
ingenuousness.

Mr Mason is my Acquaintance [he told Wharton in 1748]. He
has much Fancy, little Judgement, and a good deal of Modesty.
I like him for a good and well-meaning Creature; but then he is
really *in Simplicity a Child*, and loves every body he meets with:
he reads little or nothing, writes abundance, and that with a Design
to make his Fortune by it.[23]

A further year's acquaintance with Mason did not lead him to
alter his verdict, except on the issue of Mason's modesty,
never one of his more conspicuous qualities. In the summer of
1749 he wrote:

[Mason] grows apace into my good Graces, as I know him more:
he is very ingenious with great Good-Nature and Simplicity.
A little vain, but in so harmless and comical a Way, that it does not
offend one at all; a little ambitious, but withall so ignorant in the

6 81 K-C

World and its Ways, that this does not hurt him in one's Opinion. So sincere and so undisguised, that no Mind with a Spark of Generosity would ever think of hurting him, he lies so open to Injury. But so indolent, that if he can not overcome this Habit, all his good Qualities will signify nothing at all.[24]

In his own college Gray continued to be somewhat isolated. Even Henry Tuthill, one of the few congenial people there, had moved across the street to Pembroke in 1746. Gray himself was not on good terms with the Master, Dr Whalley—there had been some dissension in the College about an election to a fellowship—and in 1748 their hostility led to a curious imbroglio:

[The Master] thought fit to intimate to a large Table full of People, that I was a kind of Atheist. I wrote to him partly to laugh at, and partly to reprove him for his Malice; and (as what he said was publick) I shew'd my Letter to several of those, who had heard him; and threaten'd (not in earnest, you may imagine) to have it hawk'd about the Streets. They took me literally, and by Way of Anticipation my Letter has been consign'd to one Etoffe (a Fiend of a Parson, that you know) to shew about here, and to carry to Town, if any one will read it. He makes Criticisms on it, and has found out a false Spelling, I'm told.[25]

This fiendish parson, the Rev. Henry Etough, was undoubtedly one of the most disagreeable figures of eighteenth-century Cambridge. He was supposed to have begun his career as a Presbyterian minister in Scotland, but had done some service for Sir Robert Walpole and was rewarded with substantial preferment in the Church of England. He lived not far from Cambridge at his rectory of Therfield in Hertfordshire, and often visited the university with what Gray described on a later occasion as 'his Budget of Libels (for it is his constant Practice twice in a year to import a Cargo of Lyes, and scandalous Truths mix'd)'.[26] It seems to have been Gray who first gave him the nickname of Tophet, which is more or less an anagram of Etough. Cole wrote about him frequently and with even greater abhorrence, as 'a pimping, tale-bearing dissenting teacher', 'a busy impertinent meddler in everyone's affairs', and much else in his usual uninhibited strain.[27] Now that Sir Robert was dead, Etough had attached himself to his brother Horace Walpole of Wolterton, who was on bad terms with his nephew Horace Walpole of Strawberry Hill; and he played a part in the violent quarrel which broke out between the two Horaces in 1751. His diabolical aspect, stunted, round-shouldered, with a huge head 'so hot and reeking that when he entered a room he often hung up his wig on a peg and sat bare-headed',[28] was recorded for posterity about this time by Mason, in a drawing which was etched for private circulation many years later by Michael Tyson of Corpus Christi College. Gray was delighted with the drawing, and inscribed beneath it some lines in the vein of trenchant satire which he exploited all too seldom:

> Thus Tophet look'd; so grinned the brawling fiend,
> While frighted prelates bow'd and called him friend;
> I saw them bow, and while they wish'd him dead,
> With servile simper nod the mitred head.
> Our mother-church, with half-averted sight,
> Blush'd as she bless'd her griesly proselyte:
> Hosannas rung through hell's tremendous borders,
> And Satan's self had thoughts of taking orders.[29]

Gray had become, in fact, an unexpectedly militant figure in certain Cambridge affairs at this period. Besides his differences with Whalley and the formidable Etough, he was involved in a controversy which had violently disturbed the society of Pembroke, to which so many of his friends belonged. At this time, and for many years to come, the Master of Pembroke was a richly eccentric figure named Roger Long. He was a Norfolk man by birth, a Tory in a society predominantly Whig, obstinate and cantankerous in temper, an astronomer and a musician with a lifelong addiction to scientific experiments of every kind. Among his constructions were a huge revolving planetarium, which remained in the college precincts until late in the nineteenth century; a musical instrument called a lyri-chord, which he presented to the King and Queen when he reached the age of eighty; and a water-velocipede on which he used to paddle himself around 'a beautiful and large Bason' in his garden.[30] He was constantly at odds with the Fellows, in particular over the right of veto in college affairs which he claimed to possess and indeed constantly exercised. In 1746 Henry Tuthill had migrated from Peterhouse to Pembroke, where Wharton had thought highly of him and caused him to be nominated for a fellowship. At a college meeting that autumn Tuthill received the votes of all seven Fellows present; but the Master exercised his veto, writing beneath their signatures in the college register his inexorable '*Ego non consentio. R. Long*' at the foot of the page, and nothing further could be done.[31] Next year another fellowship fell vacant. Gray suggested to his friends in Pembroke the name of William Mason as a suitable candidate, and he too received the votes of every Fellow present at the next college meeting. 'I was at this time scholar of St John's College, and Batchelor of Arts, personally unknown to the gentlemen who favoured me so highly', he wrote many years afterwards: 'therefore that they gave me this mark of distinction and preference was greatly owing to Mr Gray.'[32] But once again the Master used his veto, this time on the ground that the college had suitable candidates within its own walls and did not want a stranger. The deadlock continued until 1749, with the Fellows united under the leadership of James Brown, whom Gray described as 'fixed and obstinate as a little Rock',[33] and the Master refusing to yield an inch. Gray naturally took the deepest interest in the efforts of his Pembroke friends on behalf of the two young men in whom he saw such promise; and the letters which he sent to Wharton, who had now married and vacated his fellowship, reflect all the hopes and disappointments of the protracted struggle. At last the Master yielded, though not before the reputation of the college had seriously declined and its intake of undergraduates fallen almost to nothing. He withdrew his opposition to Tuthill and Mason, and in March 1749 both were elected Fellows of Pembroke, together with a third candidate.[34]

Wharton's marriage in the spring of 1747, when he gave up

ROGER LONG, MASTER OF PEMBROKE

From an engraving by Edmund Fisher, after a painting by Benjamin Wilson

his fellowship and left Cambridge to practise as a doctor in his native city of Durham, deprived Gray of his closest friend in the university. No one else could offer him that sturdy common sense allied to quick intuitive sympathy; no one else was so entirely dependable in moments of perplexity or depression. His place in Gray's confidence gradually came to be filled by James Brown, more purely academic in temperament, but sensible and reliable as Wharton had been. Besides Mason and Tuthill, the likeable William Trollope was sometimes to be found at Pembroke; but increasing ill-health kept him much away, and he died in 1749. Gray's friends in other colleges included the newly elected Master of Magdalene, Thomas Chapman, whose behaviour he described in his letters to Wharton with more amusement than respect, and Henry Coventry, also a Fellow of Magdalene. Coventry was an aristocratic young man—'the best Sort of Man in this Place', Gray called him on one occasion—with a conspicuous Roman nose and a fondness for gay clothes and gold lace.[35] Gray had some acquaintance, which did not ripen into friendship until some years later, with Richard Stonhewer, the son of a Durham clergyman and an undergraduate of Trinity. Another friend was Nicholas Bonfoy, a former Pembroke man some years older than Gray, who had encountered him both at Paris and at Florence during his Grand Tour. Bonfoy later became Serjeant-at-Arms in the House of Commons, and was the squire of Abbot's Ripton near Huntingdon, where Gray and Brown used often to spend a few days with him and his mother. Gray was much attached to this lady, and many years later he was to write sadly to Wharton that 'Mrs Bonfoy (who taught me to pray) is dead'. She had certainly not known him in his childhood, and any explanation of this remark must be purely conjectural.[36]

Finally, there was among the Fellows of Pembroke at this time a noisy, drunken, excitable little man named Christopher Smart. He was something of a poet, and first appears in Gray's letters as the author and producer of a play called *A Trip to*

Cambridge, or The Grateful Fair, which was acted in 1747 by a party of undergraduates with Stonhewer officiating as prompter. Gray regarded him as an unmitigated nuisance, and complained more than once of his 'Lies, Impertinence and Ingratitude'. Like everyone else who knew Smart, however, he did what he could to extricate him at intervals from his tangle of debts and disreputabilities; and he asked Wharton, at one moment of particular crisis, to intercede for Smart with a powerful north-country family who had befriended him and whose allowance was in danger of being withdrawn.[37] Smart for his part undoubtedly admired Gray's writings; he composed several poems in the stanza first introduced in the *Ode on the Spring* and the *Eton Ode*, and referred to him as

> . . . our great Augustan *Gray*. . .
> With sweet, with manly words of woe,
> That nervously pathetic flow.[38]

A joke about Gray's manner of walking, first attributed to him long after both were dead, is almost certainly apocryphal.[39] But there can have been no personal sympathy or liking between them; and in Smart's years at Cambridge no one could suppose that long afterwards, tried in the fires of adversity and madness, he would create those strange and lovely masterpieces *A Song to David* and *Jubilate Agno*.

IV

In the early hours of 25 March 1748 a fire broke out in the house of a peruke-maker in an alley off Cornhill. It spread rapidly through the surrounding shops and houses until close upon a hundred premises had been destroyed. The London Assurance Office was entirely consumed, together with several inns and coffee-houses, half a dozen booksellers' shops, and a long row of the buildings fronting Cornhill. Among these last was the house with its shop below, now occupied by a milliner named Mrs Sarrazin, in which Gray had been born and had passed so many years of his life. By some family arrangement the ownership of this property had now passed from Mrs Gray to her son. It proved to be considerably under-insured; he only received £485 in settlement of his claim, and calculated that the rebuilding and other expenses would cost him £650, apart from the loss of income in the meantime. It was hardly an overwhelming calamity, but the shock was considerable. With his unfailing kindness Wharton wrote offering a loan, and he found it necessary next year to accept the modest sum of twenty guineas.[40] The worry and perplexity of the business seem to have depressed him more than the actual loss, and enhanced the dread of fire which preyed upon his mind. He could not forget the scenes of desolation along those familiar streets and alleys, and the six people who had died in the flames.

He was obliged to spend several weeks in London, where his friends tried to cheer him by every means except, as he remarked to Wharton, the obvious one of offering him financial help:

Their methods of Consolation were indeed very extraordinary: they were all so sorry for my Loss, that I could not chuse but laugh. One offer'd me Opera-Tickets, insisted upon carrying me to the Grand-Masquerade, desired me to sit for my Picture. Others asked me to their Concerts, or Dinners and Suppers at their Houses; or hoped, I would drink Chocolate with them, while I stayed in Town. All my Gratitude (or if you please, my Revenge) was to accept of every Thing they offer'd me: if it had been but a Shilling, I would have taken it. Thank Heaven, I was in good Spirits; else I could not have done it. I profited all I was able of their Civilities, and am returned into the Country loaded with their Bontés and Politesses, but richer still in my own Reflexions, which I owe in great Measure to them too.[41]

Such undertones of bitterness and self-pity were unusual in Gray at this time, and show how violent the shock had been. In normal circumstances he would undoubtedly have regarded an offer of money, except from so privileged a friend as Wharton, as a deep affront.

The friend who asked him to sit for his picture was Walpole, and John Giles Eckhardt was the artist. Eckhardt was a

German of mediocre talent, much employed by Walpole at various times to make portraits of his family and friends for his newly acquired house at Twickenham. Some whim induced him to have all these people portrayed in attitudes and dresses suggested by paintings of an earlier age—his sister and her husband and son after a Rubens at Blenheim; Henry Conway and his wife and daughter after a picture by Watteau; Gray, Richard Bentley and Walpole himself in seventeenth-century costume, in imitation of certain portraits by Van Dyck. Gray's pose and dress were taken from a painting by Van Dyck of a musician, in the collection of the Duke of Grafton.[42] This idealised vision of a languid young poet with carefully dis-ordered hair and shirt open at the throat, with the manuscript of the *Eton Ode* held negligently in his hand, can have borne little resemblance to his actual appearance and none to his customary attire. It is unfortunate that his only portrait between childhood and late middle age should show him in an admittedly fanciful disguise.

Horace Walpole had now given up his house at Windsor, and bought another at Twickenham in the spring of 1747. A dull little building in itself, it was delectably placed in a landscape of tranquil meadows, close to the Thames and looking across to the trees of Richmond Park. Walpole revived its forgotten name of Strawberry Hill, and before long was deep in the pleasures of planting and gardening, and projecting a series of alterations and additions in the Gothic style. Gray was one of his earliest guests; he stayed at Strawberry Hill a few weeks after Walpole first acquired the place, and again in the summer of 1748. After the second of these visits Walpole wrote to his friend George Montagu that 'Gray has been here a few days and is transported with your story of Madame Bentley's diving and her white man, and indeed with all your stories'.[43] Richard Bentley, the son of the great Master of Trinity, was at this time Walpole's chief adviser on artistic and architectural matters, and his intrusive wife was a favourite laughing-stock at Strawberry Hill.

THOMAS GRAY AS A YOUNG MAN
From a painting by John Giles Eckhardt, in the National Portrait Gallery

It may be recalled that Montagu, in company with George Selwyn, had spent some weeks with Walpole and Gray in the autumn of 1739 at Rheims. He had now become a cheerful, indolent, gossip-loving bachelor, living by preference in the country but still in touch with the great world, and one of Walpole's most favoured correspondents. He and Gray occasionally met in Walpole's company, but there was little sympathy between them, however amusing Gray may have found his stories about Mrs Bentley as retailed to him by Walpole. Montagu for his part appears to have regarded Gray as a bore, and evidently said something of the sort; for in his next letter Walpole wrote:

I agree with you most absolutely in your opinion about Gray; he is the worst company in the world—from a melancholy turn, from living reclusely, and from a little too much dignity, he never converses easily—all his words are measured, and chosen, and formed into sentences; his writings are admirable; he himself is not agreeable.[44]

These gusts of slightly petulant criticism—Gray complaining of Walpole's lack of true sympathy in his misfortunes, and Walpole grumbling about Gray's reticence and dullness —need not be regarded too seriously. Temperamentally they had never been in complete accord; and as in earlier years, each would on occasion find himself irritated by the faults or the mannerisms of the other. The mood would be confided to some other friend, Wharton or Montagu, in a letter or a conversation, and would quickly pass away. At no time was their reconciliation seriously threatened by these passing clouds.

All the same, Walpole's critical sketch of Gray at this juncture was not overdrawn. Despite the liveliness of his letters, and his enjoyment of visits to London and Twickenham, and the deceptive air of youthful grace in the Eckhardt portrait, he does appear to have given the general impression of a man growing old before his time. The defensive dignity, the reticence of manner, the careful precision of speech—they were disconcerting in someone barely thirty years of age. The melancholy, of whose oppressive influence he had always been so conscious, was enhanced by the slow pace of an academic life. His horizon was bounded by his books, his walks, the friendships and hostilities of his little circle; and when he spent a few weeks away from Cambridge, he seldom strayed far from the quiet house at Stoke Poges, where his coming was eagerly awaited by those three fond old ladies, his mother and his aunts. It was all peaceful and safe and rather tame. There appeared no likelihood of a renewal of the sudden lyrical flowering of 1742, or of the emotions which had prompted it. His creative power seemed almost dead, and he spoke of his earlier poems with indifference. In the first years of their acquaintance Mason thought he set a greater value on his Latin than on his English poems,[45] but he was disinclined to carry into execution his more aspiring projects in either language. *De Principiis Cogitandi* had long since been consigned to oblivion, and likewise his drama of *Agrippina*.

He did, however, embark in the summer of 1748 upon an ambitious didactic poem in heroic couplets. 'What Name to give it I know not', he told Wharton, 'but the Subject is, the Alliance of Education and Government; I mean to show that they must necessarily concur to produce great and useful Men.'[46] He planned the poem carefully; many notes relating to it, and fragmentary maxims and aphorisms which bear upon its arguments, were preserved among his papers; he completed an opening passage of rather more than a hundred lines, describing, in the loftiest strain, the influence of environment and circumstance upon national character; and then he suddenly abandoned the whole scheme. According to Mason this was the result of the publication of Montesquieu's *L'Esprit des Lois*, in which he found that many of his best thoughts had been forestalled. According to Mason, again, he toyed later with the idea of completing the poem and dedicating it in an introductory ode to Montesquieu, but gave up this project also when the latter died in 1755.[47] Like all his age he admired

Montesquieu's great work, and welcomed it with delight when it first appeared—the style, he said, was 'the Gravity of Tacitus, temper'd with the Gayety and Fire of a Frenchman'[48]—but he himself gave a more probable explanation of his abandonment of *The Alliance of Education and Government* many years later to Norton Nicholls.

> I asked him [Nicholls wrote] why he had not continued that beautiful fragment beginning 'As sickly plants betray a niggard earth.' He said, because he could not; when I expressed surprise at this, he explained himself as follows: That he had been used to write only Lyric poetry in which the poems being short, he had accustomed himself, and was able to polish every part; that this having become habit, he could not write otherwise; and that the labour of this method in a long poem would be intolerable; besides which the poem would lose its effect for want of Chiaro-Oscuro; for that to produce effect it was absolutely necessary to have weak parts.[49]

The eighteenth-century didactic poem, like the eighteenth-century poetic drama, is little esteemed today; but even an unsympathetic age can appreciate the excellence of Gray's attempt in this form—its vigour, its eloquence, the perfect marshalling of its stately couplets. When it first appeared in Mason's biography, a few years after the poet's death, it was one of the sensations of the book, and was ranked by some critics beside the *Elegy* itself. Gibbon called it 'an exquisite specimen of a philosophic poem', and lamented its unfinished state.[50] Fox would declaim to his friends, with rising voice and heightened colour,[51] the lines with which the fragment closed:

> What wonder, in the sultry climes, that spread,
> Where Nile redundant o'er his summer-bed
> From his broad bosom life and verdure flings,
> And broods o'er Ægypt with his wat'ry wings,
> If with advent'rous oar and ready sail
> The dusky people drive before the gale;
> Or on frail floats to neighb'ring cities ride,
> That rise and glitter o'er the ambient tide.

And countless lovers of a concise and brilliant epigram have delighted in that solitary couplet, intended for a later passage on the Reformation in England, which Mason salvaged from amongst Gray's notes:

> When Love could teach a monarch to be wise,
> And Gospel-light first dawn'd from Bullen's eyes.*

Since the close of 1742, then, Gray's entire poetic output had been the ode on Walpole's cat, these opening lines of *The Alliance of Education and Government*, and the 'few autumnal verses' which may or may not have been a part of the *Elegy*. Otherwise his solitary hours had been spent, month after month and year after year, in reading and making notes of what he read. 'My life', he had told West in 1742, 'is like Harry the fourth's supper of Hens. "Poulets à la broche, Poulets en Ragoût, Poulets en Hâchis, Poulets en Fricasées." Reading here, Reading there; nothing but books with different sauces.'[52] And so he continued, ranging in the seclusion of his rooms at Peterhouse over the entire field of classical antiquity—philosophy and oratory and drama, history and geography and chronology—the steady accumulation of a stupendous mass of knowledge. In his undergraduate days he had acquired a folio volume of more than 400 pages, which he started to use as a commonplace book in accordance with 'the Method of Mr Lock'. Later he abandoned the system of arranging his entries which Locke had recommended, and gradually filled up the pages of the volume (and in due course a second volume, and part of a third) with notes upon his reading. Here and there, among the notes on Plato and the extracts from Athenaeus and Aulus Gellius, he would sometimes transcribe one of his own poems.

The three volumes are now in the library of Pembroke College. It is an absorbing exercise to follow Gray's unfailingly clear and beautiful hand through those crowded pages, and trace the course of his tireless reading.[53] Sometimes he

---

* Another striking couplet from this poem, sadly applicable to the present times, runs:
> 'While European freedom still withstands
> Th'encroaching tide, that drowns her lessening lands.'

would use subsidiary notebooks for his extracts from some particular author. He told Wharton in 1747 that he had lately read the whole of Pausanias, Athenaeus and Aeschylus again, and 'am now in Pindar and Lysias, for I take Verse and Prose together, like Bread and Cheese'; and subsequent research has found his notes on Lysias in one of these smaller notebooks, those on Pindar in a second, and copious extracts from Athenaeus in the main Commonplace Book.[54] He was, in fact, taking the whole of the ancient world for his province; and his reading and note-taking ranged from the sublimities of philosophy and poetry to the smallest details of domestic life —the wines and vineyards of the Greeks and Romans, their vehicles and furniture, food and medicine, clothing and footgear and pottery. These studies led to a particular interest in early geography, and he is said to have contemplated at one time a new edition of Strabo.[55] He carried his investigations of oriental geography into later times, and filled many pages with descriptions of Persia and India, Egypt and the Levant by medieval and modern travellers.

Yet another special interest was Greek chronology; and always at hand during these years, along with the Commonplace Books, lay his 'great Chronological Table, the Wonder and Amazement of Mr Brown'.[56] Only a few fragments of this production now survive. It was a most elaborate affair, with nine columns to each page—one for the Olympiad, the next for the Archons, the third for the public affairs of Greece, three more for the philosophers and three for the poets.[57] And in addition to the notebooks and the chronological table, Gray indulged his love of annotation still further by writing copiously in his own books and those which he borrowed from other sources. Even at this date he seems to have used the library at Pembroke in preference to that of his own college of Peterhouse. The catalogue at Pembroke records his constant borrowings of books, and in several of them his notes may still be seen.

In letter after letter, to the end of his days, Gray would tell his friends that 'to be employed is to be happy'; that 'to find oneself business is the great art of Life'; that 'the whole matter is to have always something going forward'.[58] Patient and methodical reading, long hours devoted to the transcribing of notes and extracts, industrious compilation of tables and catalogues and calendars—such were the barriers which he had raised against his encroaching melancholy, against the insidious promptings of indolence and *accidie*. And they were not adversaries to be regarded lightly. 'The Spirit of Lazyness (the Spirit of the Place), begins to possess even me, that have so long declaimed against it; yet it has not so prevail'd, but that I feel that Discontent with myself, that *Ennuy*, that ever accompanies it in its Beginnings.' So he wrote to Wharton in the spring of 1749, continuing in a lighter vein:

Time will settle my Conscience, Time will reconcile me to this languid Companion: we shall smoke, we shall tipple, we shall doze together. We shall have our little Jokes, like other People, and our long Stories; Brandy will finish what Port begun; and a Month after the Time you will see in some Corner of a *London Evening Post*, 'Yesterday, died the Rev^nd Mr John Grey, Senior-Fellow of Clare-Hall, a facetious Companion, and well-respected by all that knew him. His death is supposed to have been occasion'd by a Fit of an Apoplexy, being found fall'n out of Bed with his Head in the Chamber-Pot.'[59]

Beneath the rueful humour lay a resigned acceptance. He thought that in all likelihood the future did not hold much else in store for him. This sequestered life of reading and reflection was not the ideal existence; but it had its compensations, and to a certain extent it fulfilled his sober wishes. His temperament and his circumstances alike forbade him to expect a different lot. The ebb and flow of the creative impulse are wholly unpredictable; and he can have had no inkling, as the quiet months of 1749 passed by, of the achievement and the fame which were so soon to come.

CHAPTER VI

THE 'ELEGY'

1749-1753

I

In the eighteenth century the village of Stoke Poges lay deeply secluded in the Buckinghamshire countryside. The rich landscape of the Thames valley, with its elm-shaded meadows, spreading beechwoods and high-banked winding lanes, extended for miles around. The large parish included several widely dispersed groups of houses, little isolated centres of population; and in one of these, West End, stood the home of Gray's mother and aunts. It was a modest but comfortable two-storied dwelling known as West End House, secluded in its own garden and grounds. In the nineteenth century both house and grounds were enlarged, and the place received the more exalted name of Stoke Court; but some of the rooms remained much as they had been in Gray's own day. An ivy-covered summer-house, and a tree-shaded walk round a neighbouring meadow, were traditionally associated with his memory.*

A mile or so away was the parish church. It was a small building of flint and rubble, with a roof of red tiles covering both nave and aisles in an unbroken sweep. The low square tower was then surmounted by a shingled spire. Against the south wall of the chancel, and exceeding it in size, a chapel of red Tudor brick had been erected in the sixteenth century by the family of Hastings, Earls of Huntingdon, the lords of the manor.

---

* When I last visited Stoke Court the trees of 'Gray's Walk' had just been felled, and the house was being used for the storage of television sets. The little rooms supposedly occupied by Gray were crammed to their ceilings with the boxes containing these appliances, and similar boxes were being conveyed on an elevator-belt to the floors above.

This chapel was intended to serve as their place of burial, and also for the devotions of the inmates of an almshouse which they had built close by. The untidy turf of the churchyard was shaded by ancient elms and yews. Two great yew-trees, which Gray probably knew well, still stand close to the south porch of the church.

A little distance north of the church rose a stately Tudor house, its walls and gables and tall chimney-stacks already mellowed by time. It had likewise been built by the Earls of Huntingdon, and was bought from them towards the close of the sixteenth century by Sir Edward Coke, the future Lord Chief Justice. Coke's second wife was the widow of the nephew and heir of Queen Elizabeth's admired favourite Sir Christopher Hatton; and in Gray's time there was an unfounded but persistent tradition, to which he gave further currency, that the mansion had once been the home of Sir Christopher himself. It was now occupied by the Dowager Viscountess Cobham, who had come to live there after her husband's recent death. At present her humbler neighbours knew little about her. The sisters at West End House may have had a glimpse of a fashionable figure driving through the lanes, or rustling on Sundays through the private door from the grounds of the Manor House into her great pew beneath the church tower; but that was all.

To these tranquil scenes Gray withdrew every May or June; and apart from a week or two in London, and a few days at Strawberry Hill, he would remain there until the autumn. Day after day he would take his slow contemplative walks through the fields and lanes, so different, in the full luxuriance of summer, from the sober levels around Cambridge. It was the landscape which he had painted in the *Ode on the Spring*, the heavy-foliaged oaks, the noble beech woods, the butterflies dancing in the hot sunshine, the cattle drowsing in the shade. Away from his bookshelves and the college libraries, he began to observe the life of the little rural community of which he was temporarily a part. His eyes watched the ripening of the hay, the gradual changing of the cornfields from green to pale or tawny gold. His thoughts turned to the men who laboured in those fields and woods, whose whole existence was bounded by them and who would lie forgotten under the churchyard turf when their work was done.

The man of reading and reflection often feels an envious admiration for the man of physical skill. It need not be supposed that because he did not care for dogs and could not ride a horse, Gray was indifferent to the life of the English countryside. He must often have paused in his walks to admire the handling of scythe or sickle, axe or plough. For a town-dweller he knew a good deal about agriculture, and loved to note down the events of cornfield, orchard and garden. And he watched with sympathy and understanding, though never with sentimentality, the daily life of the people of Stoke Poges, the men working from dawn to dusk on the farms, the women in their smoky cottages. Theirs was the ordinary lot of most of the human race—poverty and toil, a measure of domestic happiness, the usual vicissitudes of fortune, and then oblivion. In his earlier odes he had written of the brevity of life, the certainty of pain and death, the helplessness of man confronted by his fate. Summer after summer, the same thoughts filled his mind as he watched the whole village busy in haymaking and harvest, or mused among the simple headstones at twilight in the churchyard. But now his meditations took on a deeper and more universal significance, as he slowly fashioned and perfected the greatest of all his poems.

II

It is unlikely that the exact dates of the composition of the *Elegy written in a Country Churchyard* will ever be known. Unless some fresh and conclusive evidence is forthcoming, opinion on the matter will always be divided, and controversy will be profitless. The poem may have been begun, and indeed in Mason's view the greater part of it was written, during the sad and eventful summer of 1742. But it seems more probable, in my own submission, that Gray merely wrote a few of the opening stanzas in 1742, and continued to work upon the poem at irregular intervals during the next eight years.* At one stage he brought it to a tentative conclusion, and in this form it possessed a unity of structure and of sentiment which the final version does not retain. At some later date he began to work on it again, and introduced for the first time a deeply personal note, which dominated the poem to its close and greatly altered its mood. Again we have no details or dates; we do not know whether these final additions were a sudden inspiration, or the outcome of months and perhaps years of labour. We only emerge from conjecture into certainty in the summer of 1750, when Gray wrote to Walpole from Stoke on the twelfth of June, enclosing a manuscript of the completed *Elegy*, and telling him that 'having put an end to a thing, whose beginning you have seen long ago, I immediately send it you'.[1]

The original impulse of the *Elegy*, as of so much more of Gray's earlier poetry, must surely have been the death of West; and a quatrain in one of West's own poems—

> Ah me! what boots us all our boasted power,
> Our golden treasure, and our purpled state?
> They cannot ward th'inevitable hour,
> Nor stay the fearful violence of Fate:

—may conceivably have suggested its stanza, its diction and even something of its mood.[2] It is possible also that Gray's impulse to bring the poem to a close, after so many years of hesitation, was connected with the death of his aunt Mary Antrobus in the previous autumn. Her loss affected him deeply; he could never forget how much he owed in the past to her devotion and self-sacrifice. She was one of the few people who throughout his life had never failed to give him kindness, reassurance and support. But whatever part these two bereavements may have played in the inspiration of the *Elegy*, the poem transcends the private sorrows of its writer. In the words of Samuel Johnson, it 'abounds with images which find

* I have reserved a fuller discussion of the composition of the *Elegy* for an appendix (pp. 271–3).

a mirrour in every mind, and with sentiments to which every bosom returns an echo'.[3] By some miraculous chance this most retiring of men had built out of his lonely meditations, the musings of his obscure and secluded life, a poem which could reach the hearts of all mankind.

It is almost impossible to analyse a work which for two centuries has formed a part of the English heritage, so familiar, so constantly quoted, so universally beloved. The exquisite twilight scene with which it opens; the long series of reflections upon fame and obscurity, ambition and destiny; those stanzas, tolling like solemn bells, which seem to voice all that can be expressed of sadness, resignation and hope—since childhood they have been a part of our consciousness, exerting upon us the same irresistible spell as they did upon our forefathers. For all its familiarity the *Elegy* retains to an extraordinary degree its original eloquence and mystery, its power to move the heart with those 'divine truisms that make us weep'.[4]

(Gray told his readers more about himself in the *Elegy* than in any other poem. Yet this introduction of his own personality was an afterthought; and some critics have felt that by his final additions to the *Elegy*, and by the epitaph in particular, he destroyed the symmetry of something that was already perfect. In its original form, the poem consisted of the first eighteen stanzas as they exist at present, stanzas in which the mood is unaltered and the argument moves steadily forward without a check or digression. The poet's attention was fixed throughout on the rude forefathers of the hamlet, their simple virtues, their destiny remote from the splendours and miseries of greatness. Then he brought his poem to a close with four more stanzas, rejected in the final version, in which he briefly touched upon his own perplexities and reconciled them to the common lot of humankind:)

> The thoughtless World to Majesty may bow
> Exalt the brave, & idolize Success
> But more to Innocence, their Safety owe
> Than Power & Genius e'er conspired to bless

And thou, who mindful of the unhonour'd Dead
Dost in these Notes their artless Tale relate
By Night & lonely Contemplation led
To linger in the gloomy Walks of Fate,

Hark how the sacred Calm that broods around
Bids ev'ry fierce tumultuous Passion cease
In still small Accents whisp'ring from the Ground
A grateful Earnest of eternal Peace

No more with Reason & thyself at Strife
Give anxious Cares & endless Wishes room
But thro' the cool sequester'd Vale of Life
Pursue the silent Tenour of thy Doom.[5]

Such was the poem as it was originally conceived, a perfect
artistic whole, completely harmonious in form and context
alike. But Gray was still not satisfied, and at some later date
he resumed work upon it once more. He rejected the sixteen
lines which had provided so superb a close, only incorporating
some scattered fragments from them in the five new stanzas
which now took their place. These were the famous 'Far from
the madding crowd's ignoble strife...', and then the stanzas
of which Johnson was to say that 'I have never seen the notions
in any other place; yet he that reads them here, persuades
himself that he has always felt them'. Amid the sober philosophic musings a fresh note begins to be heard, a sudden note
of human loneliness and anguish in the face of death:

For who to dumb Forgetfulness a prey,
This pleasing anxious being e'er resign'd,
Left the warm precincts of the chearful day,
Nor cast one longing ling'ring look behind?

On some fond breast the parting soul relies,
Some pious drops the closing eye requires;
Ev'n from the tomb the voice of Nature cries,
Ev'n in our Ashes live their wonted Fires.[6]

It is easy to see why such poetry went to the heart of Johnson,
another profoundly lonely man, and a man preoccupied as
Gray never was by the horror of death, the dread of leaving
this warm familiar world.

The next stanza introduces the figure of the poet himself.
At the close of the earlier version he had briefly appeared,
murmuring the lesson of calmness and resignation in his own
worldly cares which his twilight musings had taught him,
content to pursue the silent tenour of his doom. Now he
becomes the central figure of the poem, and occupies that place
until the end:

> For thee, who mindful of th'unhonour'd Dead
> Dost in these lines their artless tale relate;
> If chance, by lonely contemplation led,
> Some kindred Spirit shall inquire thy fate,
>
> Haply some hoary-headed Swain may say...

and then follows a strangely dramatised description of a poet
in aspect and behaviour the complete antithesis of Gray, and
of his untimely death. The language loses nothing of its
beauty; but in the figure conjured up by the swain,

> Now drooping, woeful wan, like one forlorn,
> Or craz'd with care, or cross'd in hopeless love,

it is impossible not to feel that a sacrifice has been made to
theatrical effect.

The poet dies, and is buried in the churchyard with those
whose artless tale he has related. The three final stanzas
represent his epitaph. Certain writers have condemned the
Epitaph as an artistic blunder;[7] but a biographer may be
forgiven for regarding it with gratitude. It has little of the
theatrical air of the stanzas which immediately precede it;
and it may reasonably be held to embody, without an undue
measure of poetic licence, what Gray in 1750 felt about himself *sub specie aeternitatis*. It has been suggested that these
may have been among the earliest lines of the *Elegy* to be
composed, that they were in fact intended as an epitaph on West
and were written shortly after his death. There is surely no
justification for any such view, nor can any overt reference to
West be found apart from one single line. On the contrary, the
Epitaph is intensely subjective. At the close of his greatest
poem Gray was led to describe, simply and movingly, what

sort of man he believed himself to be, how he had fared in his
passage through the world, and what he hoped from eternity:

> Here rests his head upon the lap of Earth
> A Youth to Fortune and to Fame unknown.
> Fair Science frown'd not on his humble birth,
> And Melancholy marked him for her own.
>
> Large was his bounty, and his soul sincere,
> Heav'n did a recompence as largely send:
> He gave to Mis'ry all he had, a tear,
> He gain'd from Heav'n ('twas all he wish'd) a friend.
>
> No farther seek his merits to disclose,
> Or draw his frailties from their dread abode,
> (There they alike in trembling hope repose,)
> The bosom of his Father and his God.

III

Gray had no thoughts of publishing the *Elegy*,[8] and did
not even send a copy to Wharton, his most intimate friend,
for several months to come. But Walpole, delighted and
astonished by the poem, and triumphantly confirmed in his
estimate of Gray's genius, was quite unable to keep it to
himself. He gave copies away to all his circle, and the copies
were handed about and swiftly multiplied. During the summer
one of them found its way down to the Dowager Viscountess
Cobham at the Manor House of Stoke Poges. She was presently surprised to learn from the Rev. Robert Purt, the tutor
of a young nobleman at Eton and an acquaintance of Gray's, that
the scene of this much-discussed masterpiece was the little
churchyard just outside her garden, and that the author himself was at that moment living in the parish.

Lady Cobham had been Anne, daughter of Edmund Halsey,
a wealthy brewer and Member of Parliament for Buckingham.
She had married Sir Richard Temple, first Viscount Cobham,
a distinguished soldier and politician, best remembered now as
the recipient of splendid compliments in verse from Pope and
Congreve, as the builder of Stowe and the patron for whom

Kent created its wonderful landscapes and gardens. He had died only a few months before, in the autumn of 1749; and Lady Cobham had withdrawn, a childless widow, from the Palladian magnificence of Stowe to the sombre Elizabethan halls and galleries of the Manor House at Stoke, which had descended to her from her father. With her came a relation whom she and her husband had brought up, a lively and attractive young woman of twenty-two named Henrietta Jane Speed, whose father, Colonel Samuel Speed, had died when she was a small child.

Lady Cobham did not know the two elderly widows who lived so quietly at the other end of the parish, and could not at first decide how to make the acquaintance of their equally re-tiring son and nephew. There happened to be staying with her at the time a certain Lady Schaub, the wife of Sir Luke Schaub, a naturalised Swiss who had filled a number of posts in the British diplomatic service, and had finally risen to be ambas-sador at Paris. Lady Schaub was herself a Frenchwoman, gay, good-natured, the subject of a certain amount of gossip at all times. She was a friend of Lady Brown, the hostess of the 'travelling and travelled calves', with whom, it may be re-membered, Gray was also acquainted. It was decided that this would provide a sufficient introduction, and accordingly she and Miss Speed set out one September afternoon to track down the author of the *Elegy*. They found Mrs Gray and Mrs Rogers at home, but Gray concealed himself—or later professed to have done so—in a place of refuge where ladies would not in any circumstances have intruded. So they returned home, leaving on the table this note:

Lady Schaubs compliments to Mr Gray
She is sory to have not find him to tell him that Lady Brown, is very well.[9]

Gray duly returned the call, and his reticence soon melted before Lady Cobham's warm-hearted friendliness and Miss Speed's irresistible gaiety. Before long he was a constant guest at the Manor House. He found himself welcomed on the

easiest footing into a household where everyone seemed cheerful and free from care, where nothing was taken too seriously,
where he was always sure of good company and a gratifying
measure of regard. And he found himself, probably for the
first time in his life, on terms of equal friendship with an attractive woman. The tone of *A Long Story*, the poem which he
wrote in October to commemorate the momentous visit to his
mother's house, shows how intimate that friendship had become in less than a month after their first meeting.

A Long Story was thrown off with a facility which bears out
Walpole's view that 'Gray never wrote anything easily but
things of humour: humour was his natural and original turn'.[10]
It was an airy and delectable piece of burlesque, written in a
lilting stanza copied directly from Prior's poem *The Dove*.
Gray first describes the 'Great House' and its historic background, both actual and fictitious, the Huntingdons and Hattons
and especially the redoubtable Sir Christopher:

> His bushy beard, and shoe-strings green,
> His high-crown'd hat, and sattin-doublet,
> Mov'd the stout heart of England's Queen,
> Tho' Pope and Spaniard could not trouble it.

From this mansion issue forth Lady Schaub and Miss Speed on
their search for 'a wicked Imp they call a Poet':

> The first came cap-a-pee from France
> Her conqu'ring destiny fulfilling,
> Whom meaner Beauties eye askance,
> And vainly ape her art of killing.

> The other Amazon kind Heaven
> Had arm'd with spirit, wit and satire:
> But Cobham had the polish given,
> And tip'd her arrows with good-nature.

> To celebrate her eyes, her air....
> Coarse panegyricks would but teaze her.
> Melissa is her Nom de Guerre.
> Alas, who would not wish to please her?

So the mellifluous nonsense ripples gaily on, as if the beauty
and kindness of Henrietta Speed had suddenly unfrozen a spring
in Gray's heart. The lovely warriors, 'rustling in their silks
and tissues', invade the parlour of the two old ladies, and ran-
sack the house in their quest for the poet; but

> On the first marching of the troops
> The Muses, hopeless of his pardon,
> Convey'd him underneath their hoops
> To a small closet in the garden.

The intruders depart baffled, but have left their spell, the
'powerful pothooks' of Lady Schaub's note, upon the table.
Trembling and apprehensive, he is irresistibly drawn to the
Great House; and there, watched by the ghosts of haughty
dames of the past, he is compelled to explain himself to the lady
of the mansion. He makes some halting excuses for the crime
of being a poet:

> The ghostly Prudes with hagged face
> Already had condemn'd the sinner.
> My Lady rose, and with a grace—
> She smiled, and bid him come to dinner.
>
> 'Jesu-Maria! Madam Bridget,
> 'Why, what can the Viscountess mean?'
> (Cried the square Hoods in woful fidget)
> 'The Times are alter'd quite and clean!
>
> 'Decorum's turn'd to mere civility;
> 'Her air and all her manners shew it.
> 'Commend me to her affability!
> 'Speak to a Commoner and Poet!'
>
> [*Here 500 stanzas are lost.*]
>
> And so God save our noble King,
> And guard us from long-winded Lubbers,
> That to eternity would sing,
> And keep my Lady from her Rubbers.

The note in which Miss Speed acknowledged the poem was carefully preserved by Gray, and kept, together with the 'spell', to the end of his days:

Sr Sunday morning.

I am as much at a loss to bestow the commendations due to your Performance as any of our modern Poets wou'd be to imitate it, Ev'ry body that has seen it is charm'd and Lady Cobham was the first (tho not the last) that regreted the loss of the 500 stanzas. All that I can say is, your obliging intention in sending it has fully answer'd as it not only gave us amusement the rest of the Evening but always will upon reading it over. Lady Cobham and the rest of the company hope to have yours to morrow at Din'er

I am S^r
Your most oblig'd and obed^{nt}.
HENRIETTA JANE SPEED[11]

As Walpole had given away copies of the *Elegy*, so the house-party at Stoke passed on *A Long Story* to their friends. News of it, and of Gray's friendship with Lady Cobham and Miss Speed, had apparently reached Wharton at Durham a couple of months later.

The Verses you so kindly try to keep in countenance were wrote to divert that particular Family, and succeeded accordingly [Gray told him] but, being shew'd about in Town, are not liked there at all. Mrs French, a very fashionable personage, told Mr W[alpole] that she had seen a Thing by a Friend of his, which she did not know what to make of, for it aim'd at every Thing, and meant nothing. To which he replied, that he had always taken her for a Woman of Sense, and was very sorry to be undeceived. [He also assured Wharton that] for my Heart it is no less yours than it has long been; and the last Thing in the World, that will throw it into Tumults, is a fine Lady.[12]

Indeed, at this time any serious attachment between him and Miss Speed would have been regarded as out of the question. She was almost twelve years the younger, a brilliant girl just beginning to come before the world, the probable heiress of Lady Cobham's fortune, admired and courted by everyone. He was a quiet academic recluse without any advantages of birth or position, only known outside his own circle to a handful of

people as the author of three or four poems. She could but think
of him at this stage as the agreeable and talented neighbour
unexpectedly discovered close to her new home. For him, in
spite of those chilly words to Wharton, the encounter probably
meant a good deal more. 'Coarse panegyricks would but teaze
her. . .' and he had no thoughts of venturing upon any. But a
new element of colour and warmth had suddenly entered his life.

IV

In November he went to London, where he spent a month
'diverting myself among my gay Acquaintances'—the circle of
Walpole and Chute, and no doubt the circle of Lady Cobham,
who always spent the winter at her London house. He found
himself regarded with a new respect as the author of the *Elegy*,
which was circulating ever more widely in manuscript, and was
'so applauded, it is quite a Shame to repeat it'. In December he
returned to his cell, as he told Walpole, with all the more
pleasure.[13] But early in February he received a letter which
brought him no pleasure at all. It was addressed to him by

certain Gentlemen (as their Bookseller expresses it) who have taken
the *Magazines of Magazines* into their Hands. They tell me, that an
ingenious Poem, call'd *Reflections* in a Country-Churchyard, has been
communicated to them, which they are printing forthwith: that they
are inform'd, that the *excellent* Author of it is I by name, and that they
beg not only his *Indulgence*, but the *Honor* of his *Correspondence*.[14]

Walpole's enthusiastic patronage of the *Elegy* was bound,
sooner or later, to lead to a situation of this kind. The niceties
of copyright were not much observed in the eighteenth century.
The newspapers, and especially the monthly magazines, were
in the habit of printing any stray poetry or other material that
took their fancy, regardless of the author's sanction. Gray had
not intended to publish the *Elegy* at all, or at any rate not at the
present time. His only wish, he had told Wharton, was 'that
you and two or three more People had liked it, which would have
satisfied my ambition on this Head amply'.[15] But such reticence
was now impossible; and unless he acted very quickly, his

masterpiece would come before the world in the pages of a particularly obscure and dingy periodical.

Since it was Walpole's fault in the first place that a copy of the Elegy had found its way to the *Magazine of Magazines*, Gray did not hesitate to ask his help. 'As you have brought me into a little Sort of Distress', he wrote, 'you must assist me, I believe, to get out of it, as well as I can.' He then told him of the letter he had received from the proprietors of the magazine, and continued:

I have but one bad Way left to escape the Honour they would inflict upon me, and therefore am obliged to desire you would make Dodsley print it immediately (which may be done in less than a Week's time) from your Copy, but without my Name, in what Form is most convenient for him, but in his best Paper and Character. He must correct the Press himself, and print it without any interval between the Stanza's, because the Sense is in some Places continued beyond them; and the Title must be, *Elegy, wrote in a Country Church-yard*. If he would add a Line or two to say it came into his Hands by Accident, I should like it better.... If you behold the Magazine of Magazines in the Light that I do, you will not refuse to give yourself this Trouble on my Account, which you have taken of your own Accord before now.[16]

Walpole wholeheartedly shared Gray's dislike of the magazines and their editors—'these dirt-carts and their drivers', he called them on one occasion;[17] and as he was perpetually struggling to overcome Gray's reluctance to publish his poetry, the negotiations with Dodsley were a welcome duty. He got into touch with the friendly bookseller at once, and they carried out Gray's instructions to the letter. A quarto pamphlet was produced, printed in handsome type on good paper, with wood-cut adornments emblematic of mortality on the title-page and first page of the text—skulls and bones, hourglasses, a pickaxe and a spade. The stanzas were printed continuously, without any interval between them, as Gray had directed;* and there

---

* This arrangement was continued in all the quarto editions of the poem. But Gray altered his mind as early as 1753, and the *Elegy* was printed with intervals between the stanzas in the edition with Bentley's illustrations in that year, and likewise in the 'definitive' edition of 1768.

was no author's name upon the title page. Walpole contributed a tactful note of explanation:

The following Poem came into my hands by Accident, if the general Approbation with which this little Piece has been spread, may be call'd by so slight a term as Accident. It is this Approbation which makes it unnecessary for me to make any Apology but to the Author: As he cannot but feel some Satisfaction at having pleas'd so many Readers already, I flatter myself he will forgive my communicating that Pleasure to many more. THE EDITOR

The *Elegy* appeared on sale in Dodsley's shop, at the price of sixpence, on 15 February, only five days after its author had first learned the intentions of the *Magazine of Magazines*. So the greatest poem of the eighteenth century did not have to make its first appearance tucked away with riddles and charades in the back pages of a piratical 'dirt-cart'. But it only escaped that fate by a single day. On 16 February the *Magazine of Magazines* came out, and in it the *Elegy* was printed in full, with a good number of misprints, and with the authorship unblushingly revealed to all the world. 'Gentlemen, said *Hilario*, give me leave to sooth my own melancholy, and amuse you in a most noble manner, with a fine copy of verses, by the very ingenious Mr *Gray* of *Peter-house, Cambridge.*—They are —STANZAS written in a Country Church-yard.'[18]

Gray soon subsided into his accustomed calm. He told Walpole facetiously that 'you have indeed conducted with great decency my little *misfortune*: you have taken a paternal care of it, and expressed much more kindness than could have been expected from so near a relation. But we are all frail; and I hope to do as much for you another time.' Nor was he unduly perturbed about the misprints, of which there were several.

Nurse Dodsley has given it a pinch or two in the cradle, that (I doubt) it will bear the marks of as long as it lives. But no matter: we have ourselves suffered under her hands before now; and besides, it will only look the more careless, and by *accident* as it were. I thank you for your advertisement, which saves my honour, and in a manner *bien flatteuse pour moi*, who should be put to it even to make myself a compliment in good English.[19]

But there was to be plenty of opportunity to correct misprints, for the poem soared into popularity almost from the day of its appearance. Dodsley reprinted the original quarto four times before the close of the year, and twice in the following year, and five times thereafter.* It was also pirated by other periodicals besides the *Magazine of Magazines.* The *True Briton,* the *Scots Magazine* and the *London Magazine* all made use of it during 1751; in the last-named it was sandwiched between the epilogue to Thomson's masque of *Alfred* and a rumbustious piece of propaganda in verse against the vice of gin-drinking, entitled *Strip-Me-Naked, or Royal Gin for Ever.* It appeared during the next few years in various collections of poems printed in England, Scotland and Ireland. It was imitated, and paraphrased, and parodied, and translated into Latin and Greek. It was quoted in books and in sermons, on deathbeds and on battlefields. It bore the name of its modest and reluctant author all over the globe, wherever the English tongue was spoken and wherever English books were read. And it became more generally loved and cherished than perhaps any poem in our language had ever been, its sentiments echoed in every bosom, its images mirrored in every mind.

V

For the past two years Walpole had been transforming Strawberry Hill into a miniature Gothic castle. His most ambitious works there—Gallery and Cloister, Chapel, Round Tower, Holbein Chamber—were still far in the future. At present everything was being done on a very modest scale, and

---

* The second reprint of 1751 contained an additional stanza immediately before the Epitaph.

> 'There scatter'd oft, the earliest of the year,
> By hands unseen, are show'rs of violets found;
> The red-breast loves to build and warble there,
> And little footsteps lightly print the ground.'

Gray withdrew this lovely stanza again in 1753, and it did not afterwards reappear. According to Mason, Gray removed it because 'he thought that it was too long a parenthesis in this place'. Stokes however suggests that his reason was the unintentional similarity of the lines to the fourth stanza of Collins's *Dirge in Cymbeline.*

the cramped and fragile staircase was regarded as 'the most particular and chief beauty of the Castle'.[20] Flimsy battlements and pinnacles rose among the rich verdure of Twickenham. The little rooms had Gothic wallpapers, Gothic fireplaces copied from medieval tombs, Gothic tracery in the windows, ancient painted glass in the tracery. The general effect was odd rather than beautiful, but for Walpole the adornment of his house— 'built to please my own taste, and in some degree to realize my own visions'[21]—was an enterprise of unending delight.

All the work was carefully planned by a conclave which Walpole loved to describe as the 'Committee of Taste'—Chute, Richard Bentley and himself. Despite his love of Italy and his long residence there, Chute had been discovering unexpected Gothic sympathies since his return to England, and proved himself an architect of some ability. Walpole was no draughtsman or designer, but his antiquarian and heraldic enthusiasms were given full scope. Bentley was the most creative member of the triumvirate, an irresponsible light-hearted dabbler in architecture and painting and the more frivolous forms of literature. He had settled close to Strawberry Hill and spent the greater part of his time with Walpole, who credited him with 'more sense, judgment and wit, more taste and more misfortunes than sure ever met in any man'.[22] Virtually the whole of the early decoration of Strawberry Hill was carried out to his designs, and everywhere he introduced an air of strange and most individual fantasy, quite unlike anything that medieval architects or craftsmen had ever conceived.

Beside his designs for Strawberry Hill, Bentley had made a number of drawings—vignettes, tailpieces and so forth—for Walpole's occasional poems and historical memoirs. Walpole had no particular thoughts of publishing his poems, and his memoirs were intended for the enlightenment of posterity and could not possibly have been printed in his lifetime. But it now occurred to him that an edition of Gray's poems, with illustrations by Bentley, would make an attractive book and spread the renown of his two friends. In the early summer of 1751, after telling Montagu how exceedingly bad were the designs which William Kent had lately done for *The Faerie Queene*, he added that 'our charming Mr Bentley is doing Gray as much more honour as he deserves than Spenser'.[23] A few months later Gray sent Walpole a copy of the *Hymn to Adversity*, which with the *Elegy*, the *Long Story*, and the three odes which had already appeared in Dodsley's *Collection*, made up a slender volume of half a dozen poems.[24] Bentley worked, as always, in bursts of energy alternating with long periods of indolence; but by the summer of 1752 most of his drawings were in the hands of the engraver.

Gray felt a little doubtful about the entire scheme. He hesitated to appear in such elaborate trappings as the author of six poems, four of which were already well known to the public, and another, the *Long Story*, essentially a private *jeu d'esprit*. But he admired Bentley's graceful talent, and became more and more enthusiastic as the work progressed. He made a drawing of Stoke Manor House on which one of the illustrations to the *Long Story* was based; and finally he composed some glowing *Stanzas to Mr Bentley*, in which the artist's vivid and prolific pencil was contrasted with his own reluctant pen.

> The tardy Rhymes that us'd to linger on,
>   To Censure cold, and negligent of Fame,
> In simpler measures animated run,
>   And catch a lustre from his genuine flame.
>
> Ah! could they catch his strength, his easy grace,
>   His quick creation, his unerring line,
> The energy of Pope they might efface,
>   And Dryden's harmony submit to mine...

Dodsley undertook the printing of the volume, and the engraving of the plates was mainly done by Johann Sebastian Müller, although the illustrations to the *Elegy* were entrusted to the more delicate hand of Charles Grignion. Proofs began to reach Gray at Stoke, where his two aunts—Mrs Oliffe seems temporarily to have joined the household at this time—got hold of the *cul de lampe* for the *Elegy* and mistook it for a 'burying-ticket' or invitation to a funeral: 'and so they still conceive it to be, even with all their Spectacles on.'[25] He was impressed by the high quality of the work, which far surpassed his idea of English engraving; he carefully corrected, and in a few instances altered, the text of the poems; and everything went on happily until the eve of publication in February 1753. Then he insisted upon a last-minute alteration of the title-page. His poems, he told Dodsley, were 'only subordinate and explanatory to the drawings', and the book must be entitled *Designs by Mr R. Bentley for Six Poems by Mr T. Gray.*[26]

The alteration was duly made; but directly afterwards he heard from Walpole that at Dodsley's special request the Eckhardt portrait was being engraved by Müller as the frontispiece to the book. He took fright at once.

> Sure you are not out of your Wits! [he wrote to Walpole]. This I know, if you suffer my Head to be printed, you infallibly will put me out of mine. I conjure you to put a stop immediately to any such design.... The thing, as it was, I know will make me ridiculous enough; but to appear in proper Person at the head of my works, consisting of half a dozen Ballads in 30 Pages, would be worse than the Pillory. I do assure you, if I had received such a Book with such a frontispiece without any warning, I believe, it would have given me a Palsy. Therefore I rejoice to have received this Notice; and shall not be easy, till you tell me all thoughts of it are laid aside. I am extremely in earnest, and can't bear even the Idea![27]

Walpole at once suppressed the half-finished plate, and calmed Gray's anxieties with a charming letter of reassurance. 'You must not wonder', he concluded, 'if I am partial to you and yours, when you can write as you do and yet feel so little Vanity.'[28]

The book, a small folio, was published in the last week of March, at the price of half a guinea. Even with the text printed on one side of the leaf, it only extended to thirty-six pages. For each poem Bentley had designed a full-page illustration, a headpiece, initial letter and tailpiece. Opinions on its artistic merits have differed greatly. Sir Kenneth Clark has called it 'the most graceful monument to Gothic Rococo',[29] while Mr C. F. Bell, with the unquestionably superior productions of contemporary France in mind, dismisses it as 'a barbaric, amateurish curiosity'.[30] Amateurish it certainly was, like all Bentley's undertakings and most of Walpole's; but with all its faults the book retains a compelling originality and charm. Bentley was not successful with the more sombre poems; he was quite unfitted to deal with the grim abstractions of Gray's imagination, Melancholy and Adversity, Jealousy and Madness, 'disdainful Anger, pallid Fear, and Shame that sculks behind'. But the full-page illustration to the *Elegy*, with its blending of the chivalric and the pastoral, is a work of genuine beauty, of a quality that Gothic Rococo was never to achieve again; and the same sense of poetry is conveyed in the tailpiece to the *Eton Ode*, with the sun setting beyond the Chapel, the boys rowing on the river and a mallard rising from the sedge.

Bentley was happiest of all, however, in the designs for the lighter poems, *A Long Story* and the ode on the death of Walpole's cat, where his gay extravagance and inexhaustible fancy could run riot. The principal illustration to the *Long Story* shows Gray being escorted to his hiding-place under the hoops of two stalwart Muses, while Lady Schaub and Miss Speed sail through the air in hot pursuit, preceded by Mr Purt in the guise of Fame, blowing lustily on a double trumpet. Above and around the principal scene is an elaborate rococo border, in which Sir Christopher Hatton dances a galliard, while Queen Elizabeth and the Pope confront one another in scornful defiance. Beside them are their chosen weapons, the cannon known as the Queen's pocket pistol, and (since even in its lightest moments Strawberry Hill maintained its Whiggish postures) a Papal bull and a crucifix, a phial of poison and a dagger. In the same vein of fantasy were the decorations of the ode on poor Selima—cats mourning her death in hatbands and scarves, Destiny cutting the threads of her nine lives, mice rejoicing at her death, and the final scene in Charon's boat, where she arches her back and spits at the menacing heads of Cerberus.

The drawings were full of private jokes and allusions, some of which must now be lost. In the vignette on the title-page Bentley drew himself as a monkey sitting at an easel under a withered tree, while a nude figure representing Gray reclined, lyre in hand, under the shade of a flourishing laurel[31]—a theme which was repeated in the principal illustration of the *Ode on the Spring*. It would be interesting to know whether the three figures of the poet in the book were in fact intended to bear any close resemblance to Gray, and whether the attractive girl of the *Long Story* was actually a portrait of Henrietta Speed. In view of his manifold anxieties over the volume, and his fears of possible ridicule, it seems likely that Gray would have insisted, during one of the early consultations with Walpole and Bentley at Strawberry Hill, on the figures being drawn from the artist's fertile imagination and not from life.

In any case the reception of the book was to mean little to him. At the end of February his mother, who had been in declining health for a year or more, became gravely ill, and on 11 March she died. She was buried in the churchyard at Stoke Poges, close to the eastern end of the chancel, in the grave where her sister already lay. After the funeral Gray hastened to London, where Wharton fortunately happened to be staying. On the 29th the book appeared, but he found himself indifferent to criticism or praise, thinking only of the valiant and devoted woman whom he was presently to describe on her tombstone as ' the careful tender mother of many children, one of whom alone had the misfortune to survive her '.

CHAPTER VII

THE PINDARIC ODES AND THE MIGRATION TO PEMBROKE COLLEGE
1753-1756

I

THE course of Gray's life was little altered by his unexpected fame. It was inevitable that he should become the subject of some curiosity, and that his personality should be discussed both in Cambridge and in London. His name was being carried far and wide by the constant reprinting of the *Elegy*. The edition of the *Six Poems* consolidated his reputation within a more limited but highly influential circle. As early as the spring of 1753 he was described in *The World* as 'the sweetest of our elegiac poets', and before long was being quoted again in that most fashionable of periodicals.[1] He could not wholly escape the personal publicity which he had foreseen and dreaded; but he did all he could to avoid it, and the sudden tide of success neither enlarged his circle of friends nor affected his way of life.

This fear of intrusion no doubt enhanced the air of coldness of which strangers used to complain, the precision of manner and speech which so often struck the casual observer. Fastidious withdrawal had always come instinctively to him, and he now employed it as the best defence against the well-meaning admirer, the gossip and the bore. In the company of his chosen associates, or addressing them in his letters, he was all wit and kindness and warmth of heart; but to the world at large he presented a different aspect—frigid, reticent, finical. He seems to have been quite indifferent to the impression he made on people whom he did not like and whose opinion he did not value. His studied aloofness was not taken in good part. University gossip is never unduly charitable, and there was much comment upon the careful fashion of his clothes, his measured walk, the solicitude with which he arranged his rooms. His delicacy was represented as effeminacy; stories were exchanged, over port and tobacco in the combination rooms, about the flowers in his window-boxes and the *pot pourri* in his china jars, his tea and his apricot marmalade. In time even distant strangers such as William Shenstone came to hear of these foibles, so incongruously remote from the splendour and magnanimity of the *Elegy*, and were struck by the paradox of 'Mr Gray, of manners very delicate, yet possessed of a poetical vein fraught with the noblest and sublimest images, and of a mind remarkably well stored with the more masculine parts of learning'.[2]

A number of factors—the sadness of his mother's death, his sudden onsets of melancholy, a growing anxiety about his health—increased Gray's tendency to withdraw into the privacy of his rooms and the little circle of his trusted friends. The disturbances of childhood and the sorrows of early manhood had implanted in him a deep apprehensiveness, a longing for safety which grew in intensity with the approach of middle age. As he had written in that cancelled passage of the *Elegy*,

> The thoughtless World to Majesty may bow,
> Exalt the brave, and idolize Success,
> But more to Innocence their Safety owe
> Than Power and Genius e'er conspired to bless.

In an unfriendly world he was determined to retain what he had achieved of personal and financial security, to enjoy the comforts of scholarly retirement and even a measure of luxury. 'I love a little finery', he once wrote; and loving finery in other people, he did not see why he should not indulge in a modest degree of it himself. Such were the varied origins of the peculiarities which now brought ridicule upon him at Cambridge —the precise and defensive manner, the elegance of his dress and his surroundings, the ill-concealed timidity about fire. Most of all, however, his withdrawal was probably due to the state of his health. He had lately become the victim of a recurrent illness which was diagnosed as gout, and from 1754 onwards some of the pocket-books survive in which he recorded his symptoms.[3] In the spring of 1754 he was suffering from rheumatic pains in his feet and legs, and also from 'pain in the breast, and a sinking there frequently, which goes off by exercise and quick motion'. During 1755 the Latin entries in his pocket-book form a detailed and almost continuous narrative of ill-health. They reveal, even more clearly than the letters in which he described his condition to his friends,[4] the pain and depression, the attacks of feverishness and dizziness, the restless nights and uneasy days which he suffered during so much of that year. The physicians of the eighteenth century included a wide variety of ailments under the comprehensive term of gout, and it is now thought probable that Gray's malady was not solely of a gouty or rheumatic nature, but was also in part an affection of the kidneys, which intensified in later years.[5] These bouts of illness, and the anticipation of them, weighed heavily on his spirits. He could give no concentrated attention to his studies, still less to the writing of poetry. Depression and listlessness would enshroud him, until the black cloud lifted and he could once more take pleasure in his books and the company of his friends, and those walks in garden and countryside which were at this time perhaps his greatest solace.

As even his earliest poems show, Gray had never regarded the beauties of nature with the vague appreciation of a townsman. From his youth he had looked at trees and flowers and growing crops with something of an expert's eye, and his interest in botany and natural history continued to develop in middle age. The 1754 pocket-book is full of details about wind and weather, the earliest appearance of flowers and the progress of the crops. It also shows that the array of flowers in his rooms, the subject of occasional ridicule by his detractors, was in fact a hobby with an experimental bearing. Despite his ill-health during this spring, he must have spent some happy hours pottering among his glasses of jonquils and hyacinths, his bowls of tuberoses, the branches of plum and almond in water, the lupins and Windsor beans which he was growing in moss and the anemones on wet sponge. In the same way he loved to record what he saw in his walks; and he began to make observations for the special benefit of Wharton, whose interests lay along the same lines, of the budding and leafing of the trees, the appearance of migrant birds, the ripening of fruit, the cutting of hay and corn, the turning and fall of the leaves, and (to complete 'my Georgick in prose') the first sowing of winter wheat.[6] Whenever his health allowed he might be seen walking slowly and circumspectly in the college gardens or in the meadows around Cambridge, always ready to stop—glad indeed of an excuse to stop—to watch the sunshine of late winter upon snowdrops and aconites, or the rooks piling their nests in the elms, or the drifts of cow-parsley foaming along the dusty roadsides, or the brilliance of autumn colouring in lime and beech.

II

Little of moment had occurred in Gray's circle at Cambridge since the defeat of Roger Long and the admission of Mason and Tuthill as Fellows of Pembroke. Towards the close of 1748 the Master of Peterhouse, Dr Whalley, had died, and another of the Fellows, Edmund Keene, had been elected in his place. Edmund Keene and his elder brother Benjamin belonged to a King's Lynn family attached to the political interest of the Walpoles, and had begun their careers under the patronage of Sir Robert, Benjamin in the diplomatic service and Edmund in the Church. According to Horace Walpole, who frequently repeated the story, the new Master of Peterhouse had received a valuable living on condition that he married one of Sir Robert's natural daughters, but 'my father dying soon after, he dispensed with himself from taking the wife'.[7] For this or other reasons Gray had no great liking for Keene, but was on superficially pleasanter relations with him than with his predecessor, being 'of his Cabinet-Council' over a disputed fellowship soon after his election, and indeed 'on very good and civil Terms' with

him throughout his mastership.[8] In March 1752 Keene was
made Bishop of Chester, but retained the mastership of Peterhouse until 1754, when he resigned and was succeeded by Dr
Edmund Law. Towards the end of 1751 Richard Stonhewer at
length became a Fellow of Peterhouse, a matter of great satisfaction to Gray, who had been trying to bring it about for
several years past.[9]

One of Stonhewer's first pupils at Peterhouse was the Earl of
Euston, before long to be better known as the third Duke of
Grafton. Gray would have met him regularly at the Fellows'
table, but he says nothing about the young man in his letters at
this time. The acquaintance, however, was not forgotten; indeed, it will be seen that Stonhewer, who later became the
Duke's private secretary and confidential friend throughout his
troubled political career, did not allow him to forget it. Another
fellow-commoner at Peterhouse, whom Gray soon knew more
intimately, was Lord John Cavendish, a younger son of the
Duke of Devonshire. He was a pupil of Mason, who thought
very highly of his talents and addressed a characteristic elegy
to him when he left Cambridge:

> Ere yet, ingenuous Youth, thy steps retire
>   From Cam's smooth margin, and the peaceful vale,
> Where Science call'd thee to her studious quire,
>   And met thee musing in her cloisters pale;
> Oh! let thy friend (and may he boast the name)
>   Breathe from his artless reed one parting lay.... [10]

Lord John was small and yellow-haired, extremely studious
and at the same time gay and cheerful. George Selwyn used to
call him 'the learned canary-bird'. He too entered politics
soon after leaving Cambridge, and provided Gray with another
link with the great world until the end of his life.

About this time also Gray began to include Richard Hurd, a
Fellow of Emmanuel, in the number of his friends. Hurd had
already attracted some notice as an editor of Horace, and was
known also as the ally and champion of Warburton; but his
more important works, the *Moral and Political Dialogues* and

the *Letters on Chivalry and Romance*, had not yet appeared. In due course his career in the church was to be crowned with the bishopric of Worcester, which he held for twenty-five years and well into the next century. Gray tended to laugh at his old-fashioned mannerisms, and when asked what sort of a man he was, would only reply that he was 'the last person who left off stiff-topped gloves'.[11] But they corresponded regularly, respected each other's abilities, and always remained on amicable terms.

There was an echo of Gray's Florentine days in the spring of 1751, when Francis Whithed, the younger of his 'two Italianized friends', died in his thirty-second year. Whithed had been about to marry an important heiress, Miss Margaret Nicoll. Chute, his cousin and lifelong friend, was almost heartbroken, but overcame his grief sufficiently to attempt the transference of Miss Nicoll's affections to Walpole's spendthrift nephew, the third Earl of Orford, in the hope of repairing the declining fortunes of Houghton. Before long, however, Horace's uncle 'Old Horace' of Wolterton, aided by the sinister Etough, entered the field and tried to secure Miss Nicoll for one of his own sons. In the resulting *imbroglio* Gray somehow became involved as a partisan of Walpole and Chute, and told Walpole that there were only three methods of dealing properly with Etough, 'the Cudgel, the Blanket, and the Horse-pond. If you are present at the operation, you may venture to break a Leg or an Arm *en attendant*, and when I see you, I may possibly give you some Reasons, why you ought to have broke t'other Leg and t'other Arm also: for it is too long to stay, till he is a Bishop.'[12] It need scarcely be added that Walpole was no more likely to adopt such heroic measures, in person or by proxy, than was Etough, for all his wire-pulling and servility, to be raised to the episcopal bench. So far as is known 'the brawling Fiend' made no further appearances in Gray's life, and he died at his Hertfordshire parsonage six years later. In the end neither branch of the Walpole family secured Miss Nicoll, who was married in due course to Lord Carmarthen.

In 1753, the year of his mother's death, Gray did not spend the summer at Stoke Poges as he had done for so many years past. Instead he travelled northwards to visit Wharton at Durham, accompanied by Stonhewer who was on his way to see his father in the same county. They inspected various notable houses, including Burleigh and Belvoir Castle, in the course of their journey; met Wharton and his wife at Studley Royal; saw Ripon and Fountains Abbey with them, and went on to Durham—'one of the most beautiful Vales here in England to walk in with prospects that change every ten steps, and open something new wherever I turn me, all rude and romantic'.[13] It was the first of the sight-seeing tours which henceforward he undertook almost every summer for the rest of his life.

He spent the next two months at Durham, seeing the castles and country-houses of the neighbourhood, dining with the Bishop, accompanying Wharton's cheerful party to the assembly and twice to the races. In September he had intended to move on to Hull, where Mason was staying at his family home, but was prevented by the unexpected death of Mason's father. 'I know', he told Mason, thinking of his own mother's death, 'what it is to lose a Person, that one's eyes and heart have long been used to, and I never desire to part with the remembrance of that loss, nor would wish you should.'[14] It was presently disclosed, to the general surprise, that the elder Mason had virtually disinherited his son, leaving his whole estate to his second wife for her life, and then entailing it upon his daughter by her. On his way southward Gray met Mason at York, and was greatly impressed by the fortitude with which he bore the unexpected loss of his patrimony. 'He has absolutely no support at present but his fellowship,' he wrote to Wharton, 'yet he looks more like a Hero, than ever I knew him, like one that can stare poverty in the face without being frighted, and instead of growing little and humble before her, has fortified his Spirit and elevated his brow to meet her like a Man.'[15] Mason's character was a complex one, and many critics have found it wholly unsympathetic; but it should always be remembered that his vanity and his frequent absurdities were outweighed, in the eyes of Gray and others of his contemporaries, by very different qualities.

Gray returned to Cambridge at the beginning of October. In the stage-coach he made the acquaintance of a Lady Swinburne, 'a Roman-Catholick, not young, that had been much abroad, seen a great deal, knew a great many people, very chatty and communicative, so that I passed my time very well'.[16] Lady Swinburne was born a Bedingfield of Oxburgh in Norfolk, a family which was to be better known to Gray a couple of years later, when one of its younger members, Edward Bedingfield, an enthusiastic admirer of his poetry, visited his rooms at Cambridge during his absence and left a volume of Italian verse and a letter full of compliments. More than a year was to elapse before the two men finally met; but in due course Edward Bedingfield—who, incidentally, was married to his cousin, a daughter of the agreeable Lady Swinburne—made a second pilgrimage to Cambridge, and a friendship was established which endured to the end of the poet's life.[17]

Gray spent most of the autumn at Stoke, where the familiar landscapes were now saddened for him by memories of his mother's illness and death. Later he went to London and there saw much of Mason, who had accepted the post of private secretary to the fourth Earl of Holdernesse, a Yorkshire nobleman holding high office in Pelham's ministry. Mason only occupied this position for a few months, and then entered into holy orders, being ordained towards the end of 1754. He became Lord Holdernesse's chaplain, and in that capacity accompanied his patron next summer to the court at Hanover. He was also presented by Lord Holdernesse to the living of Aston in Yorkshire. On receiving these preferments he resigned his fellowship at Pembroke.

Gray returned to Cambridge just before Christmas, and remained there almost continuously until the following summer, suffering at intervals from the gouty and feverish symptons

which have already been described. In May, John Chute succeeded on the death of his only surviving brother to the beautiful Tudor house, The Vyne in Hampshire, which their great-
grandfather had acquired during the Commonwealth years.
The brother was an eccentric and ill-tempered character, and it
had been feared that he might leave the estate elsewhere; so the
entry of Chute into his birthright was a subject of relief as well
as of satisfaction to the whole of Walpole's circle. Gray spent
a few days at The Vyne early in July, and then he and Chute went
together on a short visit to Strawberry Hill.[18] Later, after a
period at Stoke, he set out on his usual summer tour, staying
first with William Cole in his comfortable parsonage at
Bletchley, and then with George Montagu at Greatworth in
Northamptonshire.

During this tour he explored several of the midland counties,
and saw a number of great houses—Stowe, Woburn, Wroxton,
and finally Warwick Castle. As always, the descriptions of his
travels in his letters to Wharton were full of gaiety and wit.
He was deeply impressed by the ancient dignity of Warwick
Castle, and not less amused by the architectural vagaries of its
owner Lord Brooke:

He has sash'd the great Appartment, that's to be sure, (I can't
help these things) and being since told, that square sash-windows
were not Gothic, he has put certain whim-wams withinside the glass,
which appearing through are to look like fretwork. Then he has
scooped out a little Burrough in the massy walls of the place for his
little self and his children, which is hung with Paper and printed
Linnen, and carved chimney-pieces, in the exact manner of Berkley-
square or Argyle-Buildings. What in short can a Lord do now a
days, that is lost in a great old solitary Castle, but sculk about, and
get into the first hole he finds, as a Rat would do in like case?

From Warwick Castle he walked to the celebrated viewpoint
at Guy's Cliff:

and of all improvers commend me to Mr Greathead, its present
owner. He shew'd it me himself, and is literally a fat young Man
with a head and face much bigger than they are usually worn. It was
naturally a very agreeable rock, whose Cliffs cover'd with large trees

hung beetling over the Avon, which twists twenty ways in sight of it. There was the Cell of Guy, Earl of Warwick, cut in the living stone, where he died a Hermit. . .there were his fountains bubbling out of the Cliff; there was a Chantry founded to his memory in Henry the Sixth's time. But behold the Trees are cut down to make room for flowering shrubs, the rock is cut up, till it is as smooth and as sleek as sattin; the river has a gravel-walk by its side; the Cell is a Grotta with cockle-shells and looking-glass; the fountains have an iron-gate before them, and the Chantry is a Barn, or a little House. Even the poorest bits of nature, that remain, are daily threatened, for he says (and I am sure, when the Greatheads are once set upon a thing, they will do it) he is determined, it shall be *all new*. These were his words, and they are Fate.[19]

At the close of his tour Gray returned to Stoke. On his arrival he learnt that Wharton, who had resolved to leave Durham and practise his profession for a time in London, was now comfortably settled there, and had already been inspired by a visit to Strawberry Hill with a longing to adorn his house in the Gothic manner. Although willing to admit that Walpole had achieved 'a purity and propriety of Gothicism (with very few exceptions) that I have not seen elsewhere', Gray did not feel that such embellishments were well suited to a doctor's house in the City of London, and told Wharton that 'if you project anything, I hope it will be entirely within doors; and don't let me (when I come gaping into Coleman-street) be directed to the Gentleman's at the ten Pinnacles, or with the Church-porch at his door'.[20] Shortly afterwards he was invited by the second Earl of Bristol, who was expecting to go to Lisbon as British Minister, to accompany him as his private secretary.[21] He had some acquaintance with Lord Bristol's younger brother, the Reverend Frederick Hervey, who may have suggested him for the position. A sojourn in the climate of Portugal might have been of great benefit to his health at this time; but he refused the offer, and in the event Lord Bristol did not go to Lisbon, but was sent instead as envoy to Turin.

Ill-health continued to be his portion during the whole of 1755. His pocket-book for the year is full of entries recording gouty and feverish symptons, and attacks of depression both mental and physical. After one sharp fit of gout at the beginning of July he went to stay with Chute at The Vyne, and they spent a few days exploring the southern part of Hampshire, and admiring the landscapes and seascapes of that delectable countryside:

the Fleet, the Sea winding, and breaking in bays into the land, the deep shade of tall Oaks in the enclosures, which become blue, as they go off into distance, Porchester-Castle, Carshot-Castle, and all the Isle of Wight, in which you plainly distinguish the fields, hedgerows, and woods next the shore, and a back-ground of hills behind them. I have never seen a more magnificent or more varied Prospect.[22]

At the close of this little tour he returned to Stoke, but another attack of gout prevented his usual summer visit to Strawberry Hill. In October he was still at his aunt's house, 'in a very listless, unpleasant, and inutile state of Mind'.[23] There are no references in his letters, during any of the periods which he had passed at Stoke since the gay summer of the *Long Story*, to the presence at the Manor House of Henrietta Speed. In 1752 he had told Walpole that 'I know not what you mean by hours of love, and cherries, and pine-apples. I neither see nor hear anything here, and am of opinion that is the best way.'[24] This remark was probably to do with Miss Speed; but it is more than cryptic, and for several years nothing more is heard of her at all.

III

Walpole once said that in certain years of his life Gray was 'in flower';[25] and this was certainly the case during the early seventeen-fifties, the period immediately following the completion of the *Elegy*. The flowering, as always, was slow and reluctant, and its progress was further retarded by the state of his health. But between 1752 and 1757 he achieved the two great Pindaric odes which he himself ranked high above the *Elegy*, and regarded as the most important of all his works. He also struggled for months with another poem, an ode in his earlier and less elaborate manner, which he was never able to complete.

The Pindaric Odes and the migration to Pembroke College

In the summer of 1752 Dodsley was thinking of publishing a
fourth volume of his *Collection of Poems*, and Gray wrote to
Walpole that 'I don't know but I may send him very soon (by
your hands) an ode to his own tooth, a high Pindarick upon
stilts, which one must be a better scholar than he is to understand
a line of, and the very best scholars will understand but a little
matter here and there. It wants but seventeen lines of having
an end, I don't say of being finished.'[26] This was the earliest
form of the poem which he first called *Ode in the Greek Manner*,
then *The Powers of Poetry*, and finally (though not until 1768)
The Progress of Poesy. It was not sent to Dodsley at this early
stage; indeed, he told Bedingfield some years later that it had
been 'wrote by fits and starts at very distant intervals',[27] and
no doubt it underwent a great deal of revision before it was at
last completed in 1754. At the end of that year he sent a copy
to Wharton. 'I desire you would by no means suffer this to be
copied', he told his friend: 'nor even shew it, unless to very few,
and especially not to mere Scholars, that can scan all the measures
in Pindar, and say the Scholia by heart.'[28]

The poem was uncompromisingly classical in form, uncompromisingly learned in content and allusion. It was as though
he was half-ashamed of the huge popular success of the *Elegy*,
and was now resolved to write for a more eclectic audience. He
did not expect unscholarly people like Dodsley to understand
his new ode, or 'mere scholars', however versed in the more
pedantic aspects of classical learning, to appreciate it. And
when it was eventually published, those who understood or
appreciated it proved to be very few indeed. Educated readers,
who had at least some acquaintance with Pindar in the original,
were not seriously disconcerted by the form of the poem. And
even for those without Greek, 'Pindariques' were no novelty
from the time of Cowley onwards, although no poet of the first
importance had followed the structure of Pindar's odes with
the same exactitude as Gray.[29] It was the content of this *Ode in
the Greek Manner*, not its form, that so many people were to
find perplexing. He had in fact written an extremely difficult

poem, obscure, allusive, soaring at times into rhapsody and incantation. It is not an easy poem to grasp today, even with the aid of the explanatory footnotes which he withheld until the collected edition of 1768, and then inserted with an acid little statement that he had felt 'too much respect for the understanding of his readers' to provide them before.

It may be remembered that in 1747 Gray had been deep in Pindar and Lysias, 'for I take Verse and Prose together, like Bread and Cheese'.[30] The closeness of his study of Pindar at that time is attested by the notes in one of his commonplace books; and it has been pointed out by Mr Powell Jones[31] that several of the passages which he then transcribed were vividly present in his mind when he was writing *The Progress of Poesy*. In 1747 he had noted, as 'an Example of fine Expression and poetic Painting, equal to anything I have met with', the lines in the first Pythian Ode which describe Jove's eagle calmed into repose by the power of music. In *The Progress of Poesy* he himself adapted these lines:

> Perching on the scept'red hand
> Of Jove, thy magic lulls the feather'd king
> With ruffled plumes, and flagging wing:
> Quench'd in dark clouds of slumber lie
> The terror of his beak, and light'nings of his eye.

And in his notes of 1768 he admitted their source, calling them 'a weak imitation of some incomparable lines' in Pindar's ode, from which he had likewise derived other thoughts in the first antistrophe of his own.

These notes, besides indicating Gray's sources and derivations, provided an explanation—usually couched in the most laconic terms—of the drift of each stanza. In the opening strophe 'the various sources of poetry, which gives life and lustre to all it touches, are here described; its quiet majestic progress enriching every subject (otherwise dry and barren) with a pomp of diction and luxuriant harmony of numbers; and its more rapid and irresistible course, when swoln and hurried away by the conflict of tumultuous passions'. The antistrophe describes 'the power of harmony to calm the turbulent sallies of the soul'; the epode 'the power of harmony to produce all the graces of motion in the body'. The second strophe is glossed as follows: 'To compensate the real and imaginary ills of life, the Muse was given to Mankind by the same Providence that sends the Day by its cheerful Presence to dispel the gloom and terrors of the Night.' In the second antistrophe Gray had endeavoured to portray the 'extensive influence of poetic Genius over the remotest and most uncivilised Nations: its connection with liberty, and the virtues that naturally attend on it'. And so he proceeded to the concluding sections of the ode, with their description of the progress of poetry from Greece to Italy, from Italy to England, to Shakespeare, Milton, Dryden, and the latest and least illustrious of their successors:

> Oh! Lyre divine, what daring Spirit
> Wakes thee now? Tho' he inherit
> Nor the pride, nor ample pinion,
> That the Theban Eagle bear
> Sailing with supreme dominion
> Thro' the azure deep of air:
> Yet oft before his infant eyes would run
> Such forms, as glitter in the Muse's ray
> With orient hues, unborrow'd of the Sun:
> Yet shall he mount, and keep his distant way
> Beyond the limits of a vulgar fate,
> Beneath the Good how far—but far above the Great.

This sense of exaltation, of his solemn calling as one of the English poets, was very present in Gray's mind during the writing of his two Pindaric odes. However slow and spasmodic the process of their composition, there came sudden gusts of inspiration when, as he told Norton Nicholls many years afterwards, 'I felt myself the bard'.[32] Many critics, from Gray's own time until the present day, have protested against the uplifted tone and the elaborate imagery of these poems. 'He has a kind of strutting dignity, and is tall by walking on tiptoe' was Johnson's view of the daring spirit who had assumed the lyre of Pindar. Cumbrous splendour, glittering accumulations of ungraceful ornaments, 'criticism disdains to chase a schoolboy to his common-places'—no words could be too harsh for *The Progress of Poesy* and its companion.[33] There is much to be said in favour of Johnson's critical severities. But for some of Gray's contemporaries and his readers later in the century, before Wordsworth and Coleridge, Shelley and Keats had revolutionised all conceptions of romantic poetry, *The Progress of Poesy* held a new and unexpected beauty. Such lines as

> ...Oft, beneath the od'rous shade
> Of Chili's boundless forests laid,
> She deigns to hear the savage Youth repeat
> In loose numbers wildly sweet
> Their feather-cinctured Chiefs, and dusky Loves...

must surely have conjured up strange visions of romance for those who knew nothing of *Kubla Khan* or *The Ancient Mariner*.

> Woods, that wave o'er Delphi's steep,
> Isles, that crown th' Egæan deep,
> Fields, that cool Ilissus laves,
> Or where Mæander's amber waves
> In lingering Lab'rinths creep....

Where else can this clear lyrical note be paralleled in the high eighteenth century? Where else in that age can be found the subtleties of measure and rhythm in the first epode, the passage which led Mrs Garrick, the *prima ballerina* of her day, to pronounce that Gray, who had never danced, was the only poet who ever understood dancing?

Wharton naturally urged the publication of this new poem, but Gray was unwilling to print it by itself. 'I have two or three Ideas more in my head. What is to come of them? Must they too come out in the shape of little six-penny flams, dropping one after another, till Mr Dodsley thinks fit to collect them with Mr this's Song, and Mr t'other's epigram, into a pretty Volume?'[34] Unhappily only a single one of these contemplated poems, *The Bard*, was ever to be completed.

Another, which he probably did not even begin to compose, was to be based on the following theme: 'All that men of power can do for men of genius is to leave them at their liberty, compared to birds that, when confined to a cage, do but regret the loss of their freedom in melancholy strains, and lose the luscious wildness and happy luxuriance of their notes, which used to make the woods resound.'[35] The plan of a third was thus outlined in his pocket-book of 1754: 'Contrast between the winter past and coming spring.—Joy owing to that vicissitude. —Many who never feel that delight.—Sloth.—Envy.— Ambition. How much happier the rustic who feels it, tho' he knows not how.'[36]

Of this last poem, to which Mason gave the title of *Ode on the Pleasure arising from Vicissitude*, six complete stanzas and some other fragments survive. It was to be a poem in his earlier manner; and the graceful lines, fresh, crystal-clear, almost Wordsworthian in their simplicity, form a remarkable contrast to the richness and sonority of the Pindaric odes:

> New-born flocks in rustic dance
>   Frisking ply their feeble feet.
> Forgetful of their wintry trance
>   The Birds his presence greet.
> But chief the Sky-lark warbles high
> His trembling thrilling ecstasy
> And, less'ning from the dazzled sight,
> Melts into air and liquid light.
>
> Yesterday the sullen year
>   Saw the snowy whirlwind fly;
> Mute was the musick of the air,
>   The Herd stood drooping by:
> Their raptures now that wildly flow,
> No yesterday, nor morrow know;
> Tis Man alone that Joy descries
> With forward and reverted eyes....

Gray is contrasting nature, rapturous and thoughtless nature, with the hopes and fears of humankind, as he had done in the *Ode on the Spring* a dozen years before. But throughout this wonderful fragment of a poem he strikes a note, tentative perhaps but curiously significant, of acceptance and consolation:

> Smiles on past Misfortune's brow
>   Soft Reflection's hand can trace;
> And o'er the cheek of Sorrow throw
>   A melancholy grace;
> While Hope prolongs our happier hour,
> Or deepest shades, that dimly lour
> And blacken round our weary way,
> Gilds with a gleam of distant day.

It is not known precisely when Gray was working on this ode, or why he abandoned it. His attacks of illness during 1754 may have been the cause, although in 1755, a year of more serious and persistent ill-health, he was able to compose the greater part of *The Bard*. One stanza indeed can perhaps be fully appreciated only by those acquainted with illness and pain:

> See the Wretch, that long has tost
>   On the thorny bed of Pain,
> At length repair his vigour lost,
>   And breathe and walk again:
> The meanest flowret of the vale,
> The simplest note that swells the gale,
> The common Sun, the air, and skies,
> To him are opening Paradise.

Whatever the reason, those gentle strains were put aside, and early in the following year Gray resumed the lyre of Pindar. For some considerable time he had been increasingly drawn to the study of European and more especially of English history. He had not by any means given up the Greek and Latin classics, or the narratives of oriental travel, or indeed any of his varied fields of research; but the chroniclers of England and France were now his favourite reading, and nothing pleased him better than to explore their laborious pages in the hope of identifying the figures in some ancient painting newly acquired by Walpole, or otherwise bolstering up the somewhat flimsy antiquarian enterprises of his friend.[37] Through the study of chronicles and histories, of genealogy and architecture and many other sources, he began to develop a most vivid sense of the English past, its colour and pageantry, its violence and horror. Pictures formed themselves in his mind; kings and queens, barons and abbots moved through the cathedrals and castles and monastic ruins which he loved to visit. He had dealt light-heartedly with English history in *A Long Story*. He would now display its full dignity and splendour in a second Pindaric ode, which he intended to be the greatest of all his poems.

He had lately made considerable researches into the ancient poetry of Wales, and several pages of his second large Commonplace Book are headed *Cambri* and devoted to notes on Welsh prosody and kindred subjects.[38] He mentions there the subjection of the Welsh by Edward I in 1284, and adds that ' he is said to have hanged up all their Bards, because they encouraged the Nation to rebellion, but their works (we see), still remain, the Language (tho' decaying) still lives, and the art of their versification is known, and practised to this day among them'. This tradition, which Gray found quoted from a manuscript source in Carte's *History of England*, and which does not appear to be in any way authentic, supplied him with the idea of his poem. He imagined a bard, the only survivor of this massacre, suddenly appearing high on a crag of Snowdon as the king and his victorious army made their way along the mountain-side. In an impassioned chant the bard would denounce the merciless invader, and lament his own murdered comrades. He would foretell the grisly fates that were in store for Edward's son and many another of his line, the centuries of war and disaster and misrule that lay ahead. Finally, he would tell the king ' that all his cruelty shall never extinguish the noble ardour of poetic genius in this island; and that men shall never be wanting to celebrate true virtue and valour in immortal strains, to expose vice and infamous pleasure, and boldly censure tyranny and oppression'.[39] Then, his song ended, he would plunge headlong into the foaming torrent of the Conway far below.

In spite of his ill-health during 1755, Gray composed *The*

Bard with unaccustomed speed. According to Mason the exordium was finished in March, and by August he had completed more than two-thirds of the poem. Portions were sent for the criticism of Wharton and Stonhewer, 'very rough and unpolished at present', and no doubt with considerable divergencies from their final form.[40] A few of the earlier variations have been preserved, and it is possible to feel a touch of regret that so lovely a line as

> ...scarce Religion dares supply
> *Her mutter'd Requiems, and her holy dew*

should disappear, even though the passage which included it was replaced by the splendid

> Fair laughs the Morn, and soft the Zephyr blows,
> While proudly riding o'er the azure realm
> In gallant trim the gilded Vessel goes;
> Youth on the prow, and Pleasure at the helm;
> Regardless of the sweeping Whirlwind's sway,
> That, hush'd in grim repose, expects his evening-prey.

Gray worked upon the poem with a sense of exaltation that was rare to him. 'I felt myself the Bard.' The first two sections of the ode were complete, and by the late summer of 1755 he was even working on the third and final strophe. Then inspiration deserted him, and he could achieve no progress with the poem for the better part of two years. He had intended the Bard to proclaim that 'men shall never be wanting to celebrate true virtue and valour in immortal strains'; but he now found himself thwarted, as Mason tactfully explained in his *Memoirs*, by the failure of even the greatest poets to fulfil those high ideals. Even Shakespeare—how were virtue and valour celebrated in his immortal creation of Sir John Falstaff? Even Dryden—'he was a mere court parasite to the most infamous of all courts'.[41] Unable to conclude his ode according to his original scheme, Gray laid it aside in despair; and when it was finally resumed early in 1757, the Bard's references to his successors were drastically curtailed.

Its resumption was due to the arrival in Cambridge of John

Parry, a blind harper of some celebrity and the editor of several collections of Welsh music.

Mr Parry has been here [Gray wrote to Mason] and scratch'd out such ravishing blind Harmony, such tunes of a thousand year old with names enough to choak you, as have set all this learned body a'dancing, and inspired them with due reverence for *Odikle*, wherever it shall appear. Mr Parry (you must know) it was, that has put *Odikle* in motion again, and with much exercise it has got a *tender Tail* grown, like Scroddles, and here it is.[42]

Odikle was, of course, the long-neglected *Bard*. Its tail consisted of the lines which were still needed to complete the third strophe, and the whole of the final antistrophe and epode. Scroddles was the nickname, unexplained but somehow oddly appropriate, which Gray had lately bestowed upon Mason and continued to use for the rest of his life.

The strains of Mr Parry had recalled Gray's fugitive inspiration as though by magic, and with most fortunate results. There was no further attempt to moralise upon the duty of poets to extol virtue and condemn vice. Instead, the Bard was made to descry, far in the shadowy future, the fulfilment of the prophecies of Merlin and Taliesin that the Welsh would one day regain their sovereignty over the whole island of Britain. In rapturous lines he hymned the coming glory of the Tudor monarchs:

> Girt with many a Baron bold
> Sublime their starry fronts they rear;
> And gorgeous Dames, and Statesmen old
> In bearded majesty, appear.
> In the midst a Form divine!
> Her eye proclaims her of the Briton-Line;
> Her lyon-port, her awe-commanding face,
> Attemper'd sweet to virgin-grace.
> What strings symphonious tremble in the air,
> What strains of vocal transport round her play!
> Hear from the grave, great Taliesin, hear;
> They breathe a soul to animate thy clay.
> Bright Rapture calls, and soaring, as she sings,
> Waves in the eye of Heav'n her many-colour'd wings.

With undiminished pomp the final epode brought the poem to its close. After a fleeting vision of the greatest of his successors—Spenser, Shakespeare, Milton—the Bard turned once more to denounce the 'fond impious Man' who might as soon hope to extinguish the sun as the golden flood of poetry. And so, his prophesyings ended,

> ...headlong from the mountain's height
> Deep in the roaring tide he plung'd to endless night.

Of the two Pindaric odes *The Progress of Poesy* appears to us the more difficult and recondite work; but *The Bard* seems to have caused the greater perplexity to Gray's contemporaries. They were disconcerted by this vast incantation, this torrential rhapsody of a Celtic seer, which the poet had fitted, together with its wildly romantic descriptive setting, into a classical framework of the utmost strictness. They were startled by its abrupt opening, by the unexpected internal rhymes which Gray had adopted from Welsh prosody, above all by the stream of historical allusions which only the genuinely erudite could identify. The subject was unfamiliar, and therefore unacceptable. There were plenty of people ready to agree with Johnson that 'to select a singular event, and swell it to a giant's bulk by fabulous appendages of spectres and predictions, has little difficulty; for he that forsakes the probable may always find the marvellous'.[43]

IV

Gray wrote no poetry between the summer of 1755, when he temporarily abandoned *The Bard*, and the spring of 1757, when Mr Parry paid his momentous visit to Cambridge. But the intervening year was by no means the least eventful of his life. After the bouts of illness during 1755, it opened on a cheerful note. He had been making use of a particular remedy advocated by Wharton, and wrote early in January to tell him of its good effects. Although he was not absolutely well, many of his unpleasant symptoms had disappeared, and he was in better health than for a long time past.

But he was already beset by a different kind of anxiety. It has already been mentioned that his rooms were on the second floor of the Fellows' Building of Peterhouse, with a formidable drop from their windows into Trumpington Street on the east side and the churchyard of Little St Mary's on the north. On the same staircase lived two fellow-commoners, fashionable and noisy young men, Bennet Williams on the ground floor and George Forrester next to Gray on the second floor. Their rowdy behaviour and their drunken parties filled him with apprehension. As he sat over his books at night, with shouts and songs and the crash of broken glass echoing up the wooden staircase, it was easy to imagine the consequences of an over-turned lamp, or of candles presently setting light to the bed where a fuddled youth lay snoring. He must have known Williams and Forrester fairly well, since they all dined to-gether at the Fellows' table; but any remonstrances upon which he may have ventured were without effect. So he took the only other remedy in his power.

I beg you [he wrote to Wharton] to bespeak me a Rope-ladder (for my Neighbours every day make a great progress in drunkenness, which gives me reason to look about me) it must be full 36 Foot long, or a little more, but as light and manageable as may be, easy to unroll, and not likely to entangle. I never saw one, but I suppose it must have strong hooks, or something equivalent, a-top, to throw over an iron bar to be fix'd withinside of my window. However you will chuse the properest form, and instruct me in the use of it.[44]

A rope-ladder duly arrived; and a bar to hold it was fixed outside, and not 'withinside', Gray's bedroom window, where it may be seen from the street below to this day. His precautions were not unobserved, and in fact invited the practical joke which Williams and Forrester and their friend Lord Perceval, a fellow-commoner of Magdalene, decided to play upon him. Its outcome was described in a letter written to a friend shortly afterwards by the Reverend John Sharp, a Fellow of Corpus.

Mr Gray, our elegant Poet, and delicate Fellow Commoner of Peterhouse, has just removed to Pembroke-hall, in resentment of some usage he met with at the former place. The case is much talked of, and is this. He is much afraid of fire, and was a great sufferer in Cornhill; he has ever since kept a ladder of ropes by him, soft as the silky cords by which Romeo ascended to his Juliet, and has had an iron machine fixed to his bed-room window. The other morning Lord Percival and some Petrenchians, going a hunting, were determined to have a little sport before they set out, and thought it would be no bad diversion to make Gray bolt, as they called it, so ordered their man Joe Draper to roar out fire. A delicate white night-cap is said to have appeared at the window; but finding the mistake, retired again to the couch. The young fellows, had he descended, were determined, they said, to have whipped the butterfly up again.[45]

This is the only contemporary account of the affair that has survived; and it was later corroborated by William Cole, who knew all the current gossip of Cambridge, in a note in his copy of Mason's *Memoirs of Gray*.* Nor does the tone of Sharp's letter suggest that he would have withheld any circumstance that might have added further to Gray's humiliation: it was only later that the two men became on friendly terms.[46] Before long, however, much more highly coloured versions of the story were gaining ground. It was said that Gray had actually clambered down his rope-ladder; that he had landed in a tub of water placed in readiness under his window; that as he stood shivering in the cold March air, a kindly watchman wrapped him in his greatcoat until the college porter could be aroused. There is no truth in any of these versions.† But Sir Edmund Gosse included them all, with embellishments of his own, in his life of Gray, and they were repeated by Sir Leslie Stephen in the *Dictionary of National Biography*, with the consequence that they are often believed today.

Even though the practical joke had failed in its main object,

---

* 'One of their tricks was, knowing that Mr Gray had a dread of fire, had rope-ladders in his chamber; they alarmed him in the middle of the night with the cry of fire, in hope of seeing him make use of them from his window.' (Quoted in *Works* (ed. Mitford), I, cviii.)

† The story that Gray descended the ladder, and was wrapped in the watchman's greatcoat, was printed by Archibald Campbell in his *Sale of Authors*, published in 1767. The water-tub appears to have been first mentioned in Southey's *Letters from England*, published in 1807. I owe the latter reference to Professor Jack Simmons.

Gray was extremely annoyed, and laid a formal complaint before the Master. But Dr Law and 'the Governing part of the Society' thought that he was making an unnecessary fuss, and advised him to disregard the affair as 'a boyish frolic'. Even if he had agreed to do so, there was no assurance that the persecution would now come to an end. Deeply resentful of the lack of support and sympathy from the Master and his colleagues, he decided to leave Peterhouse and take up his abode in Pembroke. It was a step that he might reasonably have taken long before. He had many friends in Pembroke and could be certain of a welcome there; in Peterhouse there was no one, apart from Stonhewer, whom he liked or even respected. It is improbable that the Master and Fellows of Peterhouse tried very hard to persuade him to change his mind. The exact date of the alarm of fire is uncertain; but his pocket-book states that he was admitted to Pembroke on 5 March, and his formal admission was recorded in the Admission Book of the college on the following day.[47]

In his next letter he told Wharton of his migration, but did not enter into details:

Tho I had no reasonable excuse for myself before I received your last letter, yet since that time I have had a pretty good one, having been taken up in quarrelling with Peterhouse, and in removing myself from thence to Pembroke. This may be look'd upon as a sort of Æra in a life so barren of events as mine, yet I shall treat it in Voltaire's manner, and only tell you, that I left my lodgings, because the rooms were noisy, and the People of the house dirty. This is all I would chuse to have said about it; but if you in private should be curious enough to enter into a particular detail of facts and minute circumstances, Stonhewer who was witness to them will probably satisfy you. All, I shall say more, is, that I am for the present extremely well lodged here, and as quiet as in the Grande Chartreuse; and that everybody (even the Dr Longs and Dr Mays) are as civil, as they could be to Mary de Valence in person.[48]

Within the walls of the venerable foundation of Mary de Valence, Countess of Pembroke, he was to pass the remainder of his life; and there, fifteen years later, he was to die.

CHAPTER VIII

THE PUBLICATION OF THE ODES
AND THEIR RECEPTION
1756-1757

I

PEMBROKE has suffered more than any other Cambridge college from the rebuildings and improvements of the nineteenth century. In 1756 it consisted mainly of two small courts, a Hall, a Library, and the Master's Lodge. Its most modern feature was the Chapel, built shortly after the Restoration by Matthew Wren, Bishop of Ely, to the designs of his gifted young nephew Christopher Wren. Portions of the ancient courts remain; the Chapel has been a little enlarged, but is still substantially as Gray knew it; the Library, beneath whose moulded plaster ceiling he spent so many tranquil hours, also survives, although it is no longer used for purposes of study. All else has undergone drastic change, and the hand of Alfred Waterhouse lies heavy over the college. That uncompromising architect was authorised to demolish the Lodge where Roger Long had diverted himself with his telescopes and his orreries, to pull down the old Hall and rebuild it on a more impressive scale, to intrude a new Library surmounted by a Gothic clock-tower, to erect a new range of buildings along Trumpington Street and a new Lodge on the north side of the Fellows' garden. But these transformations were far in the future when Gray moved to Pembroke.

He was temporarily provided with rooms in the seventeenth-century Hitcham Building which forms the south wing of Ivy Court, the innermost of the two courts of the college. A year later he moved into larger rooms close by in the same building, immediately over what is now the Senior Parlour; and these he continued to occupy until his death. The principal room was spacious and comfortable, with good panelling and broad window-sills to hold his pots of flowers. Three of the windows faced north into Ivy Court, and another on the south overlooked the Master's garden with its planetarium and its pool, as did the windows of the bedroom and another small study or closet. Quiet and seclusion reigned every where, and his comparison of his new abode with the Grande Chartreuse was amply justified.

Seven years had now elapsed since the end of the great dispute over the admissions of Mason and Tuthill, and there had been comparative peace throughout that time between the Fellows of Pembroke and 'the high and mighty Prince Roger, surnamed the Long, Lord of the great Zodiack, the Glass Uranium, and the Chariot that goes without Horses'.[1] The Master was now seventy-six years old, and underwent a serious illness a few months after Gray moved to Pembroke, while the college buzzed with intrigues for his succession. But he soon recovered and lived to see his ninetieth year, with his activity and eccentricity in no way diminished, his 'old Tory notions' unimpaired, his eyes as twinkling and his nose and cheeks as rubicund as ever.

The leading figure among the Fellows was still Gray's faithful friend, '*le petit bonhomme*', James Brown. He was President (i.e. Vice-Master) of the College and Senior Fellow; and in the eyes of most people he would be, when the time came, the Master's obvious successor. But his ability in business, his resolution and firmness—qualities which he had displayed to such effect in the affair of the disputed admissions—were combined with a singular modesty. During Roger Long's illness Gray, who was away at Stoke, did everything he could to organize support for Brown in case the Mastership should fall vacant. He wrote to Walpole, begging him to exert his political and personal influence with Henry Fox and the Duke of Bedford on Brown's behalf. He wrote to Mason—himself a potential candidate for the office, but pledged to support Brown

—outlining an elaborate manoeuvre by which it might be possible to enlist the favour of certain other interests, and thus 'gain the dirty part of the College, so as to throw it into Mr Brown's scale at pleasure'. In the meantime, while his friends were secretly working on his behalf, Brown himself had written in all innocence to Gray, 'to acquaint me of Dr Long's illness, and (if I will qualify myself by taking orders, and I know not what) offers me his utmost endeavours to serve me in the same way, and make me *his Master*'.[2] It is inconceivable that Gray would have contemplated for one moment accepting the Mastership in the unlikely event of its offer; and in any case he was trebly ineligible under the college statutes, since he was not a Fellow, and not in orders, and not even a Master of Arts. In a few days Roger Long's recovery put an end to these discussions; but Gray was left with a sense, even deeper than before, of the unselfishness and integrity of his old friend—'a Person entirely unknown to the World, whom those few, that know, love and esteem; and to whom I myself have a thousand obligations'.[3] It is symbolic of James Brown's undemonstrative progress through life that apart from a modest inscription in the ante-chapel the only relic of him at Pembroke, even though he later became Master of the college, is not the customary portrait but his favourite pair of bowls, which are still in use.

Prominent among the junior Fellows of Pembroke was Edward Hussey Delaval. He was a younger son of an ancient family in Northumberland, whose members had long been celebrated for their rowdiness and their love of practical joking. His elder brother, a fellow-commoner of Pembroke, had been sent down for bringing into the college a woman disguised as a friend in the army, who spent several days in his rooms and was finally detected by the Master in circumstances amusingly described by Gray.[4] Edward Delaval's conduct was more restrained, but he had inherited the volatility, the vehemence, the talkativeness and the resounding voice of his family. He was an able scholar, a Fellow of the Royal Society, and a scientist of considerable distinction in the fields of chemistry and experimental philosophy. He was also a gifted musician, and constructed a famous set of musical glasses on which he played so beautifully that Gray compared the sounds to 'a Cherubim in a box'. He and Gray, though never very intimate, were always on friendly terms, and there is a note of genuine liking in the poet's references to 'Mr Delly' and 'Delaval the loud'.

Mason had lately resigned his fellowship of Pembroke, on becoming domestic chaplain to Lord Holdernesse and receiving the living of Aston in Yorkshire. Tuthill was still in residence as a Fellow and tutor. The vagaries of Christopher Smart no longer disturbed the college. He had gone to London in 1749 to seek his fortune in the world of letters, and his fellowship had lapsed when he married his publisher's step-daughter four years later. By the time of Gray's migration to Pembroke he had already become virtually insane, and he was soon to enter upon the long period of confinement during which he wrote *A Song to David.*

Little is remembered about the other members of the society into which Gray was so cordially welcomed. Except for Dr Samuel May, who seems to have been an odd and difficult character, he got on well enough with them all. Francis Mapletoft had a pretty knack of cutting 'shades' or silhouettes in paper, and his portraits in this medium of Gray and Mason are still preserved at Pembroke. Humphrey Senhouse shared the fondness of Gray and Delaval for music, and owned an instrument which Gray called an 'Acoustic Warming-Pan', whose nature has so far baffled every commentator on his letters. 'Dick' Forester, who as an undergraduate had taken the part of the heroine in Smart's farce *The Ungrateful Fair*, withdrew before long to a country parsonage. Joseph Gaskarth is mentioned once or twice with regard in Gray's letters; but others of the Fellows—John Bedford, Richard Spenser, Thomas Milburn, Thomas Axton—have become the veriest shadows. They were on the whole a youthful body, and several of them were soon removed by marriage or the acceptance of livings.

As the present Master of Pembroke has pointed out, 'the personnel of an eighteenth-century high table changed much more rapidly than in later times.... When Gray moved across the road to Pembroke, his friend and sponsor, James Brown, was 47; the average age of the rest of the Fellows was 30.'[5]

The long period of estrangement between the Master and the Fellows had brought much discredit upon Pembroke, and the number of undergraduates had become sadly reduced. In 1748 only a single pensioner had been admitted, and in 1749 two sizars.[6] Gray had concerned himself about this state of things long before he moved from Peterhouse. When Mason and Tuthill were at length admitted as Fellows, he had told Wharton that 'I have hopes that these two with Brown's assistance may bring Pembroke into some Esteem; but then there is no making Bricks without Straw. They have no Boys at all, and unless you can send us a Hamper or two out of the North to begin with, they will be like a few Rats straggling about an old deserted Mansion-House.'[7] Since then his hopes had been fulfilled. The reputation of the college began to rise once more, and the vacant rooms were fewer. In 1756 six fellow-commoners dined at the high table, and at the lower table were twenty-three bachelors and undergraduates of humbler degree.[8]

The most conspicuous of the fellow-commoners was John Lyon, ninth Earl of Strathmore. His mother had been an important Durham heiress, and it was probably through Wharton and Stonhewer, both natives of that county, that he was sent to Cambridge and to Pembroke. He was a young man of intelligence and charm, 'a tall genteel figure in our eyes', according to Gray; a good scholar, and on excellent terms with his tutors Brown and Tuthill.[9] Beside him at the high table sat his brother James Philip Lyon, who later entered the service of the East India Company, and was fated to perish in the massacre at Patna in 1763. A third brother, Thomas, joined them at Pembroke in 1758, and was afterwards for some years a Fellow of the college. Gray got on well with all the Lyons, and was later to visit 'the Thane of Glamis' at his Scottish castle.

The other fellow-commoners entered little into Gray's life. The name of one of them, Edward Southwell, a rich young man from Gloucestershire, occurs now and then in his letters. They met sometimes in London after Southwell had gone down from Cambridge; and when he returned from the Grand Tour, Gray wrote approvingly that 'he has got many new tastes and knowledges, and is no more a cockscomb than when he went from hence'.[10] A scholar of the college, William Palgrave, the son of a physician at Ipswich, became a fellow-commoner in 1757, and was soon admitted to the circle of Gray's friends. He was a clever and amiable youth, small of stature, agreeable in his manners and something of a *dilettante* in his tastes. He remains a rather shadowy figure, and in 1759 he took Holy orders and vanished into the depths of the Suffolk countryside; but Gray had taken a great liking to him, and corresponded with him regularly until his death.

Finally, no survey of Pembroke in 1756 would be complete without a mention of the college butler, Richard Dunthorne. In his hand—the clearest and most elegant hand imaginable— Gray's first 'sizings' as a member of the Pembroke high table were recorded in the Sizings Book, as his last were to be fifteen years later. But Dunthorne was also a scientist and astronomer of high ability. He had assisted Dr Long, whose early *protégé* he was, in all his experiments, and had dedicated more than one treatise to him. His *Practical Astronomy of the Moon* had been published at the University Press. Valuable communications from his pen had been laid before the Royal Society and printed in *Philosophical Transactions*. And to this day he remains the only college butler whose achievements are recorded in the *Dictionary of National Biography*.[11]

II

Gray did not undertake in 1756 the summer tour which had now become his usual custom. In June he spent a few days in London with George Montagu's cousin Frederick, who had lately been a fellow-commoner of Trinity and was now reading for the bar. Then he went to Stoke Poges, where he lapsed into one of his spells of profoundest melancholy, the melancholy 'black indeed' of which he had spoken years before.

> I am at Stoke [he wrote to Mason in apology for a long period of silence] hearing, seeing, doing absolutely nothing. Not such a nothing, as you do at Tunbridge, chequer'd and diversified with a succession of fleeting colours; but heavy, lifeless, without form, and void; sometimes almost as black, as the Moral of Voltaire's *Lisbon*, which angers you so. I have had no more pores and muscular inflations, and am only troubled with this depression of mind. You will not expect therefore that I should give you any account of my *Verve*, which is at best (you know) of so delicate a constitution, and has such weak nerves, as not to stir out of its chamber above three days in a year.[12]

His inspiration had flagged for many months past; *The Bard* and the *Pleasure arising from Vicissitude* lay in his desk unfinished. And if Miss Speed was at the Manor House this summer, there is no word of it in his letters.

In August he threw off his inertia, went to London to see Chute, who was laid low with the gout, and at the end of the month accompanied him to The Vyne. There Chute's gout attacked him again with redoubled fury, so that 'for above forty hours it seem'd past all human suffering, and he lay screaming like a Man upon the rack'.[13] There was no one in the house except the servants and Walpole's *protégé* the German painter Müntz, and much responsibility devolved upon Gray. He felt obliged to remain at The Vyne for several weeks, looking after the tormented invalid and sending frequent bulletins to Walpole. But Chute was well on the way to recovery by the beginning of October, and Gray returned to Stoke, spending a few days at Strawberry Hill on the way.

From this time his friendship with Chute gradually withered. There does not seem to have been any open breach, and the two may have continued to meet occasionally at Strawberry Hill. But Gray never stayed with Chute again; and when next year he spoke in a letter to Wharton of being glad of an excuse 'for not going into the country to *a place, where I am invited'*, it may be assumed that The Vyne was meant. In rather the same tone he told Walpole in 1758 that if he was going to The Vyne 'I shall be glad to attend you thither, and *back again'*. The underlining in both letters was Gray's; and altogether it seems that he, rather than Chute, must have decided for some reason that their paths should divide.[14]

The autumn and winter passed uneventfully; but in February a trouble fell upon Gray and upon Pembroke. For the past eight years, ever since he attained his fellowship, Henry Tuthill had faithfully discharged his academic duties, and had filled a succession of college offices, such as Chaplain, Junior Treasurer and Dean. For the same length of time he had held the curacy of Brampton in Huntingdonshire, not far from the home of Gray's friends the Bonfoys at Abbot's Ripton. He spent the Christmas of 1756 in college, and then left Cambridge early in the new year, never to return. On 5 February the following entry was made in the college register: 'This day the Master in the presence of 5 Fellows, declared Mr Tuthill's fellowship to be vacant, he having been absent from the College above a month contrary to the Statutes which inflicts this punishment upon such absence.' This was signed by the Master, Brown, May and three others. A further entry was presently added, without signature or date: 'Since Mr Tuthill's absence common fame has laid him under violent suspicion of having been guilty of great enormities; to clear himself from which he has not made his appearance, and there is good reason to believe he never will.'

No details of Tuthill's enormities have ever been revealed; but there can be little doubt, from the wording of the second entry and from the embarrassment and dismay shown by his friends, that he had been accused of some homosexual offence. Naturally the matter was concealed as far as possible, and all correspondence bearing directly upon it was later destroyed; but several of Gray's letters reveal something of the distress which he suffered. He and his circle had used all their influence to secure Tuthill's admission at Pembroke, against the Master's wishes; and now the Master's opposition proved to be amply justified. His friend and *protégé* had brought discredit, and perhaps serious harm, upon the college which he loved and which had lately received him with such kindness.

On the whole, everyone took the affair a good deal more calmly than Gray had expected. He had feared, in his first agitation, that Tuthill's pupil Lord Strathmore and his brother might leave the college; but they remained unperturbed, as did Edward Southwell and the rest. In March he went to London to consult with Wharton, who had also been a friend of Tuthill's and his particular sponsor over the Pembroke fellowship, and with Mason, his former colleague. The advice of Mr Bonfoy, Tuthill's neighbour in Huntingdonshire, was also sought; and a note from Gray to Walpole survives, asking to see him on urgent business, almost certainly in the same connection. It seems likely that all these discussions had two aims, the hushing-up of the scandal of Tuthill's disappearance, and the provision of some help for the unhappy man himself.

Before long Gray returned to Cambridge, and was able to tell Wharton that 'I find nothing new to add to my uneasiness here; on the contrary it is considerably abated, and quiet, I hope, is gradually returning.' No serious harm had been done to the college, and life proceeded on its accustomed way. But the shock had affected him deeply; and although from this time not a single word about Tuthill appears in his surviving letters, he was profoundly saddened by the loss of one who had been for so many years his friend. The fate of Tuthill is unknown. There is a story, unsupported by any evidence, that he drowned himself. More probably he left the country. It is not impossible that the direction in Gray's will, that his executors should 'apply the sum of two hundred pounds to the use of a charity, which I have already informed them of', may represent the last of many contributions to the support of this pathetic figure, still living on in exile and disgrace.[15]

III

As the spring advanced, and the echoes of the Tuthill catastrophe died away, Gray's spirits began to rise a little. People went out of their way to show kindness and sympathy. Lord John Cavendish visited Cambridge, and proved so cheering an influence that Gray described him to Mason as 'the best of all Johns—I hardly except the Evangelist and the Divine'.[16] Hurd perceived that 'you want amusement at this time', and to that end sent him a translation of Aristotle's *Ode to Virtue*, intended as a footnote in his forthcoming edition of Horace, by their friend Thomas Neville, who 'I know will take a pleasure to correct it according to any hints you shall give him'.[17] And he also received an unexpected visit of homage from a stranger, Lord Nuneham, an elegant young man with a taste for the arts, who had become acquainted with Mason at Hanover and was later to be his patron and lifelong friend:

> Stonhewer [he wrote to Mason] has done me the honour to send me your friend Lord Nuneham hither with a fine recommendatory letter (written by his own desire) in Newmarket-week. Do not think he was going to Newmarket. No! he came in a Solitaire, great Sleeves, jessamine-powder, and a large Bouquet of Jonquils within twelve miles of that place on purpose not to go thither. We had three days intercourse, talk'd about the Beaux-Arts, and Rome, and Hanover and Mason, whose praises we celebrated *a qui mieux mieux*, vowed eternal friendship, embraced, and parted. I promised to write you a thousand compliments in his name. I saw also Lord Villiers and Mr Spencer, who carried him back with them, *en passant*. They did not like me at all.[18]

To Wharton he wrote a little more critically. 'Lord Nuneham is a sensible well-bred young man, a little too fine even for me, who love a little finery: he never will be popular, and it is well, if he be not very much hated.'[19]

Next month a very different visitor appeared at Cambridge, and one who made a deeper impression upon Gray than Lord Nuneham with his compliments and his easy charm—Mr Parry the blind harper, whose strains inspired him to complete *The Bard*.[20] He spent a few weeks in revising and perfecting the poem, consulting Mason by letter, and his Cambridge friends —Hurd, Neville, Bonfoy are specifically mentioned—in person. Then he went up to London, intending to arrange with Dodsley for the publication of both the Pindaric odes. But Walpole had this summer set up a printing press in a little building in his garden at Strawberry Hill, and insisted that Gray's odes should be the first production of the *Officina Arbuteana*. Dodsley should still be the publisher, and indeed he had already paid Gray forty guineas for the copyright of the poems; but Walpole would act as printer on Dodsley's behalf. It was a heaven-sent opportunity for the worthy inauguration of his press, and he would take no denial.

Gray gave his consent rather unwillingly. He had always disliked the publicity and the gossip that accompanied Walpole's enterprises, and had not forgotten his worries over the Bentley edition four years ago. He felt more deeply about these odes than he had done about any of his other writings. They were addressed to the serious and learned world, whose attention he did not wish to be distracted by the social *réclame* of Strawberry Hill. But, as he told more than one of his friends, 'it was impossible to find a pretext for refusing such a trifle';[21] and Walpole had his way.

Deeply though he admired the odes, Walpole ventured to raise with Gray the question of adding some explanatory notes. 'They are Greek, they are Pindaric, they are sublime! consequently I fear a little obscure', he wrote to Mann.[22] But Gray remained obdurate. Notes, he said, 'are signs of weakness and obscurity. If a thing cannot be understood without them, it had better not be understood at all.'[23] In the end he consented to add four brief notes to *The Bard*, but none to *The Progress of Poesy*.* He went to Strawberry Hill in mid-July for the

* I cannot accept the story in the *Diaries of Sylvester Douglas, Lord Glenbervie* (ed. Bickley), I, 135, that Gray, presumably about this time, read the manuscript of *The Progress of Poesy* to an audience consisting of Walpole,

inauguration of the press, an event celebrated by Walpole with a party at which Dodsley, Tonson and other leading publishers were present.[24] The printing of the odes was begun on 16 July, and the date of publication was 8 August. The rate of progress was slow, since only one man was employed at the press; but the edition finally consisted of two thousand copies, which were sold at a shilling apiece.[25] Gray arranged for a large parcel of copies to be sent to Brown, who was to distribute them to the Master and all the Fellows of Pembroke, and to many other dons and residents in Cambridge.[26]

Copies were also sent to Bedingfield for himself, his wife, and his mother-in-law Lady Swinburne; and he was asked to transmit a fourth copy to 'Miss Hepburn at Monkridge near Haddington, if there be any such Person, which I a little doubt'.[27] This lady provides a mystery in Gray's life. She was Margaret, the daughter of George Hepburn, a Haddingtonshire laird, and was a few years younger than Gray. There is nothing to show how he made her acquaintance, or how often they had met. In 1768, when his collected poems were being printed at Glasgow, he asked Beattie to send a copy to her 'with my respects and grateful remembrances'. He also mentioned that he had been inquiring after her for fourteen years in vain, and thought that his gift of the 1757 *Odes* had probably never reached her, 'as I was forced to direct them very much at random'. Beattie replied that he could give no certain information about her, but thought that she had died some years before, which was in fact the case.[28]

Great pains had been lavished on the book, a quarto whose sober and dignified appearance commended itself to Gray, although he complained of sundry errors in punctuation. It was entitled *Odes by Mr Gray*, and no title was given to the two poems beyond *Ode I* and *Ode II*. Immediately below the main title, and just above the attractive vignette of Strawberry Hill,

Mason, George Selwyn, Richard Lord Edgcumbe and 'Gilly' Williams. The idea of such a performance is completely at variance with Gray's character, and there are several other reasons for rejecting it.

appeared in conspicuous Greek capitals the motto ΦΩΝΑΝΤΑ ΣΥΝΕΤΟΙΣΙ. This was a quotation from Pindar's second Olympian Ode. Gray translated it, on a later occasion, as 'vocal to the intelligent alone'.[29] It was his private message to the elect, and his signal of defiance to the ignorant and unworthy.

The *Elegy* had come to be published almost by accident, and its instant success had surprised and embarrassed him. Now, on the other hand, he was deliberately submitting to the world these poems on which he had expended such long and anxious toil, and which he regarded as the summit of his achievement. He was deeply concerned that they should be approved by those whose approval was best worth having; and, for all his parade of indifference, he could always derive a sober pleasure from discriminating applause. A year before he had told Bedingfield, who had written an enthusiastic letter about his poetry, that 'I find myself still young enough to tast the sweets of praise (and to like the taste too) yet old enough not to be intoxicated with them. To own the truth, they give me spirits, but I begin to wonder, they should hurt any body's health, when we can so easily dash them with the bitter salutary drop of misery and mortality, that we always carry about us.'[30] He hoped, with a curious blend of confidence and misgiving, that the odes would really prove 'vocal to the intelligent', and eagerly awaited news of their reception. He asked Walpole to tell him 'what you hear any body say, (I mean, if any body says any thing)'; and Bedingfield to find out 'what the North says either in good or in bad—as to the South, it is too busy and too fastidious to trouble its head about any thing, that has no wit in it'; and Brown at Cambridge to report the views of '*mes Confrères*, the Learned', amongst whom there was always leisure 'at least to find fault, if not to commend'.[31] When he realised that to the majority of the intelligent his strains had not proved vocal at all, that they were being almost universally condemned on the ground of their obscurity, his disappointment was very great.

His readers were not altogether to blame. The two odes, printed so uncompromisingly without titles and without notes, were undoubtedly hard to understand. Scholars and historians might perhaps have coped without difficulty with the stream of allusions, the She-wolf of France and the agonising King, the meek Usurper and the bristled Boar; but busy politicians and preoccupied ladies of fashion could hardly be expected to solve such cryptograms. Walpole, who had urged the addition of notes, may have smiled a little at Gray's perturbation when Lord Barrington believed the last stanza of *The Bard* to refer to Charles the First and Oliver Cromwell, and Lady Holdernesse missed the allusions to Shakespeare and Milton in *The Progress of Poesy*, and Henry Fox said that after having read the poems seven or eight times he now had not more than thirty questions to ask.[32]

Opinion in the learned world was much divided. Hurd wrote from Cambridge that 'every body would be thought to admire: 'tis true, I believe, the greater part don't understand them'; and presently, more warmly, 'every body here, that knows anything of such things, applauds the Odes. And the readers of Pindar dote upon them.'[33] Gray's fellow-poets Lord Lyttelton and William Shenstone admired the odes, and Lyttelton in fact wrote to Walpole of 'the bright and glorious flame of poetical fire' which they contained;[34] but both wished, like everyone else, that they had been a little clearer. Another poet, Mark Akenside, complained that it was a solecism to 'ope the sacred source of sympathetic Tears' with the golden keys of poesy. How can a key, he grumbled, possibly open a source? Robert Wood, the dilettante politician who had written about the ruins of Palmyra and Baalbec, owned himself disappointed; he had anticipated better things from the author of the *Elegy*. All these criticisms, however trivial, Gray reported in his letters to his friends. The Συνετοί were fewer, he told them sadly, even than he had expected. 'Nobody understands me, and I am perfectly satisfied.'[35]

Their obscurity was not the only charge levelled against the odes. Many readers complained, as Johnson was to do in his *Lives of the Poets*, of their rhapsodical and incantatory style. A letter to a private friend from Benjamin Stillingfleet, a mildly eccentric poet and philosopher whose acquaintance Gray was presently to make, sums up what many other people were thinking.

As to the Odes i* think of them as you do. Mere clinquant! verbiage! without instruction or sentiment, or even ideas agreeable, for they require as much thought to understand them as a mathematical problem. The author can write for me and has done, but not in this gallimawfry stile. I every day grow plainer and plainer in my tast. There is enough in nature to furnish out description or sentiment if men will look about them and watch either men or things with inquisitive eyes; but when people applaud such stuff, there will never be wanting writers to propagate this false tast. But i expect this bold way of talking to be confin'd to yourself, for of all things i should dislike to be cited upon such an occasion. I will always endeavour to keep clear of the *genus irritabile vatum*, who would perhaps think they might reasonably impute this opinion to envy, tho' were this the case i would certainly run down the Churchyard and the Prospect of Eaton as performances i should despair of coming up to were i to attempt it, but perhaps not these made flights, which some call Pindaric, as they do many bombast attempts in blank verse, Miltonic![36]

There were favourable voices as well. David Garrick was enthusiastic in his praise of the *Odes*; and Dr John Brown, who had just published his celebrated *Estimate of the Manners and Principles of the Times*—a work for which Gray had little admiration—was heard to say that they were the best in the language. It was their championship that caused Gray to remark, in the first flush of his disappointment, that 'I have heard of nobody but a player and a doctor of divinity that profess their esteem for them'.[37] But they were not his only supporters. Hurd had continued warm in his approval ever since he first read the poems in manuscript. Walpole, although he had faults to

* It was Stillingfleet's habit to use a small 'i' for the first person singular in his letters and publications, except at the beginning of a sentence.

find with certain passages, told Lord Lyttelton that 'perhaps no composition ever had more sublime beauties than are in each'; and in answer to Lyttelton's objection to the epithet 'many-twinkling', he assured him that 'Greek as the expression is, it struck Mrs Garrick, and she says, on that whole picture, that Mr Gray is the only poet who ever understood dancing'.[38] Finally, he was able to console himself with the kindness and sympathy of Henrietta Speed. 'The family you mention near me are full as civil as ever', he told Wharton. 'Miss Speed seems to understand; and to all such, as do not, she says Φωναντα συνετοισι in so many words.'[39]

The reviews and critical journals had not yet reached the position of authority which they were later to attain; but their verdicts were of some importance, and in general they were favourable to Gray. The notice in the *Monthly Review* was by Oliver Goldsmith, then a comparative newcomer to London and the literary world. In view of the disapproval of Gray's 'rumbling thunder' which he expressed to Boswell five years later,[40] Goldsmith's treatment of the odes was balanced and fair, although the poet received with surprise his unknown reviewer's suggestion that the idea of *The Bard* was taken from the fifteenth ode of the first book of Horace.[41] The *Critical Review* was full of enthusiasm, but so verbose and foolish that Gray could not derive much satisfaction from its outpourings. The writer of the notice was supposed to be Dr Thomas Francklin, the Professor of Greek at Cambridge; and Gray was half amused and half affronted that so high an authority, mistaking the Aeolian lyre in *The Progress of Poesy* for the harp of Aeolus, should have objected that the latter instrument, 'which is altogether uncertain and irregular, must be very ill-adapted to the dance'.[42] In fact, as it turned out later, Dr Francklin was guiltless of the mistake and of the review. The most intelligent and sympathetic of all the notices appeared in the *Literary Magazine*, and may conceivably have been prompted by Mason.[43]

So the summer and autumn wore on, with varied accounts of

the reception of the *Odes* still coming in. The Speaker of the House of Commons, Arthur Onslow, had been heard to say that *The Bard* was 'a pretty good tale, but nothing to the *Churchyard*'. Bedingfield 'in a golden shower of panegyrick writes me word, that at York-races he overheard three People, whom by their dress and manner he takes for Lords, say, that I was impenetrable and inexplicable, and they wish'd, I had told them in prose, what I meant in verse, and then they bought me (which was what most displeased him) and put me in their pocket'.[44] On the other hand, the great and magisterial Warburton, when he came to London in October, was loud in praise of the *Odes* and in contempt of those who failed to understand them.[45] The sales, too, had proved satisfactory, more than two thirds of the edition having been exhausted during the first month.

Gray remained at his aunt's house at Stoke, 'alone and *ennuyé* to the last degree', having once again, to the undoubted detriment of his health and spirits, foregone his summer tour. The gout had not returned, but several minor complaints were worrying him; and the failure of the *Odes*—for such he now acknowledged it to be—intensified his melancholy. The company of Lady Cobham and Henrietta Speed still had power to cheer him; and when Garrick and his wife stayed at the Manor House as they did twice during the summer months, he could not resist the spell of their laughter and high spirits. Garrick, however, perceived his depression, and addressed to him an attractive and lively poem of consolation, which Walpole printed as a leaflet on the press at Strawberry Hill.

> Repine not, Gray, that our weak dazzled eyes
>   Thy daring heights and brightness shun;
> How few can track the Eagle to the skies,
>   Or like him gaze upon the Sun!
>
> The gentle Reader loves the gentle Muse,
>   That little dares, and little means,
> Who humbly sips her learning from *Reviews*,
>   Or flutters in the *Magazines*.

No longer now from Learning's sacred store
   Our minds their health and vigour draw;
Homer and Pindar are revered no more,
   No more the Stagyrite is Law.

Tho nurst by these, in vain thy Muse appears
   To breathe her ardours in our souls;
In vain to sightless eyes and deaden'd ears
   The Lightning gleams and Thunder rolls.

Yet droop not, Gray, nor quit thy Heav'n born art,
   Again thy wondrous pow'rs reveal;
Wake slumb'ring virtue in the Briton's heart,
   And rouse us to *reflect* and *feel*.

With ancient deeds our long chill'd bosoms fire,
   Those deeds which mark Eliza's reign!
Make Britons, Greeks again—then strike the Lyre,
   And Pindar shall not sing in vain.

Gray remained deaf to such exhortations, and to everything that his friends and admirers could say. As the year drew towards its close he ceased to mention the *Odes* in his letters, and he seldom spoke of them again. But the sense of disappointment and frustration was permanent. He had exerted his fullest powers in these two poems; all his inspiration, all his creative energies had gone to their making; he regarded them as his masterpieces, and they had been ridiculed and misunderstood. He did not grow embittered or resentful. He merely discontinued the writing of poetry, apart from a few occasional pieces, for years to come; and withdrew more resolutely even than before into private study and the private life.

CHAPTER IX

MISS SPEED:
THE YEARS IN LONDON:
THE NORSE AND WELSH POEMS
1757-1761

I

DESPITE the cool reception of the *Odes*, Gray was now beyond all question the foremost poet in Great Britain. It was a barren time for poetry. Collins had become insane; Joseph and Thomas Warton were engaged on critical and scholarly works; Johnson had long ceased to write verse, and Churchill's ferocious satires had not yet appeared. There was a particular dearth of good lyric verse, as the three later volumes of Dodsley's *Collection of Poems*, which provide the most representative anthology of this uninspiring decade, abundantly show. Here in a wilderness of monodies and didactic poems, paraphrases of Isaiah and imitations of Spenser, were printed the most recent works of Gray and his only possible rivals amongst the lyrists, Akenside and Shenstone, Mason and Whitehead. Gray's superiority to any other writer of the time could not have been for a moment in doubt; and it was obvious that when Colley Cibber, the octogenarian Poet Laureate, died at the close of 1757, he should have been suggested as his successor.

In contrast to the practice of more recent times, when the Poet Laureateship has been known to remain vacant for months and in one case even for years, the office was filled with remarkable dispatch. Colley Cibber had died on 12 December. The Lord Chamberlain, the Duke of Devonshire, knowing that his brother Lord John Cavendish was a friend of Gray's, at once

asked him to act as his intermediary in the matter; and Lord
John in his turn arranged for Mason to sound Gray before any
formal offer was made. Gray promptly and firmly declined it in
a letter to Mason which has not survived. So on 19 December,
exactly a week after Cibber's death, William Whitehead was
appointed in his stead. Whitehead was an amiable man and a
very adequate poet of the second rank. With Gray out of the
running, no better choice could have been made.

Gray explained his reasons for refusing the offer in a second
letter to Mason. He was attracted neither by the emoluments
—one hundred pounds a year and the traditional butt of canary
or sack—nor by the reputation of the office, which had been
lowered by a succession of inferior and sometimes ludicrous
appointments. Still less would he, of all people, have found it
possible to write poems to order, even though there seems to
have been some suggestion that in his case the usual conditions
might be modified or waived.

Tho' I very well know [he wrote] the bland emollient saponaceous
qualities both of Sack and Silver, yet if any great Man would say to
me, 'I make you *Rat-Catcher* to his Majesty with a salary of £300
a-year and two Butts of the best Malaga; and tho' it has been usual
to catch a mouse or two (for form's sake) in publick once a year, yet
to you, Sir, we shall not stand upon these things', I can not say, I
should jump at it. Nay, if they would drop the very name of the
Office, and call me *Sinecure* to the King's Majesty, I should still feel
a little awkward, and think every body, I saw, smelt a Rat about me;
but I do not pretend to blame any one else, that has not the same
sensations. For my part I would rather be Serjeant-Trumpeter, or
Pin-Maker to the Palace. Nevertheless I interest myself a little in
the History of it, and rather wish somebody may accept it, that will
retrieve the credit of the thing, if it be retrievable, or ever had any
credit. Rowe was, I think, the last Man of character that had it. . . .
Eusden was a Person of great hopes in his youth, tho' at last he
turned out a drunken Parson. Dryden was as disgraceful to the
Office from his character, as the poorest Scribler could have been
from his verses. In short the office itself has always humbled the
Possessor hitherto (even in an age, when Kings were somebody) if
he were a poor Writer by making him more conspicuous, and if he

were a good one, by setting him at war with the little fry of his own profession, for there are poets little enough to envy even a Poet-Laureat.[1]

Having thus rejected public office, and still smarting from what he chose to regard as his own rejection by the public taste, Gray buried himself ever more deeply in his private studies. During the last few years his enthusiasm for the Greek and Latin classics had somewhat abated, and he had been toying for a considerable time with the idea of writing a history of English poetry. Pope had once drawn up the scheme of such a history; and Warburton, as Pope's literary executor, had passed this document on to Mason, who in turn communicated it to Gray. The suggestion was at first made that the two friends should collaborate in the undertaking.[2] It is possible that Mason's energy and ambition, allied to Gray's scholarship, might have brought it to a successful conclusion; but Mason had other schemes on hand, and Gray confined himself to the accumulation of more and still more notes in his Commonplace Book. 'I hope you don't forget, among your other amusements this summer,' wrote Hurd in 1757, 'your design for a history of the English poetry. You might be regulating your plan, and digesting the materials you have by you. I shall teaze you perpetually, till you set about the project in good earnest. It is a wonderful favourite with me, and will, I am certain, in your hands be a work of much use as well as elegance.'[3] His persuasions were of no avail. Gray continued to fill the pages of his notebooks with details of Welsh and Norse prosody, with extracts from Lydgate and considerations upon the 'Pseudo-Rhythmus'; but no amount of teasing, from Hurd or anyone else, would have prevailed upon him to 'digest' them.

He embodied the results of these researches principally in three long articles in his second Commonplace Book. Under the heading *Metrum* he considered the whole range of English metre and prosody, from the remotest sources and the earliest times. Under *Cambri* he ranged the Welsh studies which he used to such effect in *The Bard*. Under *Gothi* he collected notes upon Scandinavian and Germanic poetry.[4] It was all done in the most elaborate and painstaking detail, with references to an immense number of works in a wide variety of languages, and with divagations along any interesting bypath that might happen to tempt him aside. He continued to meditate a history of English poetry for several years to come; and if the few pages which he wrote on Lydgate, with their easy and almost conversational air, can be regarded as a fair specimen of what he might have produced in this line, his abandonment of the project is much to be regretted.[5] But, as always, his interests turned elsewhere; and he began in 1758 to direct his main attention towards English antiquities and the more specifically antiquarian aspects of English history.

The results of these new studies soon appeared in the Commonplace Book. Fresh articles were begun in place of *Cambri* and *Gothi* and the rest—*Sepulchra*, which dealt with the monuments of the Royal Family and of the nobility, together with their places of residence; and *Ecclesia*, containing notes on the cathedrals of England and Wales. He also drew up, on the blank pages of his copy of Kitchen's Atlas, a list of all the sights in England that were worth the seeing, 'whether it be building, ruin, park, garden, prospect, picture or monument; to whom it does, or has belong'd, and what has been the characteristick, and taste of different ages'.[6] His recourse to these unexacting labours of compilation, in place of more strenuous research into the remotest background of our poetry, was due in part to the listlessness and depression from which he suffered throughout the early months of 1758.

It is indeed for want of spirits, as you suspect, that my studies lie among the Cathedrals, and the Tombs, and the Ruins [he told Wharton]. To think, though to little purpose, has been the chief amusement of my days; and when I would not, or cannot think, I dream. At present I find myself able to write a Catalogue, or to read the Peerage book, or Miller's Gardening Dictionary, and am thankful that there are such employments and such authors in the world. Some people, who hold me cheap for this, are doing perhaps what is not half so well worth while. As to posterity, I may ask, (with some body whom I have forgot) what has it ever done to oblige me?[7]

For the first time in several years he had no major poem in progress or in contemplation. 'I by no means pretend to inspiration', he wrote, 'but yet I affirm, that the faculty in question is by no means voluntary. It is the result (I suppose) of a certain disposition of mind, which does not depend on oneself, and which I have not felt this long time.'[8] Nevertheless, he was able to write graceful and feeling epitaphs at the request of two of his oldest friends. The first of these epitaphs was in memory of the wife of Dr John Clerke, whom he had known so well at Peterhouse in earlier days, and with whom he still corresponded. Mrs Clerke had died in childbirth in the previous year, and Gray wrote for her memorial tablet in Beckenham Church the lines which begin 'Lo! where this silent marble weeps,' and which close with a touching reference to the bereaved husband,

> Whom what awaits, while yet he strays
> Along the lonely vale of days?
> A pang, to secret sorrow dear;
> A sigh; an unavailing tear;
> Till time shall every grief remove,
> With life, with memory, and with love.

The other epitaph was written at the wish of Wharton and his wife, who had just lost their beloved Robin, at that time their only son:

> Here, freed from pain, secure from misery, lies
> A child, the darling of his parents' eyes:
> A gentler lamb ne'er sported on the plain,
> A fairer flower will never bloom again:
> Few were the days allotted to his breath;
> Now let him sleep in peace his night of death.

There is a temperate stoicism in both these epitaphs. Neither contains any reference to a future state or to the possibility of ultimate reunion, not even the 'trembling hope' of the epitaph which concluded the *Elegy*. Gray's letters of comfort to Wharton were in the same strain. He longed to afford his friend 'that consolation, which I have often received from you, when I most wanted it'; but his consolation was soberly rational, as he urged the virtues of fortitude and self-command, the unwisdom of surrendering overmuch to grief.[9] Despite the onslaughts of melancholy, in the face of bereavement and private sorrow, he had himself achieved a philosophy of life amounting to a moderate and chastened optimism. His clearest expression of this attitude of mind was confided to Mason, who had been lamenting some minor misfortune of his own:

A life spent out of the World [he wrote] has its hours of despondence, its inconveniences, its sufferings, as numerous, and as real (tho' not quite of the same sort) as a life spent in the midst of it. The power we have, when we will exert it, over our own minds, join'd to a little strength and consolation, nay, a little pride, we catch from those, that seem to love us, is our only support in either of these conditions. I am sensible I can not return to you so much of this assistance as I have received from you. I can only tell you, that one, who has far more reason, than you (I hope) will ever have, to look on life with something worse than indifference, is yet no enemy to it, and can look backward on many bitter moments partly with satisfaction and partly with patience, and forward too on a scene not very promising with some hope and some expectations of a better day.[10]

II

In the early summer Gray went for a short tour of the cathedrals and monastic remains in the fen country—Ely, Peterborough, Thorney and other places. In July he joined Lady Cobham and Miss Speed in London, and went with them to some house at Hampton, possibly the villa of their friends the Garricks. They visited all the sights of the neighbourhood —Hampton Court, Sion, Oatlands—and Gray confessed to Wharton that he would gladly have stayed there longer, 'but for the reason we talk'd about'.[11]

It has been suggested that this guarded phrase refers to a scheme, which Lady Cobham is thought to have cherished at this time, of bringing about a marriage between Gray and Miss Speed. On the other hand, if they were all staying with the Garricks it may just as well be connected with a quarrel which can had lately occurred between Garrick and Mason. But there be no doubt that, although Miss Speed is so seldom mentioned in Gray's surviving letters, his intimacy with her and Lady Cobham had steadily increased, and that he was now one of their closest and most valued friends. Eight years had passed since the enchanting girl of the *Long Story* had made her sudden appearance in the poet's secluded life, and drawn him into the light-hearted company at the Manor House. Melissa was now a woman of thirty, but she remained still the same embodiment of 'spirit, wit and satire'. She was well known and very popular in the world of London, a brilliant and lively talker, passionately fond of theatres and balls and parties of every kind, certain to bring gaiety and animation wherever she went. But she had not married, and does not appear to have been greatly sought in marriage. She remained, as was probably her own choice, the devoted and inseparable companion of Lady Cobham. The older woman's health was now beginning to fail; and she may have wished to see her ward and heiress safely engaged to a man whom she knew and liked so well.

Gray went on from Hampton for a few days with Walpole at Strawberry Hill, and then returned to Stoke. He spent much time at the Manor House, where the Garricks came for a week in August. He found means to compose the quarrel between Garrick and Mason; but it was all rather a strain, and he breathed a sigh of thankfulness after the vivacious pair had gone. 'I grow so old that, I own, People in high spirits and gayety overpower me, and entirely take away mine. I can yet be diverted with their sallies, but if they appear to take notice of my dullness, it sinks me to nothing.'[12] He found life pleasanter when Lady Cobham and Miss Speed were alone; and it may have been during this summer that a small boy from Eton, the son of Mr Duckworth, the vicar of Stoke Poges, saw the eminent poet being driven by Miss Speed about the country lanes in a butcher's cart, a spectacle which lingered in his memory for half a century.*

---

* The small boy became Admiral Sir John Thomas Duckworth, and he contributed this reminiscence to an edition of Gray's *Poems* published in 1821.

Gray's aunt Mrs Rogers had been seriously ill during much of the year, and died at the end of September. She left five hundred pounds to her favourite nephew, and the bulk of her remaining property was divided between him and her sister Mrs Oliffe, now the last survivor of her generation of the Antrobus family, and the only disagreeable character amongst them. She and Gray were joint executors of the will, and he was driven to describe her to his friends in such terms as 'an old *Harridan*, who is the spawn of Cerberus and the Dragon of Wantley'.[13] The house at Stoke, his summer retreat for so many years past, was put up for sale, and such furniture and china as he wished to keep was despatched to Wharton's house in London. The duties of his executorship prevented him from returning to Cambridge until early in 1759, and then he only stayed there for a few weeks. He had in fact made up his mind to leave Cambridge and settle for an indefinite period in London.

There were several reasons for this step, which must have seemed even more of a revolution in his quiet life than the move from Peterhouse to Pembroke. The prospect of a change of air was the least of these, for during the spring of 1759 the gout assailed him both in London and in Cambridge. A change of scene was a more important consideration, especially since he was in more affluent circumstances after Mrs Rogers's death, able to afford comfortable London rooms and to keep a man-servant. But the principal reason was the opening that year of the British Museum, with its great collections of almost unexplored historical manuscripts, at Montagu House in Bloomsbury. In July he hired rooms in the house of a Mr Jauncey in Southampton Row, close to Montagu House, filled them with the familiar furniture from Stoke, and prepared to enjoy his London life.

I am now settled [he wrote to Palgrave] in my new territories commanding Bedford Gardens, and all the fields as far as Highgate and Hampstead, with such a concourse of moving pictures as would astonish you; so *rus-in-urbe-ish*, that I believe I shall stay here, except little excursions and vagaries, for a year to come. What tho'

I am separated from the fashionable world by broad St Giles's, and many a dirty court and alley, yet here is air, and sunshine, and quiet, however, to comfort you.[14]

He was at first looked after by Mrs Rogers's manservant Graves Tokeley, who presently got married and had to be replaced by a certain John, 'a lad that cannot do any earthly thing'. Finally, he engaged an admirable character named Stephen Hempstead, who was to remain his loyal and diligent servant for the rest of his life.

Almost every day he strolled across to the Museum. The first rush of eager sightseers had now abated, and only a trickle of researchers and *literati* made their way past the whale's skeleton and the stuffed crocodiles into the inner sanctum. 'I often pass four hours in the day', Gray wrote, 'in the stillness and silence of the reading-room, which is uninterrupted by any thing but Dr Stukeley the Antiquary, who comes there to talk nonsense, and Coffee-house news.' The officials were all quarrelling violently among themselves; they were as disputatious, he thought, as the Fellows of a college. The keepers were not on speaking terms, and the Principal Librarian had blocked up the passage to the privy used by his colleagues, because they had to pass the windows of his house on their way to it. The Trustees were over-spending their income so recklessly that Gray expected the whole collection would soon have to be put up to auction.[15]

Week after week Gray investigated the Harleian and Cottonian manuscripts, transcribing a great variety of documents which threw fresh light on English history and antiquities. He discovered all sorts of 'odd things unknown to our Historians'. Certain material connected with Richard III was later passed on to Walpole, to be used in his *Historic Doubts* about that monarch. Another paper which he copied, the defence of Sir Thomas Wyatt at his trial in 1541, was printed by Walpole in his *Miscellaneous Antiquities* at the Strawberry Hill Press a year after Gray's death. And when he returned home to his lodgings, further labours of historical research would await him. Walpole had lately been entrusted by his cousin Lord Hertford with a mass of papers from Ragley relating to the Conway family in the seventeenth century. Gray had undertaken to sort and docket these, which he did with his usual scrupulous care.[16]

Wharton had lately abandoned London and the practice of physic, and was now settling down to a country life at Old Park in his native county of Durham. Gray wrote to him regularly and confidentially as always, and resumed his habit of sending him meteorological and botanical observations. They arranged to note the reading of their respective thermometers at certain hours each day; and Gray also described the fruit available in the shops, the blooming of jessamine in the surrounding gardens, the kinds of flowers—'Scarlet-Martagons, Ever-lasting-peas, Double-stocks, Pinks, and flowering Marjoram' —which were included in his nosegays from Covent Garden. He paid his usual visit to Strawberry Hill, and told Wharton all about Walpole's latest addition to the house, the Holbein Chamber, which he rather surprisingly regarded as 'in the best tast of any thing he has yet done'.[17] Otherwise he saw few of his friends, since almost everyone he knew was out of London during the hot summer months.

These months were among the most stirring in the whole of English history. The early disasters of the Seven Years War were at last being retrieved. Rodney destroyed the preparations for invasion which the French had been making at Le Havre, and the English and Hanoverian forces put their army to flight at Minden. Tidings were soon to come of the triumphs of British armies and fleets all over the world, in India and Africa, Canada and the Caribbean. As Walpole exultantly wrote, 'our bells are worn threadbare with ringing for victories'.[18] It was during this memorable time that there took place, far away across the Atlantic, an incident of which the precise details will always remain in doubt, but which has come to be regarded as perhaps the supreme example of the power of Gray's *Elegy* to move the hearts of men.

In one of the ships which formed part of Wolfe's expedition to Quebec there had been a young man named John Robison, who acted as companion and tutor, with the nominal rank of midshipman, to the Admiral's son, and also made himself useful as a surveyor and draughtsman. In the course of time he became Professor of Natural Philosophy in the University of Edinburgh, a position which he held until his death in 1805. He would sometimes relate to his students a story which one of them, James Currie, recorded in a letter to his father a few days after he heard it from the Professor at supper one evening in 1804.

He told me that General Wolfe kept his intention of attacking Quebec a most profound secret; not even disclosing it to the Second-in-Command, and the night before the attack nothing was known. The boats were ordered to drop down the St Lawrence, and it happened that the boat which Professor Robison, then a midshipman, commanded, was very near the one General Wolfe was in. A gentleman was repeating Gray's *Elegy* to the latter, and Mr Robison heard him (the General) say 'I would rather have been the author of that piece than beat the French tomorrow;' and from this remark guessed that the attack was to be made the next day.

This is the most authentic version of Professor Robison's anecdote, written down by young Currie almost straight from his lips. But the Professor had also told the story to others, and notably to Sir Walter Scott, who passed it on many years afterwards to Robert Southey in a much more romantic and appealing form:

On the night when Wolfe crossed the river with his small army they passed in the men-of-war's long boats and launches, and the General himself in the Admiral's barge. The young midshipman who steered the boat was John Robison. . . . I have repeatedly heard the Professor say that during part of the passage Wolfe pulled out of his pocket and read to the officers around (or, perhaps, repeated), Gray's celebrated *Elegy in a Country Churchyard*. I do not know if the recitation was not so well received as he expected, but he said, with a good deal of animation, 'I can only say, Gentlemen, that, if the choice were mine, I would rather be the author of these verses than win the battle which we are to fight tomorrow morning.'

In this latter version the story has been constantly repeated, and further embellishments have been added—for example, that Wolfe laid especial emphasis upon the line *The paths of glory lead but to the grave.* There are sufficient improbabilities even in the earliest account, which after all was committed to paper during Robison's lifetime. It is obviously absurd to suggest that Wolfe concealed from his second-in-command, or indeed from the other principal officers, his intention of attacking Quebec next day. More important is the well-attested fact that he had enjoined, on penalty of death, the strictest silence in the boats as they dropped down the river in the darkness of that September night. It was no moment for even the most subdued declamation of the sublimest poetry. Finally, it is very unlikely that Robison, whose status was that of a civilian, would have commanded or steered or indeed occupied a place at all in one of the boats engaged on this vitally important operation.

On the other hand, there was nothing in Robison's character to suggest that he would or could have invented such a story. He may perfectly well have heard Wolfe express his admiration of Gray's poem, or perhaps even recite it, during some other part of the day which preceded his glorious death. During the afternoon of 12 September it is known that Wolfe made a reconnaissance by boat; and it is not unreasonable to suppose that Robison, who had been engaged in surveying the river, may have been present on that occasion. In the words of the late Professor Temperley, describing a visit to the spot on a later 12 September:

Beneath Wolfe lay the broad green breast of the St Laurence, opposite the cliffs crowned with green bushes and patches of scarlet in the maple, beyond them the faint blue outlines of the far Laurentian hills. It is a scene which would make anyone quote poetry; and Wolfe was still young, ardent, sensitive, ill, melancholy, full of the thought that his time was not long, full also of the sense of the peace of nature to-day, and of what might happen to him and to so many of his men on the morrow.

The *Elegy* had been lately in his thoughts, since Katherine Lowther, whom he hoped to marry, had given him a copy of the poem before he left England for the last time—a copy which still exists, with his inscription and annotations. We may surely believe the substance of Robison's story, however uncertain the details may be. It was not the first nor the last instance in our history of the deep instinctive sympathy that can unite the hero and the recluse, the man of reflection and the man of action.[19]

It is unlikely that Gray ever heard of the splendid tribute which had thus been paid to his genius. At the time when his words were on the lips and in the hearts of the men who were to take Quebec, he was more prosaically occupied with the troubles of his uncle's widow, Mrs Antrobus, the postmistress at Cambridge. Attempts were being made to deprive her of that office, and he was obliged to invoke the aid of Lord John Cavendish in her defence.[20] If he made any comment when the news of Wolfe's victory and death first arrived in England, the letter containing it has not survived. And it is with a sense of anticlimax that we read his description of Pitt's speech—admittedly a very bad one—on the subject of Wolfe's monument, in the course of which 'he wiped his eyes with one handkerchief, and Beckford (who seconded him) cried too, and wiped with two handkerchiefs at once, which was very moving'.[21] As Professor Temperley remarked, it was not thus that the dead hero had spoken of Gray and his *Elegy*.

III

In the meantime Lady Cobham and Miss Speed were down at Stoke, and were missing the visits that Gray used to pay them from the little house at West End. He had written more than once to inquire after Lady Cobham's health and send them the news of the great world, and at the end of August they suggested that he should join them in their country retirement.

My dear Sir [wrote Miss Speed] I wonder whether you think me capable of all the gratitude I really feel for the late marks you have given me of your friendship, I will venture to say if you knew my heart you wou'd be content with it, but knowing my exterior so well as you do You can easily conceive me Vain of the Partiallity you show me; in return for puting me in good humour with myself I will give you pleasure by assuring you Lady Cobham is surprizingly well and most extremely oblig'd to you for the Anxiety you express'd on her account.—we now take the Air ev'ry day and are returned to our old way of living and hope we shall go on in the same way many Years.

We are both scandaliz'd at your being in Town at this time of year, not because (as you may think) that it is unfashionable, but because we think it very unwholesome from the heat of the Season— now I know you are insensible to heat or cold, not but that your Body suffers by either extreme, but you have not attention enough to your self to seek a remedy, we beg now to point out one against the Excessive heat of London, by desiring you wou'd come down to Stoke where you will find Ev'ry thing cool but the reception we shall give you—there is always a Bed Air'd for you and one for your Servant; indeed I can make use of the Strongest argument to tempt you which is that at this time it will be a deed of Charity as we are absolutely alone. . . . If you are at present an invalide let that prompt you to come, for from the *affected creature* you knew me, I am nothing now but a comfortable nurse.[22]

Her letter continued further in this strain, with thanks for the news he had sent them—'it was vastly good of you to give us a detail of what passes in the World for few People will be at that trouble'—and comments on her friend Lord George Sackville, about whose forthcoming court-martial on charges of cowardice at Minden she was '*au désespoire*'. But enough has been quoted to show the affection and solicitude with which she had now come to regard Gray. In spite of the warmth of her invitation, however, he did not go down to Stoke for almost a month. In the interval Lady Cobham was taken ill again, and at one time was thought to be dying. He stayed with them at Stoke until they returned to London late in October, and then, at Lady Cobham's particular request, continued with them for a further month at her house in Hanover Square. By this time he was certain that she had not many weeks to live, and that the doctors could do nothing more for her. His presence in the house did not pass unnoticed; as he told Wharton later on, 'the World said before her death, that Miss Speed and I had shut ourselves up with her in order to make her Will, and that afterwards we were to be married'.[23] He returned to his own lodgings towards the end of November, but remained in constant touch with the household in Hanover Square until Lady Cobham died in the following March.

She was found to have bequeathed virtually her whole estate to her ward, who was named sole executor and residuary legatee.* Miss Speed thus became an important heiress, the owner, in Gray's words, of 'at least £30,000 with a house in Town, plate, jewels, china, and old-japan infinite'.[24] Gray was left twenty guineas for a ring, and had no expectations of anything more considerable.[25] It is useless to speculate whether the dying woman may have uttered any private injunction or expression of hope as to their marriage. But during the spring they were certainly much together; and at the end of June, after various delays due to what Miss Speed described as her business affairs and Gray as her vagaries,[26] they went off to stay with her old friend Mrs Jennings, who lived at Grovelands near Shiplake in Oxfordshire. The party consisted only of Mrs Jennings, a middle-aged widow, and her daughter Susannah. They were both well known to Gray, who had written to them confidentially about Lady Cobham's health in the previous autumn.[27] If the attachment between Gray and Henrietta Speed could ever have developed into something more, this might have proved the time and the place—the sunny days and long twilight evenings of July, in a house of chosen friends, set on a hill whose wooded slopes fell steeply to a noble reach of the Thames.

IV

Many years later, perhaps even after the turn of the century, the second Earl Harcourt amused his leisure by composing

---

* If Miss Speed died without issue, the property was to pass to Henry Thrale the brewer, Lady Cobham's cousin and the father of Johnson's friend of the same name.

character sketches of some remarkable women whom he had known; and amongst his chosen subjects was Henrietta Jane Speed. He has already appeared in this book as Lord Nuneham, the young man with the jessamine powder and the bouquet of jonquils, whose enthusiastic homage had diverted Gray in 1757. At that time he already knew and corresponded on familiar terms with Miss Speed,* and he remained in touch with her throughout her life. His vivid sketch is by far the most detailed account of her character that exists, and throws important light on her relationship with Gray.

She possessed, Lord Harcourt wrote,

the most brilliant parts, she was good humoured, full of vivacity, and had an inexhaustible fund of original and engaging wit; strong sense, united with observation, and penetration the most acute, more than supplied the want of literary knowledge, for which she had not the least relish; and, without having ever given herself the trouble of learning anything, she appeared to know everything. Mr Gray has slightly sketched her portrait in four lines in the *Long Story*. Her person was tall, but not slender, her complexion dark, and, although she had no pretensions to beauty, yet an easy and graceful air with fine eyes and teeth, united to render her altogether extremely pleasing.... In truth she was as incapable of the feeling of affection as of those of hatred or dislike; she could extract entertainment even from folly or insipidity, and no company displeased her, but she really loved nobody. Yet, such was the fascinating power she derived from her invariable good humour and vivacity, and the witty playfulness of her conversation, that to live with her in intimacy without becoming attached to her was impossible.[28]

A biographer should never accept without some reserve the verdict passed upon a human being by one single observer. But it is reasonable to take account of Lord Harcourt's view that Miss Speed was incapable of strong affection, that 'she really loved nobody'. His words suggest that other men, less sensitive

* There is a long and amusing letter from Miss Speed to Lord Nuneham, written from Stoke on 26 October 1755, in *Harcourt Papers*, VIII, 3–10. She describes a visit to Tunbridge Wells, where 'it is the fashion to divide into cotteries, and I was of a very jolly one, we had more men than women of it, as in general they are less troublesome and more entertaining...'.

than Gray, may likewise have perceived an essential coldness of heart beneath her gaiety and her exuberant charm. And to Gray himself, sensitive in every fibre of his being, such coldness would have been particularly apparent. A more normal woman, genuinely in love with him, might conceivably have overcome his fundamental indifference to her sex, the barriers of shyness and reserve with which he had excluded all strong emotion from his life. But they could never be overcome by Henrietta Speed; and there was to be no other woman in his life. 'Thy joys no glittering female meets. . . .' He had written the prophetic words almost twenty years before in the *Ode on the Spring*; and they remained true until the end.

So nothing came of the three summer weeks in the house above the Thames, except a final realisation on Gray's part that for him there was no possible alternative to the life of study and retirement. He found himself shut up with 'three women that laughed from morning to night, and would allow nothing to the sulkiness of my disposition. Company and cards at home, parties by land and water abroad, and (what they call) *doing something*, that is, racketting about from morning to night, are occupations, I find, that wear out my spirits, especially in a situation where one might sit still, and be alone with pleasure.'[29] There was no respite from the talk and laughter of his companions. They dragged him with them on visits to fashionable neighbours, to the Stapletons at Greys Court, to Lady Ailesbury and her husband Henry Conway—who had tried to reconcile him with Walpole all those years ago—at Park Place across the river from Henley. On these occasions he became more than ever morose and silent. 'My Lady Ailesbury', wrote Walpole to George Montagu, 'has been much diverted, and so will you be too: Gray is in their neighbourhood—my Lady Carlisle says *he is extremely like me in his manner*. They went a party to dine on a cold loaf,* and passed the day; Lady A. protests he never opened his lips but once, and then only said, "Yes, my Lady, I believe so."'[30]

* 'To dine on a cold loaf' was an eighteenth-century expression for a picnic.

174

It may have been during these weeks also, though there is no direct evidence of it, that Gray gratified Miss Speed's ambition to 'possess something from his pen on the subject of love'. He produced a mechanical and insipid little song whose very dullness, in comparison with the high spirits of the *Long Story*, suggests the stagnation into which their relationship had drifted:

> Midst Beauty and Pleasure's gay triumphs, to languish
> And droop without knowing the source of my anguish:
> To start from short slumbers, and look for the morning—
> Yet close my dull eyes when I see it returning:
>
> Sighs sudden and frequent, looks ever dejected,
> Sounds that steal from my tongue, by no meaning connected!
> Ah say, Fellow-swains, how these symptoms befell me?
> They smile, but reply not. Sure Delia will tell me!

At the close of this exhausting visit Gray returned to London, and presently went down to Cambridge, where he had arranged to spend the next few weeks with Brown at Pembroke. Here he subsided thankfully into long-accustomed surroundings, the little world of High Table and Fellows' Parlour, the familiar atmosphere of academic gossip and intrigue. His letters deal no longer with the caprices of women of fashion, but with aspirants to bishoprics, and a private tutor for Lord John Cavendish's nephew, and the death of the Master of Magdalene, his old acquaintance Dr Chapman, after consuming five large mackerel and a turbot.[31] There had been no breach of friendship between him and Miss Speed. He was to meet her again in London often enough during the coming months, and Mrs and Miss Jennings as well. Next year he gave her another song, the complaint of a forsaken shepherdess, the charming lines beginning

> Thyrsis, when we parted, swore
> Ere the spring he would return...

which he had written to an air of Geminiani. But by now she must have realised, as clearly as he had always done, that there could be no question of marriage between them.

V

The first week of October saw Gray back in London, settled once more in his Bloomsbury rooms, resuming his studies at the Museum and his long evenings of solitary reading. There was much activity in the literary world throughout 1760, and a good deal of it was reflected in his letters. The new books and pamphlets ranged from Lord Lyttelton's *Dialogues of the Dead* down to the latest ribaldry of John Hall Stevenson. The first volumes of *Tristram Shandy* made their sensational appearance, and their author hastened up from Yorkshire to enjoy the fruits of his success. 'One is invited to dinner, where he dines, a fortnight before', wrote Gray, without making it clear whether he had himself been present at any of those dinners. He found *Tristram Shandy* full of good fun, and was not displeased with the two volumes of *Sermons* with which Sterne promptly followed up his novel. 'They are in the style I think most proper for the Pulpit, and show a very strong imagination and a sensible heart: but you see him often tottering on the verge of laughter, and ready to throw his perriwig in the face of his audience.' Then there were new or recent books by Buffon and D'Alembert; and at the close of the year appeared the six volumes of *La Nouvelle Héloïse*. Gray failed to share the general enthusiasm which greeted Rousseau's emotional masterpiece, although many of his friends, including Mason and Hurd, helped to swell the chorus of praise. He ploughed through it when confined to his rooms for three weeks with a severe cold, and could see nothing in its throbbing pages but insipidity and absurdity.[32]

He had been amused rather than perturbed by a satire against himself and Mason which appeared early in the summer. Two young men of letters, George Colman, who had been largely responsible for *The Connoisseur*, and his friend Robert Lloyd published a slender pamphlet containing an *Ode to Obscurity*, which burlesqued the style of Gray's recent Pindarics, and an *Ode to Oblivion*, in imitation of Mason's *Ode to Memory*. In neither case were the parodies at all skilful or exact. The

principal vices of Gray's poetry, as the authors explained in an
unsigned newspaper puff of their own pamphlet, were 'a wilful
obscurity, a species of false sublime, and a pedantic imitation of
Pindar'. They did their best to pillory these faults; but it was
only once or twice, when they closely followed the text of the
original, that their hits were at all effective:

> O Steed Divine! what daring spirit
> Rides thee now? tho' he inherit
> Nor the pride, nor self-opinion,
> Which elate the mighty Pair,
> Each of Taste the fav'rite minion,
> Prancing thro' the desert air;
> By help mechanick of Equestrian Block
> Yet shall he mount, with classick housings grac'd,
> And all unheedful of the Critick Mock,
> Drive his light Courser o'er the bounds of Taste.

No one could have taken much offence at this second-rate and,
on the whole, good-natured fooling; even Gray, who was
under the impression that Colman was the sole author, thought
that 'he makes very tolerable fun of me', and felt no resentment. 'I believe his Odes sell no more than mine did', he
wrote a little later, 'for I saw a heap of them lie in a Bookseller's
window, who recommended them to me as a very pretty thing.'[33]

His main literary preoccupation in this year was with Erse
and in a lesser degree with Welsh poetry. A young Scotsman
named James Macpherson had lately been arousing much
interest in his own country by what purported to be his translations from the ancient poetry of the Highlands, and in
particular from the compositions of a bard of royal race, Ossian
the son of Fingal. These were circulated in manuscript, and in
the spring of 1760 some examples were sent to Horace Walpole by Sir David Dalrymple, who suggested that Gray also
might be interested to see them. Gray was deeply impressed
with them, and yet felt doubtful of their authenticity. He asked
Walpole to make further inquiries of Dalrymple, and presumably wrote himself to Macpherson. The result left him more
perplexed than before. The translations, in their simple

rhythmical prose, appeared to him quite marvellous. 'I am gone mad about them...*extasié* with their infinite beauty', he wrote. Yet Macpherson's letters to him were 'ill-wrote, ill-reason'd, unsatisfactory, calculated (one would imagine) to deceive one, and yet not cunning enough to do it cleverly. In short, the whole external evidence would make one believe these fragments (for so he calls them, tho' nothing can be more entire) counterfeit: but the internal is so strong on the other side, that I am resolved to believe them genuine, spite of the Devil and the Kirk.'[34]

In the summer Macpherson published a volume of *Fragments of Ancient Poetry collected in the Highlands*. Private doubts as to their genuineness gave place to public controversy, which broke out again in later years on the appearance of *Fingal* and *Temora*, two lengthy epic poems. In these disputes Gray took no part. While retaining his doubts about Macpherson, he continued to admire the prose-poems which this mysterious and faintly disreputable figure continued to produce in the name of Ossian. His commendation was welcomed in Scotland. 'It gives me pleasure', wrote David Hume, one of Macpherson's early champions, 'to find that a person of so fine a taste as Mr Gray approves of these fragments; as it may convince us, that our fondness of them is not altogether founded on national pre-possessions, which, however, you know to be a little strong.'[35]

Macpherson had certainly not discovered complete epics, or dramatic poems in dialogue, in the remoter Highlands. He merely adapted and transformed to his own purposes such fragmentary legends, ballads and songs as he may have found there. Gray suspected all this; nevertheless, the supposed translations had the power to move him almost beyond words, in such passages, for example, as that strange dialogue between the chief and the five bards, who leave his house in succession and return to describe to him the changing aspects of the night.[36] The Ossian poems contained in extravagant measure the mystery and romance for which he had been delving, toilsomely and with varying success, in the Norse and Welsh originals only a few years before. Here were mountains and moorlands, eagle-haunted rocks and mist-enshrouded seas, mighty warriors and maidens with floating hair, the voices of ghosts and the incantations of bards. 'The chief of Urlor had come to Gormal with his dark-bosomed ships. He saw the daughter of Annir, white-armed Foina-brâgal. He saw her! Nor careless rolled her eyes on the rider of stormy waves. She fled to his ship in darkness, like a moon-beam through a nightly vale. Annir pursued along the deep; he called the winds of heaven....'[37] Such strains, claimed to be handed down from remote antiquity—for Fingal, Ossian's father, was supposed to have warred valiantly against the Roman masters of Britain—made the same emotional appeal to Gray as to later romantics all over Europe, to Goethe and Byron, Pushkin and Chateaubriand.[38]

Gray's interest in Welsh poetry was likewise renewed in 1760, when he was shown a Latin discourse, *De Bardis Dissertatio*, written by a Denbighshire curate of antiquarian tastes, the Rev. Evan Evans, together with some translations by the same hand. Although he had been studying Welsh poetry and prosody some years before, with results which were triumphantly evident in *The Bard*, he does not seem to have made any great progress in the language. He found these versions, some of which were in Latin and one at least in English, a good deal less striking than Macpherson's wild outpourings; but Aneurin and Gwalchmai were authentic bards, centuries removed from the magnificent phantom of Ossian, and he spoke of Evans's work with interest and gratitude.[39]

Gray's ambition to write a history of English poetry was temporarily revived by these impressive glimpses, both occurring in the same year, into its Erse and Welsh backgrounds. They inspired him, moreover, with the idea of rendering into his own verse 'some specimens of the Style that reigned in ancient times among the neighbouring nations, or those who had subdued the greater part of this Island, and were our Progenitors', and including them in the early chapters of his book.[40] To this end he drew up a list of suitable poems for translation from Old Norse, Anglo-Saxon, Welsh and Erse. The full scheme was never carried out. He made no translations from the Anglo-Saxon, and none from the five Ossianic pieces of his choice, which he cautiously labelled 'very ancient if genuine'.⁴¹ But in 1760 he adapted two sizeable poems from the Norse, and four fragments of varying length from the Welsh. Since the completion of *The Bard* in 1757 his entire poetic output had consisted of two epitaphs and a song. Now his friends rejoiced to learn that his inspiration was astir once more, and Walpole wrote to George Montagu that 'Gray has translated two noble incantations from the Lord knows who, a Danish Gray, who lived the Lord knows when'.⁴²

These new productions were *The Descent of Odin* and *The Fatal Sisters*, which Gray at first entitled *The Song of the Valkyries*. Their originals were in fact Icelandic, and were widely separated in date, the first poem being taken from the *Vegtams Kviða*, a work of great antiquity, and the latter from *Darraðer Lioð* or *The Lay of Darts*, which belonged to the eleventh century. Gray found the texts of these and other Norse poems, together with Latin translations, in Thomas Bartolin's *Antiquitatum Danicarum de causis contemptae mortis*, printed at Copenhagen in 1689, substantial extracts from which were copied into a second article headed *Gothi* in his Commonplace Book. It seems clear that in his Icelandic as in his Welsh renderings he had little knowledge of the language itself, and relied for the meaning of the poems mainly upon the Latin translation; but his ear was quick to catch the rapid beats, the hurrying urgent rhythm of the originals, and to reproduce such effects in his own versions.⁴³

It is easy to understand why Walpole described these poems as 'noble incantations'. To him and to his contemporaries the abrupt and almost gnomic dialogue between Odin and the Prophetess at the portals of 'Hela's drear abode', and the grim song of the Valkyries as they wove their web of human entrails, were profoundly impressive. Gray had conjured up an atmosphere of darkness and doom, of battles on desolate moors and spirits crying in the mist, which was the very essence of northern romanticism:

Now the storm begins to lower,
(Haste, the loom of Hell prepare,)
Iron-sleet of arrowy shower
Hurtles in the darken'd air.

Glitt'ring lances are the loom,
Where the dusky warp we strain,
Weaving many a Soldier's doom,
Orkney's woe, and *Randver's* bane.. . .

The generation which had welcomed Ossian so warmly could scarcely fail to be enraptured by this.

The versions from the Welsh would also appear to have been written some time in 1760 or 1761, and were derived from the translations by Evan Evans which Gray had seen in manuscript. The longest was *The Triumphs of Owen*, a passage of 36 lines from Gwalchmai's *Ode to Owen Gwynnedd*, describing a battle in which that monarch routed an invading force of Irish, Danes and Normans. The three remaining fragments, *The Death of Hoel*, *Caradoc* and *Conan* were all taken from the *Gododin* of Aneurin:

Have ye seen the tusky boar,
Or the bull, with sullen roar,
On surrounding foes advance?
So Caradoc bore his lance.

There is such vigour in even the smallest of these fragments that Gray's failure to continue his projected series of translations was indeed regrettable. But the poetic impulse soon flagged once more, the *History of English Poetry* was laid aside, and none of the translations was published for several years to come.

VI

Gray's life in London during these years was not unsociable. He went occasionally to the opera and to the play, but the time which he spared from study and reading was mainly devoted to a few old friends such as Walpole, Miss Speed, Lord John Cavendish and Frederick Montagu. Now and then he would

spend a few days at Strawberry Hill, on one occasion with
Mason, when Walpole, happy in the company of the two
distinguished poets, 'spent Sunday as if it was Apollo's birthday
...we listened to the nightingales till one o'clock in the
morning'.[44] He made one or two new acquaintances, among
them Benjamin Stillingfleet, who had criticised his *Odes* so
severely in private when they first appeared.[45] Stillingfleet,
the leading English disciple of Linnaeus, used to attend the
assemblies of learned ladies wearing blue worsted stockings,
an eccentricity which led to the name of 'Bluestocking' being
applied to the assemblies and finally to the ladies themselves.
He and Gray were drawn together by their interest in botany
and natural history, and by the fact that both, unknown to one
another, had for some years past kept calendars of the seasons,
the weather, the crops and so forth. 'I have lately made an
acquaintance with this Philosopher, who lives in a garret here
in the winter, that he may support some near relations, who
depend upon him. He is always employ'd, and always cheerful,
and seems to me a very worthy honest Man.' So Gray wrote to
Wharton, enclosing calendars of the foliation of trees, the
flowering of plants and the arrival of migrant birds, all by a
curious coincidence drawn up in 1755, by himself at Cambridge,
by Stillingfleet at Stratton Strawless in Norfolk, and by the
Swedish botanist Berger at Upsala. Wharton was desired 'to
observe, as you tend your plantations and take your walks, how
the Spring advances in the North, and whether Old-Park most
resembles Upsal, or Stratton'.[46]

Gray returned to Cambridge for most of the summer of 1761.
He spent a few days with Palgrave at his parsonage of Thran-
deston in Suffolk, and explored the surrounding countryside,
including the romantic castles of Wingfield and Framlingham.
At the beginning of September he made the acquaintance of
Thomas Percy, who was then assembling the material for his
Reliques of Ancient English Poetry, and had come to Cambridge
to inspect the matchless collection of ballads at the Pepysian
Library. Gray called upon him at Magdalene, and they spent an

afternoon together at Pembroke, drinking tea and absorbed in wide-ranging discussion of ancient poetry, English, Welsh and Erse. It may be, as Mr Powell Jones has surmised, that at this meeting Gray 'with his customary inertia and aversion to publicity' suggested to Percy the publication of certain other Norse poems which he had himself listed among his intended translations. It is certainly significant that with one exception these poems were to appear in Percy's *Five Runic Pieces* in 1765. For some reason the acquaintance between these two enthusiasts for ancient poetry was not destined to flourish. When the *Reliques* were published Percy was eager to know what Gray thought of them; but later he took offence when Gray failed to reply to some inquiry about a manuscript, and announced that in future 'I do not chuse to apply to him for any favour of any kind'.[47]

During the summer Frederick Montagu asked Gray to write an epitaph for the monument to his friend Sir William Williams, a young soldier of great talent and personal charm, who had been killed in the attack on Belleisle in April. Gray had known Williams a little as an undergraduate of Clare some years before, and had met him by chance on the road to London during the previous autumn. They had discussed the coming expedition, and Gray felt a curious premonition, sadly to be fulfilled, that 'perhaps he may lay his fine Vandyke-Head in the dust'. The slightness of his acquaintance with Williams made him hesitate to undertake the epitaph, but Montagu was 'so friendly a Person, and his affliction seem'd to me so real, that I could not refuse him'. His own feelings were little engaged in the task; but a touch of pathos softens the twelve rather stiff and stilted lines which resulted:

> ... From fortune, pleasure, science, love, he flew,
>   And scorn'd repose, when Britain took the field.
>
> With eyes of flame and cool intrepid breast,
>   Victor he stood on Bellisle's rocky steeps:
> Ah gallant youth!—this marble tells the rest,
>   Where melancholy Friendship bends, and weeps.[48]

Early in September 1761 Gray returned to London, which

was buzzing with excitement over the coming Coronation and the arrival of the new Queen. The Coronation took place on the 22nd, and Lord John Cavendish obtained him one of the coveted seats in the box of his brother the Duke of Devonshire, the Lord Chamberlain, in Westminster Hall. Here he sat all day while the long and elaborate scenes of pageantry were unfolded below. He described all the splendours and absurdities of the occasion in an immense letter to Brown—the brilliance of dress and jewellery in the crowded boxes, the stately or ludicrous aspect of individual peers and peeresses, the blunders of prelates and heralds, the good square meal which the Duke had provided for his guests while the actual crowning was taking place in the Abbey, and finally the culminating glory of the royal banquet, 'the most magnificent spectacle I ever beheld'. It is a wonderful letter, and may be compared and contrasted with Walpole's account of the same scenes and personages in a letter to George Montagu. Two abler pens have perhaps never depicted one single occasion.[49]

For more than two years Gray had been living in his quiet rooms in Bloomsbury, and he now decided to return to Cambridge. His landlord, Mr Jauncey, had told him in May that he wanted to let the whole of his house to a single tenant, and Gray had then lamented the trouble of finding another lodging, but does not seem to have contemplated leaving London. However, his plans had changed; and at the end of October he despatched twenty-eight packages—tables and sofas, chairs and feather-beds and chests of books—of which James Brown was asked to take charge. He followed his possessions down to Cambridge on 19 November.

Just a week before he left London, a ceremony took place at the Chapel of the Sardinian Embassy in Lincoln's Inn Fields, about which he does not seem to have heard until some time later.

My old Friend Miss Speed has done what the World calls a very foolish thing [he wrote to Wharton next January]. She has married the Baron de la Peyrière, son to the Sardinian Minister, the Comte de Viry. He is about 28 years old, (ten years younger than herself) but looks nearer 40. This is not the effect of debauchery, for he is a very sober Man; good-natured and honest, and no Conjurer. The estate of the family is about 4000 £ a-year. The Castle of Viry is in Savoy a few miles from Geneva, commanding a fine view of the Lake. What she has done with her money, I know not: but (I suspect) kept it to herself. Her religion she need not change, but she must never expect to be well-received at that Court, till she does; and I do not think she will make quite a *Julie* in the country.[50]

It is perhaps hardly necessary to mention that Julie was the country-loving heroine of *La Nouvelle Héloïse*, and that the expression 'no conjuror' was applied in the eighteenth century to persons of less than average intelligence. But a few of Gray's statements in this letter require correction. It is true that there was a difference of ten years between the ages of Henrietta Speed and her husband; but at the time of their marriage she was nearly 34 and he was 24. And the register of the Chapel states that 'the very noble Joseph-Maria Baron de la Peyrière and the most illustrious Henrietta-Joan Speed were joined in wedlock according to the rites of the Holy Roman Catholic Church, both professing its orthodox faith'.[51] The bride is later said to have been 'an occasional Conformist' for some while after her marriage, and at one time to have returned to the Church of England; but before long the displeasure of the King of Sardinia impelled her to enter finally 'into the Pale of the Romish Church', exactly as Gray had predicted.

It is of course possible that Gray knew of this marriage before it took place, but for some reason did not mention it earlier to Wharton, the closest of all his friends. His description of the Baron's appearance suggests that they had met; but he may equally well have taken it at second hand from some mutual acquaintance, possibly Walpole or Cavendish. In any case Henrietta Speed mattered little to him now. She had brought a measure of warmth and gaiety into his life for a few years, and he was always grateful to her and wished her well. But that was all. Their roads had parted; and he did not in any way repine that she should have bestowed her kind heart and her large fortune upon this mediocre young nobleman from Savoy.

CHAPTER X

LIFE AT CAMBRIDGE:
FRIENDS AND OCCUPATIONS:
THE VISIT TO SCOTLAND
1761-1765

I

ALTHOUGH he had at no time wandered far afield and had often revisited Cambridge during the past two years, there was an air of homecoming about Gray's return in the winter of 1761. Outside the walls of Pembroke lay the rainswept streets, the leafless elms and tossing willows, the mists rising in the early dusk. Within the college were old friends such as Brown and Delaval to welcome him back, and junior Fellows eager to make his closer acquaintance; the blazing fire in the quiet sociable parlour, the comforts of his own familiar rooms. For awhile he was deeply content, and his contentment is evident in the earliest letter written after his return, a happy nonsensical note addressed to Mason:

Of all loves come to Cambridge out of hand, for here is Mr Dillival and a charming set of Glasses, that sing like nightingales, and we have concerts every other night, and shall stay here this month or two, and a vast deal of good company, and a Whale in pickle just come from Ipswich. And the *Man* won't die, and Mr Wood is gone to Chatsworth, and there is no body but you, and Tom, and the curl'd Dog, and don't talk of the charge, for we will make a subscription: besides we know, you always come, when you have a mind.[1]

Gray was never again to be away from Cambridge for so lengthy a period. He could no longer spend the summers and autumns at Stoke Poges, as he had done for so many years past. Instead his annual tours grew more varied and more enterprising, and began to include long visits at the houses of his friends. Almost all the members of his circle had originally been associated with him at Cambridge, but they were now scattered throughout the kingdom. And since no man was ever more dependent upon his friends than Gray, or was more affectionately regarded by them in return, it may be fitting at this stage to pass them in review and see how they had fared as the years went by.

Wharton, the good and kindly and reliable, must always come first in any list of Gray's friends. He had now given up the practice of medicine and settled at Old Park near Durham, an estate which he had lately inherited. There he led the life of a country gentleman, busied with his farm and garden, improving his house and laying out his modest grounds. A second Robin had taken the place of the son whose epitaph Gray had written, and the family steadily grew in numbers. Gray was fond of the children and used to send messages to them all, Robin and Peggy and Debo and Dicky and Betty and Kee. The sight of his old friend's country contentment gave him unfeigned pleasure. 'Happy they', he once wrote to Wharton, 'that can watch the brood of a hen, or see a fleet of their own ducklings launch into the water! It is with a sentiment of envy I speak it, who never shall have even a thatch'd roof of my own, nor gather a strawberry but in Covent-Garden.'[2]

Mason had been steadily making his way in the Church, and was just in the act of receiving sufficient preferment 'to shut', as Gray expressed it, 'his insatiable repining mouth'.[3] He had for some years been rector of Aston in Yorkshire, a prebendary of York Cathedral and chaplain to Lord Holdernesse. In 1757 he had been appointed, through the Cavendish interest, one of the chaplains in ordinary to King George II, and the appointment was renewed under his successor. And now at the beginning of 1762 the friendly influence of Frederick Montagu, whose sister was married to the Dean of York, obtained for him a residentiary canonry of the Cathedral, and soon afterwards the Precentorship as well. He was thus established almost permanently in the north, living at his rectory of Aston except for his periods of obligatory residence at York, and only coming to London when his duties as a royal chaplain required his attendance.

It is difficult to be quite fair to Mason. 'Nobody likes him, and nobody trusts him', says Professor Garrod bluntly.[4] Reflecting on his vanity, his ambition, the striving after wit and the depressing lapses into vulgarity that characterise his letters to Gray, one cannot but agree. Yet Gray liked him and trusted him, to such an extent that he chose him out of a wide circle of friends as the custodian of his papers and the guardian of his fame. He even approved of Mason's poetry, with reservations, and his kindness and patience were never more conspicuous than in the pains which he took to improve it. He corrected *Elfrida*; he polished *Caractacus*; he hinted that such a line as 'See mitred Drummond heave the heartfelt groan' was not entirely adequate as a description of an Archbishop's sorrow at the loss of his daughter.[5] A great deal of Mason's posthumous unpopularity is due to the liberties which he took with the text of Gray's letters, a matter upon which he could have said something in his own defence.[6] Despite all the criticism that has been justifiably levelled at him, he played an essential part in Gray's life and filled an important place in his affections; and there can be no doubt of his absolute fidelity to the elder poet

> Whose lofty genius bears along
> The conscious dignity of Song;
> And, scorning from the sacred store
> To waste one note on Pride or Power,
> Roves through the glimmering twilight gloom,
> And warbles round each rustic tomb.[7]

Stonhewer's activities at this time are a little vague. He occupied a modest position on the fringes of the Court and the political world, holding such minor offices as Historiographer to the King, and Knight Harbinger, and Interpreter of Oriental Languages, in which last capacity he had to go to Portsmouth on one occasion to welcome an ambassador from Morocco.[8]

WILLIAM MASON
From a painting by Peter Falconet, in the possession of Viscount Harcourt

His ability and his charm of manner won him many friends—
'he was one of the prettiest Figures of a Man I ever saw', said
William Cole, 'and was as pretty a Scholar'[9]—but he remained
firmly attached to his old pupil the Duke of Grafton, whose
political fortunes were to rise before long in a spectacular
manner and with important consequences for Gray.

Walpole continued to lead his gay, busy and immensely
varied life. At this time he was occupied in compiling his
Anecdotes of Painting from the chaotic manuscripts left behind
by George Vertue the engraver, and availed himself freely of
Gray's learning and his services as a researcher and transcriber. The *Anecdotes*, the first two volumes of which appeared
in 1762, rank highest among those of Walpole's works which
could be published during his lifetime, as a really valuable con-
tribution to the history of English art. Gray often called on him
in London and stayed with him at Strawberry Hill; and in
Cambridge he always looked forward to the arrival of his
letters, with their news and gossip of the great world and the
irradiation of their incomparable wit.

Of his younger friends, Lord John Cavendish and Frederick
Montagu were both returned to Parliament again at the
general election of 1761, but neither had yet achieved any
political distinction. They were members of the group of
Whigs who faithfully followed Lord Rockingham, and in due
course obtained office during the brief administrations of their
leader. Cavendish was to be twice Chancellor of the Exchequer
and to receive at his death a noble eulogy from Burke, who
wrote with admiration and grief of his 'great integrity, great
tenderness and sensibility of heart, with friendships few and
unalterable; perfect disinterestedness; the ancient English
reserve and simplicity of heart'. But this was all far in the
future. In 1761 Cavendish and Montagu were two lively and
agreeable young men of the world, whose friendship meant a
good deal to Gray, and whose influence was exerted occasionally
on his behalf and constantly on behalf of Mason.

Lord Strathmore now spent most of his time in the north,

managing his wide estates in Scotland and in Durham. His youngest brother Thomas Lyon had just become a Fellow of Pembroke, to Gray's great satisfaction, and remained there for several years. William Palgrave was still at his Suffolk parsonage, and John Clerke at his home in Surrey. With all these friends Gray kept in touch, and the names of new acquaintances appear now and then in his letters. One of them was Sir Henry Erskine, a Scottish baronet of poetical inclinations, a soldier of some note and now a member of Parliament high in the confidence of Bute. Another was Christopher Anstey, the squire of Trumpington, who had translated the *Elegy* into Latin and was soon to achieve celebrity with *The New Bath Guide*. A third was 'Billy Robinson', the Rev. William Robinson, a brother of that rich and learned lady Mrs Elizabeth Montagu. Gray had known him for some time as a Fellow of St John's, but became more closely acquainted with him after his marriage and the consequent vacation of his fellowship in 1760. In London he used occasionally to see Thomas Pitt of Boconnoc in Cornwall, later created Lord Camelford, a Member of Parliament and amateur architect; a friend, until they quarrelled on political issues, of Walpole's, and often called into consultation over the adornment of Strawberry Hill. He also knew, probably through Stillingfleet, the Hon. Daines Barrington, a fellow-enthusiast in the pursuit of natural history, and interested also in Evan Evans and his translations of Welsh poetry. Apart from Billy Robinson all these remained more or less on the fringes of his acquaintance, pleasant and intelligent people to meet and talk with, but nothing more.

In the summer of 1762, however, he met by chance at the rooms of William Lobb, a Fellow of Peterhouse, a young pensioner of Trinity Hall named Norton Nicholls, whose friend and mentor he was to remain until the end of his days. The early life of Nicholls had been a little like his own. His father, a London merchant, had deserted his mother soon after their marriage, and she had brought up their only child and educated him at Eton. But there the resemblance ended. No cloud of melancholy ever weighed upon the spirits of Norton Nicholls. He was a vivacious, enthusiastic, sociable young man, passionately fond of music and poetry, and a little reluctant to pursue the career in the Church which had already been marked out for him. He had long hoped for an introduction to Gray, whom he regarded with admiration and awe; and he at once described their meeting in a letter to another hero-worshipping young man in London, his friend William Johnson Temple:

My dear Temple

Now I give you leàve, nay insist on it, that you Envy me! Last Friday I had the Happiness of drinking Tea with the great Mr Gray at Lobb's Room. I assure you after the first Quarter of an hour which was quite little enough for me to compose my Spirits, and get Courage enough to be happy I was as much so as it is possible for you to conceive me in such circumstances. I did not find him as you found Johnson, surly, morose, Dogmatical, or imperious. But affable, entertaining and polite. He had no other opportunity of showing his superior abilities but such as naturally presented itself from the subject of Conversation, which however he never propos'd.

Conceive if you can how happy I find myself when he told me he hop'd to have the Pleasure of my Company some Afternoon at Pembroke. He has not yet fix'd on any. I am under a thousand Anxieties whether or no he will. But Lobb assures me I may depend on more of his Acquaintance. I assure you the whole afternoon, and ever since I have been employ'd with this Idea. That I should be acquainted with one of the greatest Men who ever existed in the World! That he should (as it is probable he may!) visit me at my own Room!

We had some Discourse about Dante and he seem'd very much astonished that I should have read any of it. He speaks of it in the highest Terms and particularly desir'd me to read one part of it, the Story of Count Ugolino; as you may imagine, I read it the next morning, and found it what I expected one of the finest Things I had ever read in my Life.

What I could chiefly observe in him, was vast politeness, great Good-nature, and the most elegant accuracy of Phrase in the World.

The Bell rings for Chapel and I can't bear to defer sending this by the Post.

Adieu my most dear Friend!   N.N.[10]

Many years later, when writing his *Reminiscences of Gray*, Nicholls enlarged upon one point in his account of their first meeting. 'The conversation turned on the use of bold metaphors in poetry; and that of Milton was quoted—"The sun was pale, and silent as the moon" &c.,* when I ventured to ask if it might not possibly be imitated from Dante, *mi ripingeva là dove il sol tace*. Mr Gray turned quickly round to me and said "Sir, do you read Dante?" and entered into conversation with me.'[11]

Nicholls seems almost invariably to have made this excellent first impression upon strangers. A year later James Boswell, to whom he was introduced by Temple, wrote in his journal that 'I never saw anybody who engaged me more at the very first than this gentleman. He discovered an amiable disposition, a sweetness of manners, and an easy politeness that pleased me much.'[12] He did not have to endure for very long his anxieties as to whether Gray really meant to pursue the acquaintance further. The relationship of master and disciple was soon established between them—Gray directing the young man's studies, suggesting his reading, advising him on conduct and morals; Nicholls following every precept with humility and gratitude, and at the same time delighting his mentor with his intelligence, his high spirits, his youthful sensitiveness and charm. Gray was describing him before long as 'a young man worth his weight in gold'; and Nicholls was to be thankful to the end of his days for the great poet's 'kindness and condescension to which I owe all that is not bad in every part of my character'.

These were not empty words. Nicholls stood much in need of a steadying influence, an older man whom he respected and whose example could curb his volatile temperament. Even in later years his vivacity and loquacity were sometimes felt to be out of keeping with his clerical profession, and once he seriously shocked James Boswell. But he responded to Gray's steady insistence upon upright conduct, and the duties of religion, and the quality which is called virtue:

* The quotation from *Samson Agonistes* should of course begin 'The sun to me is dark...'.

Ability, talents, genius, the highest acquisitions of science and knowledge were in his opinion of little account compared with *virtue*, which he often used to quote to me from Plato is nothing but 'the exercise of right reason.' I remember in the early part of my acquaintance with him saying that some person was 'a clever man' —he cut me short and said 'Tell me if he is good for any thing?' In the choice of his acquaintances he certainly often preferred persons of excellent moral character to those of superior ability; and had an aversion for those who were vicious, profligate, and unprincipled, which no admiration of their Genius could subdue, or even soften.

Gray has sometimes been described as a deist, and it is certain that at one period the views of Conyers Middleton, so fashionable among the younger men at Cambridge, had a considerable influence upon him. It may be—and the supposition is borne out by the epitaphs which he wrote upon Mrs Clerke and Wharton's little boy—that during his middle years his positive convictions even fell short of the 'trembling hope' of the *Elegy*; but towards the close of his life there are many indications in his letters of a strengthening of faith, a more complete acceptance of the teachings of his Church. And at no time could he forgive the deliberate fostering of irreligion, which he regarded as 'taking away the best consolation of man without substituting any thing of equal value in its place'. He lost no opportunity of warning younger men against the writings, whatever their literary brilliance, of professed atheists such as Hume and above all Voltaire. 'Atheism', he once remarked to Walpole, 'is a vile dish, tho' all the cooks of France combine to make new sauces to it.'[13] He could enjoy, as much as anyone else, most of the works of 'that inexhaustible, eternal, entertaining Scribler Voltaire'; but he never tired of voicing his detestation of his character. He seemed, thought Nicholls, 'to know even beyond what had appeared of him, and to see with the eye of a prophet his future mischiefs: he said to me, "No one knows the mischief that man will do"'.[14]

It was thus towards the highest ideals of virtue that Gray sought to direct the thoughts of his new disciple. But his relationship with Nicholls did not invariably move upon this solemn plane. Happily both sides of their correspondence have largely survived; and their letters reveal, often through a veil of cheerful badinage, a degree of sympathy and understanding which shows how fortunate an event in both their lives was that chance meeting in the rooms of Mr Lobb at Peterhouse.

II

Gray spent most of the spring of 1762 in London, seeing Walpole and his other friends, and suffering two slight attacks of gout. He had been free of this malady for almost two years, and it did not seriously affect him now. At the beginning of July he set out for a long sojourn in the north. He spent a fortnight at York with Mason, who was sunning himself in his new ecclesiastical splendours.

The Precentor [he wrote to Brown] is very hopefully improved in dignity; his scarf sets the fullest about his ears: his surplice has the most the air of lawn-sleeves you can imagine in so short a time; he begins to complain of qualms and indigestions from repose and repletion: in short *il tranche du Prélat*. We went twice a day to church with our vergers and all our pomp.

Then he went on to stay with Wharton at Old Park, and found himself in a very different establishment. His friend was still altering and improving his house, and everything was in a cheerful state of confusion, with workmen indoors and out, the books stored away, only one pen and ink to be found, no newspapers or magazines, poultry crowing and clucking under the windows, but incomparable cream and butter from the farm. Gray was perfectly happy at Old Park; even the frequent presence in the house of Jetty and Fadge, Wharton's two favourite sows, did not disturb his equanimity; and he remained there for nearly four months.[15]

Early in November he left this congenial household and journeyed southward again, sight-seeing as he went. He saw Richmond, Ripon, Fountains a second time, Wentworth Castle, the parish church at Sheffield, Chatsworth, and finally Hardwick, which impressed him most of all.

One would think Mary, Queen of Scots, was but just walk'd down into the Park with her Guard for half-an-hour. Her Gallery, her room of audience, her antichamber, with the very canopies, chair of state, footstool, Lit-de-repos, Oratory, carpets, and hangings, just as she left them. A little tatter'd indeed, but the more venerable; and all preserved with religious care, and paper'd up in winter.[16]

He stayed two or three days with Frederick Montagu at his house near Nottingham, and thence went straight to London.

On his arrival he learnt that Shallet Turner, the Professor of Modern History at Cambridge, had died a fortnight before. This Chair, founded by King George I, was worth £400 a year, a stipend far in excess of any other in the university. Its holders were not required in practice to deliver lectures, or to reside at Cambridge, or to do anything beyond paying an exiguous salary to humble teachers of the French and Italian languages, such as the Signor Piazza who had instructed Gray in his undergraduate days. Gray had long desired to succeed to the professorship. It was, indeed, the one object of worldly ambition that he ever sought. More than ten years before, on a rumour of Turner's death, he had made known his hopes to Chute, whom he told that 'I certainly might ask it with as much, or more Propriety, than any one in this Place'. In 1759, when Turner's health again appeared to be failing, he was sounded about his intentions, and told his questioner that 'I should not *ask* for it, not chusing to be refused'. But now he was encouraged by his friends to make the application, and he allowed his name to be submitted to Bute. Sir Henry Erskine, whose influence with Bute was very considerable, put forward his claims with zeal; but the all-powerful Minister's reply was a refusal, 'join'd with great professions of *his desire to serve me* on any future occasion, and many more fine words, that I pass over'. It was at first rumoured that Delaval, whom Gray would have preferred next to himself, was to be the successful candidate; but the professorship was finally bestowed upon Laurence Brockett, a drunken and disreputable Fellow of

Trinity who had had the advantage of being private tutor to Bute's son-in-law, Sir James Lowther.[17]

Although the choice of Brockett was somewhat humiliating, Gray was well aware of the reasons for it and bore his disappointment calmly. The stipend of the professorship would have been welcome enough; but his income was now considerably larger than it had been ten or twelve years before, and sufficient for all his needs. Moreover he took a pride in his detachment from the squalor and jobbery of the political world, and felt some shame at having dabbled in those muddy waters even to the modest extent of his application to Bute. In the previous year he had jotted down in one of his pocket-books some lines intended as a sketch of his own character:

> Too poor for a bribe, and too proud to importune,
> He had not the method of making a fortune:
> Could love, and could hate, so was thought somewhat odd;
> No very great Wit, he believ'd in a God.
> A Post or a Pension he did not desire,
> But left Church and State to Charles Townshend and Squire.[18]

Charles Townshend, so dexterous, fickle and unscrupulous, embodied all that Gray most hated in contemporary politics. Dr Samuel Squire, chaplain to the Duke of Newcastle, for years his toady and chief adviser on university affairs, and lately rewarded with the bishopric of St David's, was the symbol of everything he detested in the Church. Now that he had for once departed from his principles and had not shown himself 'too proud to importune', he felt a little tarred with the same brush.

The year 1763 passed without much incident. In February there opened a stately and protracted exchange of compliments between Gray and Count Algarotti, a writer and philosopher of European celebrity, best known in England by a youthful treatise in which he had expounded Newton for the benefit of the ladies. William Taylor How, an acquaintance of Gray's and a former fellow-commoner of Pembroke, had lately made friends with this cosmopolitan figure at Pisa, and introduced him to the odes of Gray and the dramas of Mason. The

Count's expressions of admiration were at first conveyed to Gray in a letter from How to Brown. Before long, however, he was writing to Gray direct, and assuring him in flowery Italian that England, which had already produced a Homer, an Archimedes and a Demosthenes—Shakespeare, Newton and Pitt—could now also boast its Pindar.[19] Gray in reply expressed his pride in the admiration of the author of *Il Newtonianismo per le Dame*, 'having no relish for any other fame than what is confer'd by the few real Judges, that are so thinly scatter'd over the face of the earth'.[20] There was even a suggestion that Algarotti should revisit England, which he had known well in his younger days; but an end was made of all such plans by his unexpected death in the following year.

In July a figure from the past flits across Gray's correspondence with Mason in the person of Christopher Smart. After some years in confinement, during which he had written *A Song to David* and *Jubilate Agno*, Smart had recovered and was about to publish his *Translation of the Psalms of David*. Mason had seen the *Song to David*, 'and from thence conclude him as mad as ever'; and one wonders uneasily if Gray's view of that miraculous poem was any more sympathetic. But both were doing what they could to help Smart, Mason collecting subscribers for the *Psalms* and Gray putting down his name for two copies of the book.[21] It would seem that no recollection of Gray had ever drifted through Smart's clouded brain while he was composing *Jubilate Agno*. All sorts of Cambridge figures appear, mysteriously transfigured, in those extraordinary pages, including Mason himself: 'Let Mason, house of Mason rejoice with Suberies the Capitol Cork Tree. Lord be merciful to William Mason.' Other acquaintances of Gray's are remembered in the same strange formula, or find places elsewhere in the poem: for example, 'Let Anstey, house of Anstey rejoice with Eumeces a kind of Balm. Lord have mercy on Christopher Anstey and his kinswoman.'[22] But there is nowhere any word of Gray, beyond the possibility that Smart was recalling a stanza of the *Elegy* when he wrote the words, 'For many a genius being lost at the plough is a false thought, the divine providence is a better manager.'[23]

This summer Gray did not undertake one of his longer tours, but contented himself with a few weeks in London and a visit to John Clerke at his home in Surrey. He also spent a few days at Strawberry Hill. Walpole had lately been lent the original manuscript of the autobiography of Lord Herbert of Cherbury, and was hoping to persuade its owner to allow him to print that remarkable work at his own press. His favourite niece Lady Waldegrave, who had lost her husband a few weeks before, was also staying in the house. She was still overwhelmed with grief, and Walpole and Gray tried to cheer her by reading Lord Herbert aloud, only to find that 'we could not get on for laughing and screaming'.[24] Walpole was able to print the book during the autumn, with Gray as usual helping with the editorial work, and it was published next year.

The two friends met again in July, when Walpole suddenly appeared at Cambridge on his way home from an antiquarian tour in the company of William Cole.* They dined and drank tea with Gray; and Walpole, who had not set foot in Cambridge for twenty-four years, 'seem'd mighty happy for the time he stay'd, and said he could like to live here'.[25] Cole was so impressed with the fragrance of Gray's big jar of *pot pourri* that he wrote next year to ask him for the recipe. Gray's answer illustrates his loving attention to detail in these small matters. It was essential, he said, to use coarse brown bay salt, which was obtainable in London but not in Cambridge, 'where under the name of Bay Salt they sell a whitish kind of salt, that will never do for our Purpose, and will spoil all: at London the true Sort is common in every Shop, and a Pennyworth of it is enough to make a Bushel of Perfumes'. Then follow careful

* Walpole described the visit in a letter to Montagu. The University, he said, 'revived many youthful scenes, which, merely from their being youthful, are forty times pleasanter than other ideas. You know I always long to live at Oxford—I felt I would like to live even at Cambridge again. The Colleges are much cleaned and improved since my days, and the trees and groves more venerable; but the town is tumbling about their ears' (Walpole to Montagu, 25 July 1763).

directions as to the blending and stirring of the ingredients—
damask roses, orange flowers, cloves, 'Tops of Lavender,
Myrtle-Leaves bruised, Rose-Geranium, Angelica, Shavings
of Orrice Root'—so that before long Cole's parsonage at
Bletchley must have been as agreeably scented as Gray's rooms
in Pembroke.[26]

Gray had known Cole since their Eton days, and Cole had
always kept in touch with the life of Cambridge. He had developed into a portly and combative country parson, a rigid High
Churchman and outspoken Tory, an industrious antiquary
who perpetually filled huge notebooks and never published
anything. He and Walpole were close friends despite the complete divergence of their political and religious views, and Gray
also was fond of 'Old Cole'. His liking was reciprocated; and
when at the end of 1767 Cole left Bletchley and came to live
nearer to Cambridge, first at Waterbeach and then at Milton,
they used constantly to meet. But even during his Bletchley
days Cole knew Gray well enough to ask him to 'shew the
curiosities of the place' to a neighbouring clergyman and his
sister when they visited Cambridge; and he readily complied
and was indeed most obliging. The familiar picture of Gray as
a supercilious recluse begins to alter a little when we see him
acting as guide to a couple of obscure strangers, at the request
of one who was not in the circle of his more intimate friends.[27]

From Cole's rambling and repetitive notes about Cambridge
people which he called *Athenae Cantabrigienses*, and from the
marginalia in his copy of Mason's biography, it is possible to
collect many details about Gray. A picture begins to form of a
little man with a double chin, aquiline nose and bright lively
eyes, 'well put together and latterly tending to plumpness',
looking smaller perhaps than he really was by contrast with the
bulk of Cole, sitting in a scrupulously tidy room with vases
full of flowers and window-boxes fragrant with mignonette.
'I am apt to think', says Cole, 'that the characters of Voiture
and Mr Gray were very similar. They were both little men, very
nice and exact in their Persons and Dress, most lively and

agreeable in conversation (except that Mr Gray was apt to
be too satyrical) and both of them full of Affectation.' One of
Gray's affections which especially shocked Cole was his refusal
to wear spectacles—'his delicacy was such, and his dislike of
appearing old, that he only made use of an hand glass to help
him to read with. I often told him of the comfort of spectacles,
but he deferred the use of them'.* The room was full of books as
well as flowers; Gray's library overflowed into two if not three
other rooms in Ivy Court, and he was always ready to lend his
books to Cole. It was more difficult to persuade him to play or
sing; but after much hesitation he would sometimes sit at the
harpsichord, or at the pianoforte which succeeded it—a gift
from Stonhewer—and accompany himself in an air of Pergolesi
or Bononcini. According to Mason 'he so modulated the small
powers of his voice, as to be able to convey to the intelligent
hearer no common degree of satisfaction. This, however, he
could seldom be prevailed upon to do, even by his most
intimate acquaintance.' It is an indication of Gray's esteem
for 'Old Cole' that he was prepared to overcome his scruples in
this way.[28]

III

So the year 1763 passed away, one of the least eventful in
Gray's life. In August he had lost his old friend Mrs Bonfoy,
'who taught me to pray'; in September he was busied with
research on Walpole's behalf in connection with Lord Herbert
of Cherbury; in October he wrote Mason a charming letter in
expectation of his marriage, though Mason was not to be
married for almost two years, and then perhaps to a different
lady. But towards the close of the year came the first rumblings
of a storm which was to shake the Cambridge world to its depths.

The Duke of Newcastle had been Chancellor of the university
since 1748. With his unique talent for party management and
political intrigue, he had interfered in university affairs more

---

* Nevertheless the 1767 pocket-book contains the entry:

Green Spectacles & Case	7	0
Two Lenses	3	0

persistently and more effectively than any previous holder of the office. Bishoprics, deaneries, high academic appointments, important livings, the whole of the Crown patronage had been at his disposal, and for years past his word at Cambridge had been law. But in the great political upheaval soon after the accession of George III he had fallen from power, and his influence in the university was now seriously endangered. Throughout his Chancellorship the second most important dignity, the High Stewardship, had been held by the Earl of Hardwicke; and at this juncture, in the last months of 1763, the health of this faithful ally began to fail. Newcastle hoped that his influence as Chancellor would still be strong enough to secure the unopposed return of Hardwicke's son Lord Royston as his successor; but the Earl of Sandwich, a leading member of the new Ministry, announced his intention of standing as a candidate, and began a canvass of the university. It would have been hard to find anyone less suited than Sandwich to preside over the interests of an institution devoted to godliness and good learning. His private life was discreditable in the extreme, and he had lately given a sensational display of hypocrisy by publicly denouncing his old companion Wilkes for printing the *Essay on Woman*. At a performance of *The Beggar's Opera* the words of Macheath, 'that Jemmy Twitcher should 'peach I own sur-prizes me', had been applied to Sandwich by a hilarious audience on account of this episode; and as Jemmy Twitcher he was known for the rest of his days.

Gray had at no time taken an active part in university politics, as distinct from the affairs of the two colleges in which he resided. Indeed he had not even a vote in the Senate, since he never became a Master of Arts. He remained aloof from all these high matters, except when he contemplated with indigna-tion the activities of the Duke of Newcastle. This was not the result of any political antagonism, since the Duke's brand of Whiggery was broadly speaking his own. Nor is he likely to have been much influenced by the bitter personal hatred with which Walpole regarded him, as one of the principal agents of

Sir Robert's fall from power. But he detested the whole atmosphere which Newcastle had created at Cambridge during his years as Chancellor—the jobbery and toadying and wire-pulling, the struggles for notice and preferment—and he felt a deep contempt for the bustling, managing, ludicrous old creature himself. He did attend one of his levees, and 'had a very affectionate squeeze of the hand, and a fine Compliment in a corner'; but subsequently he took some pains to avoid those ceremonial occasions, even to the extent of going away from Cambridge when they impended. Both he and Mason—although the latter had written a highly obsequious ode to be sung at the Duke's installation as Chancellor—always spoke of him as Fobus; and such phrases as 'that owl Fobus', and 'that old fizzling Duke' occur frequently in his letters.[29]

Lord Hardwicke lingered until the beginning of March 1764, but for many weeks before his death the contest for his High Stewardship raged furiously in Cambridge. Lord Royston did not himself take a prominent part in the struggle—in fact his vigorous and ambitious younger brother Charles Yorke was far more active throughout—but Newcastle exerted on his behalf the full weight of his still powerful influence. Sandwich had the whole-hearted backing of the Court party. His foremost local supporters were two of Gray's particular aversions, Laurence Brockett, his successful rival for the professorship of Modern History, and Roger Long, the Master of Pembroke, 'whose old Tory notions, that had long lain by neglected and forgotten, are brought out again and furbish'd for present use, tho' rusty and out of joint, like his own Spheres and Orreries'.[30] However much Gray disapproved privately of the Duke of Newcastle, in such a contest as this he was emphatically on his side. His sympathies lay entirely with the 'Anti-Twitcherites', and he gave expression to them in a brilliant lampoon. He had been struck by the large number of clergymen, pillars of virtue and sobriety, who had expressed their conviction that 'Jemmy Twitcher' was peculiarly fitted to hold high office in their university; and he described how that maligned nobleman,

when his advances had been rejected by the faculties of Medicine
and Jurisprudence, found solace at last in the arms of Divinity.

When sly Jemmy Twitcher had smugg'd up his face
With a lick of court white-wash, and pious grimace,
A wooing he went, where three Sisters of old
In harmless society guttle and scold.
    Lord! Sister, says Physic to Law, I declare
Such a sheep-biting look, such a pick-pocket air,
Not I, for the Indies! you know I'm no prude;
But his nose is a shame, and his eyes are so lewd!
Then he shambles and straddles so oddly, I fear—
No; at our time of life, 'twould be silly, my dear.
    I don't know, says Law, now methinks, for his look,
'Tis just like the picture in Rochester's book.
But his character, Phyzzy, his morals, his life;
When she died, I can't tell, but he once had a wife.
They say he's no Christian, loves drinking and whoring,
And all the town rings of his swearing and roaring,
His lying, and filching, and Newgate-bird tricks:—
Not I,—for a coronet, chariot and six.
    Divinity heard, between waking and dozing,
Her sisters denying, and Jemmy proposing;
From dinner she rose with a bumper in hand,
She strok'd up her belly, and stroked down her band.
    What a pother is here about wenching and roaring!
Why David loved catches, and Solomon whoring.
Did not Israel filch from th'Ægyptians of old
Their jewels of silver, and jewels of gold?
The prophet of Bethel, we read, told a lie:
He drinks; so did Noah: he swears; so do I.
To refuse him for such peccadilloes, were odd;
Besides, he repents, and he talks about G——.
    Never hang down your head, you poor penitent elf!
Come, buss me, I'll be Mrs Twitcher myself.
D——n ye both for a couple of Puritan bitches!
He's Christian enough, that repents, and that ——.

Most people at Cambridge would never have believed that
this hard-hitting and extremely personal satire was the work
of 'delicate Mr Gray'. But they were given no opportunity

of judging. Gray wrote it for the private amusement of a few friends, and had no thoughts of printing it or otherwise engaging in the fray.* Indeed, his caution was such that no version of the poem survived among his papers, and it was only preserved by means of a single copy in Walpole's possession.[31] The justice of Walpole's remark quoted on an earlier page, that 'Gray never wrote anything easily but things of humour', is once again borne out by the fluency with which he was able to dash off these lampoons, in contrast to the anguish and frustration which accompanied the writing of his graver poems. He produced several other works of this lighter sort which were denied to posterity by Mason's over-watchful care. Only their titles remain, and we do not even know whether they were in prose or verse. It is tantalising to think what we may have lost when his conscientious executor committed to the flames *A Character of the Scotch*, and *The Mob Grammar*, and *A History of Hell*, of which Mason himself said to Walpole, 'Pray take notice of the conclusion concerning *King-craft*, and tell me whether he was not a prophet as well as poet'. And what wit and mockery may have perished with *The Duke of Newcastle's Journal going to Hanover*![32]

The long-anticipated election took place on 30 March, three weeks after Hardwicke's death. In both Houses of the Senate, the Regents and the non-Regents, the voting was almost exactly even. Owing to certain technical issues, and in particular the question of one disputed vote, no immediate decision could be made, and in June the whole question was transferred to the Court of King's Bench. Negotiations, intrigues and attempts at compromise followed in bewildering succession, and it was not until April 1765 that judgement was given in favour of the new Lord Hardwicke. Nor does the settlement appear to have been achieved without certain concessions as to future patronage being made by the victorious side. 'I do believe', wrote Gray, 'the two Pretenders had (privately)

---

* I hesitate to accept Joseph Cradock's statement that Lord Sandwich said to him, at the time of the election, 'I have my private reasons for knowing Gray's absolute inveteracy' (Cradock, IV, 223).

agreed the matter beforehand, for the House of Yorke have undoubtedly been long making up to the Court'. And it can hardly be doubted that he was right.[33]

IV

Gray had been unwell throughout the early part of 1764, and as usual was filled with the gravest apprehensions. Finally, in July he underwent an operation, painful enough but not so terrifying as he had expected, which revealed only 'the piles in an extreme degree' and effectively disposed of that ailment. Wharton had offered to support him through the ordeal, but he was content with the advice of Dr Plumptre, the Regius Professor of Physic, and the skill of the well-known Cambridge surgeon Thomas Thackeray, great-uncle of the novelist.[34]

His acquaintance with Nicholls continued to flourish; and an amusing picture of their relationship, and of a typical Cambridge evening, is given in a letter written by Nicholls to his friend Temple during these months:

I have seen Mr Gray several times, at his own room you may be sure, for I believe he fears some deadly infection in mine. I drink tea there when I please and stay till nine....He has Fitzwilliam's Harpsichord, and we sing Duetts, Marcello's Psalms, in great privacy, an hour or two....Afterwards sit and talk about what, you know, I never remember, except in scraps (or tatters, or rags, or any word you like better)—and then we go in great form to the coffee-house, where we dose over the news and pamphlets as usual till the last stroke of eleven; I now and then interrupt my own slumbers with a word or two of very sensible, solemn nonsence (my fort you know); and Mr Gould's incessant, impertinent Babble, will not let me sleep quietly, nor Mr Gray talk, which I should prefer....At the last stroke of eleven we rise, take our lanterns we who have them, Mr Talbot his galaches, and proceed in procession down stairs (Mr Gould you know stops to talk bawdy to the Nels in the coffee-room), and so, after leave duly taken at Pembroke gate, home as usual.[35]

By now Temple had also made the acquaintance of Gray. He had been up at Trinity Hall, Nicholls's own college, a few years before, and had begun to read for the bar, but family misfortunes had compelled him to look for a more immediate livelihood, and he returned to Cambridge to prepare for holy orders. Nicholls had been delighted that Gray should have admitted Temple into his circle. 'I am most sincerely glad', he wrote, 'and congratulate you on having made a Friend of a man whom I admire, and reverence with the most awful respect for his sublime Genius, and profound knowledge; and whom I am persuaded that I should esteem, love and confide in, for his disposition, and goodness, if everything else were out of the question. I think it, and always will think it the most fortunate event of my life, that he admitted me to his acquaintance'.[36] And Temple, although he never became very intimate with Gray and settled before long at a rectory in Devonshire, felt much the same about him. 'He is very civil', he wrote to James Boswell, 'and my idea of his greatness is not at all diminished by knowing him. He is the best bred man and the most agreeable companion in the world. I long to know him more.'[37]

Temple was already Boswell's most intimate friend, and was to be the lifelong repository of all his dreams and ambitions, his backslidings and repentances. Boswell's imagination was fired by everything that Temple and Nicholls told him about their venerated poet, and he added Gray to the oddly assorted celebrities upon whom he tried at intervals to model his own life. 'The contemplation of such a man must rouse every noble principle', he told Temple; and in the privacy of his journal he exhorted himself to 'Be Gray. Be *retenu* and worship God.'[38]

Full of the happiness of restored health, Gray went in the autumn of 1764 for a tour in Hampshire and Wiltshire. He had not been in those parts since he last stayed with Chute at The Vyne; and he did not now make any attempt to see his old friend. For some while he took lodgings in Southampton, from which he could walk or drive about the countryside in the soft October weather. In particular he found Netley Abbey as beautiful as his memories of it from nine years before, and he described it to Nicholls in a passage of charming fantasy.

In the bosom of the woods (conceal'd from profane eyes) lie hid the ruins of Netteley-abbey. There may be richer and greater houses of religion, but the Abbot is content with his situation. See there at the top of that hanging meadow under the shade of those old trees, that bend into a half-circle about it, he is walking slowly (good Man!) and bidding his beads for the souls of his Benefactors, interr'd in that venerable pile, that lies beneath him. Beyond it (the meadow still descending) nods a thicket of oaks, that mask the building, and have excluded a view too garish, and too luxuriant for a holy eye, only on either hand they leave an opening to the blew glittering sea. Did not you observe how, as that white sail shot by and was lost, he turn'd and cross'd himself, to drive the Tempter from him, that had thrown that distraction in his way.... [39]

The improvement in his health continued throughout an uneventful winter. There was one mild though rather protracted fit of the gout, and some trouble with his eyes. Apprehensive as always of the worst that might befall, he feared that this would probably end in blindness. But these worries vanished in the spring, and he felt well enough to travel, in the course of 1765, farther afield than he had ever done since his return from the Grand Tour.

He set out for the north at the end of May, and stayed a fortnight with Mason at York. Here he wrote another of his lighter pieces, the engaging lines called *William Shakespeare To Mrs Anne, Regular Servant to the Reverend Mr Precentor of York*. Here also he learnt of Mason's forthcoming marriage to Mary Sherman, the daughter of the garrison store-keeper at Hull, an amiable and gentle young woman with a modest fortune and uncertain health. From York he went on to Old Park, where he spent many weeks with Wharton and made two short expeditions to Hartlepool to enjoy the sea air. And finally, towards the end of August, he joined Lord Strathmore at his Durham house of Hetton, and next day set out with him for Scotland.

V

Lord Strathmore was still a bachelor: it was not until two years later that he married the great Durham heiress Mary Eleanor Bowes, and thus became one of the richest men in Great Britain. The belated news of the death of his second brother, James Lyon, in the massacre of Patna, had only reached the family a year before. The youngest brother, Thomas, the Fellow of Pembroke, and their cousin, a Major Lyon, were also of the party which set out for Scotland.

They travelled post, with none of the casual sightseeing which Gray always loved, until they reached Edinburgh. He spent a busy day exploring the Castle, and Holyroodhouse, and the other remarkable features of 'that most picturesque (at a distance) and nastiest (when near) of all capital Cities'.[40] A small supper-party of the Edinburgh intellectuals was arranged in his honour at the house of Dr John Gregory, the physician and author. It was not a success. In the words of Dr Alexander Carlyle, who was amongst those invited, Gray 'had not justice done him, for he was much worn out with his journey, and, by retiring soon after supper, proved that he had been taken at a time when he was not fit to be shown off'.[41] When his host complimented him on the *Elegy* he replied, 'with a good deal of acrimony', that its popularity was due entirely to the subject, and the public would have received it just as well if it had been written in prose.[42] And many years afterwards the most distinguished of the guests, William Robertson the historian, hurt the feelings of Norton Nicholls by telling him that 'when he saw Mr Gray in Scotland he gave him the idea of a person who meant to pass for a very fine gentleman'.[43] In fact, neither on this nor on any other occasion would Gray consent to be 'shown off'; and Dr Gregory's little party failed sadly in its purpose. Next morning the travellers crossed the Firth of Forth in rather boisterous weather, slept at Perth that night, and were at Glamis by dinner-time on the following day.

Gray was profoundly impressed by the beauty and romance of the great castle, with its towers, its spreading wings, its courts and parterres and avenues of ancient trees. All around lay the woods and meadows of the rich valley. Beyond them, to north and west, he could see the mountains, with Schiehallion towering above all. Strathmore farmed two thousand acres of his own land, and was among his husbandmen and labourers all day long. Walls were being built, the river-bed widened, and Gray could hear the workmen from the Highlands, many of whom knew no English, singing their Gaelic songs from morning till night. The autumn weather was so mild that the party would sit talking by the open windows for an hour after the sun had set.

Presently Gray was taken by Major Lyon for a five days' expedition into the Highlands, into the very land of Ossian, among lakes and mountains, precipices and cataracts, vast rocks 'like the sullen countenances of Fingal and all his family frowning on the little mortals of modern days'. They visited Taymouth and Blair Athol and the Pass of Killiecrankie; they gazed at the vast bulk of Schiehallion, and at Ben More, high above the tomb of Fingal; they passed through the glorious wooded landscapes all along the Tay and the Tummel, and saw Loch Tay lying tranquil among the mountains in the autumn sunshine. No experience for years past had so greatly moved him as these five days. 'Since I saw the Alps I have seen nothing sublime until now', he wrote, as the emotions of the Grande Chartreuse came flooding back once more. 'The mountains are extatic, and ought to be visited in pilgrimage once a year. None but those monstrous creatures of God know how to join so much beauty with so much horror.'[44]

The news of his presence in Scotland had been passed on from Edinburgh to James Beattie, Professor of Moral Philosophy and Logic in Marischal College at Aberdeen, and already a poet of some note. A letter in the most exalted strain was the result. Beattie had long passionately admired Gray's writings. The opportunity of seeing him and conversing with him was the object of his most ardent wishes. 'Will you permit us to hope, that we shall have an opportunity at Aberdeen, of thanking you in person, for the honour you have done to Britain, and to the poetic art, by your inestimable compositions, and of offering to you all that we have that deserves your acceptance, namely, hearts full of esteem, respect, and affection?'[45] Gray was not disposed to set out on another expedition before his return to England, so Lord Strathmore invited Beattie to come to Glamis. There the young Professor spent two days; and unlike the Edinburgh *literati*, he was not in the least disappointed with the great man. 'I found him possessed of the most exact taste, the soundest judgement, and the most extensive learning', he told his friend Sir William Forbes. 'He is happy in a singular facility of expression. His conversation abounds in original observations, delivered with no appearance of sententious formality, and seeming to arise spontaneously without study or premeditation. I . . . found him as easy in his manner, and as communicative and frank, as I could have wished.'[46]

Gray was also well pleased with Beattie, and was concerned afterwards lest he might have thrown a chill upon his poetical enthusiasms:

All I intended to say was, that if either Vanity (that is, a general and undistinguishing desire of applause) or Interest, or Ambition has any place in the breast of a poet, he stands a great chance in these our days of being severely disappointed: and yet after all these passions are suppress'd, there may remain in the mind of one, *ingenti perculsus amore* (and such a one I take you to be), incitements of a better sort strong enough to make him write verse all his life both for his own pleasure, and that of all posterity.[47]

Shortly afterwards Marischal College offered Gray the degree of Doctor of Laws. In his reply to Beattie he expressed his due sense of the honour, but pointed out that although he had been a Bachelor of Laws of his own university for more than twenty years, he had neglected to take his Doctor's degree. 'Judge therefore, whether it will not look like a slight and some sort of contempt, if I receive the same degree from a Sister-University. I certainly would avoid giving any offence to a set of Men, among whom I have pass'd so many easy, and (I may say) happy hours of my life.'[48]

Gray said farewell to his warm-hearted hosts in October, and returned southward alone. He had found the crossing of the Forth so alarming that he now preferred to go round by Stirling, and so experienced to the full the discomforts of Scottish travel. Next year he wrote out a detailed itinerary for the benefit of Brown, who was in his turn about to venture upon the journey to Glamis. He included one charmingly fussy paragraph, warning him of the tribulations which middle-aged Cambridge dons might expect to undergo in Caledonian inns. 'See your sheets air'd yourself. Eat mutton or hard-eggs. Touch no fried things. If they are broil'd, boil'd or roasted, say that from a child you have eat no butter, and beg they would not rub any over your meat. There is honey, or orange-marmalade, or currant-jelly, which may be eaten with toasted bread, or the thin oat-cakes, for breakfast. Dream not of milk. Ask your landlord to set down, and help off with your wine. Never scold at any body, especially at Gentlemen, or Ladies.'[49] The last cryptic sentence probably relates to some private joke, of which he and Brown shared many.

VI

Gray spent a fortnight with Wharton on his way southwards, and then stayed in London until early in December. He had now deserted Bloomsbury for St James's, returning to some lodgings which he had occasionally occupied in earlier years at the house of a hosier named Roberts in Jermyn Street. In those rooms—or, if they happened to be occupied, at the house of an oilman named Frisby just across the street—he continued to lodge on his visits to London until the end of his life. It was probably here, if we are to believe that amusing but unreliable gossip Samuel Rogers, that he customarily 'had a nice dinner from the Tavern brought to his lodgings, a glass or two of sweet wine, and as he sipped it talked about great People'.[50]

He called as usual at Walpole's house in Arlington Street, but was told that he was in Paris and had been seriously ill with the gout. It was the first time that Walpole had been to France since their Grand Tour a quarter of a century before; and the memory of those distant days, combined with his natural

211   14-2

anxiety about his friend's illness, imparted to Gray's letter of inquiry an unexpected note of tenderness. Drawing upon his own experience of the gout in all its moods, he showered Walpole with advice on regimen and diet, and with urgent warnings to proceed slowly and cautiously during his convalescence. 'The pain in your feet I *can* bear; but I shudder at the sickness in your stomach, and the weakness, that still continues. I conjure you, as you love yourself; I conjure you by Strawberry, not to trifle with these edge-tools.' Walpole was touched by his solicitude, and replied in two of the longest and most attractive letters in his whole vast correspondence. He described the social life of Paris, and the numerous ways in which it had altered for the worse since he and Gray had first encountered it together. He talked of his new friends, Madame du Deffand and her circle of elderly wits, and her detested rival Madame Geoffrin; and he explained with delightful humour his unexpected popularity, and the circumstances in which he had come to be 'sent for about like an African prince or a learned canary-bird'. Despite these immense letters he reminded Gray that 'you know my volubility, when I am full of new subjects, and I have at least many hours of conversation for you at my return'.[51]

It might have been hoped that the sight of mountains and torrents would move Gray to fresh flights of poetry. But the springs of his inspiration now seemed frozen for ever. He spent the entire winter 'neither happy, nor miserable, but in a gentle stupefaction of mind, and very tolerable health of body hitherto'.[52] His main preoccupation was now, as it had increasingly become during the last few years, the study of natural history, and in particular the elaborate annotation of an interleaved copy of the *Systema Naturae* of Linnaeus. The three large volumes lay always on his table, well known to all his friends, and a constant source of irritation to those who would have preferred to see him otherwise employed. Many years later Walpole was to describe to Lady Ossory how 'Mr Gray often vexed me by finding him heaping notes on an interleaved *Linnaeus*, instead of pranking on his lyre'.[53]

His interest in natural history had been a constant resource to him, ever since he first watched the flowers and insects in the Buckinghamshire meadows. He loved to grow plants in water or damp moss in his rooms, and sometimes extended his researches to the animal world, as when he reared the larvae of insects in a cup of water,[54] and kept an owl, 'as like me as it can stare', in the college garden.[55] His microscope was as often in use as his harpsichord; and during his summer tours he delighted to collect all kinds of herbs and roots, butterflies and beetles and the creatures of the rock-pools by the sea. His observations and experiments were recorded in Latin in his pocket notebooks, and most of them were later transferred to the interleaved Linnaeus—details of the hermit crab whose behaviour he watched on the beach at Hartlepool, and the young pelican which he saw at Glamis, and the eggs of the scavenger beetle which he discovered in the dead body of a mole at Cambridge.

The notes throughout the Linnaeus, some in English, but the greater part in Latin, are astonishing in their number and their detail. They are written with exquisite clarity, and illustrated by drawings in the most delicate penmanship. Nevertheless, it is easy to understand Walpole's exasperation. Here was the greatest poet of the day devoting the precious hours to beetles and their larvae, the writer of the *Elegy* composing a series of Latin verses upon the Orders and Genera of Insects.[56] Surely he could find some more profitable exercise for his powers than describing, no matter how elegantly, the habits of the domestic cat—*docilis, subdolus, adulatorius, domino dorsum, latera, caput affricare amat: junior mire lusibus deditus et jocis, adultus tranquillior*—and giving details about the gestation of its kittens and the number of its teeth, and setting down its name in Greek, French, Italian, German, Spanish, Swedish, Mongol, Welsh, Polish and Russian.[57] It was all a preposterous waste of time, thought Walpole, indifferent to the excuse which Gray would undoubtedly have made, that 'to be employed is to be happy'.[58]

VII

Fifteen years had now passed since the summer when *A Long Story* was written, and four since the marriage of its heroine. Madame de la Peyrière had travelled far afield—to the Sardinian court at Turin, where her father-in-law had lately become First Minister and Foreign Secretary; to her husband's ancestral home in Savoy; and to the Hague, whither his father had sent him as Sardinian Minister.* Now he had been appointed to represent his country at the Court of St James's; or rather, as Gray put it, 'Madame de la Peyrière is come over from the Hague to be Ministress in London'. Gray did not fail to pay his respects to his old friend before he returned to Cambridge for the winter. 'I sate a morning with her before I left London', he wrote to Wharton. 'She is a prodigious fine lady, and a Catholick (tho' she did not expressly own it to me) not fatter than she was: she had a cage of foreign birds and a piping Bullfinch at her elbow, two little Dogs on a cushion in her lap, a Cockatoo on her shoulder, and a slight suspicion of Rouge on her cheeks. They were all exceeding glad to see me, and I them.'[59]

It was a happy meeting, with no regrets on either side for the past: but Madame de la Peyrière does not appear again in Gray's life or in his letters. Her husband became Comte de Viry on his father's death at the end of 1766, and was soon transferred to Madrid and finally to Paris. As the years went by her corpulence steadily increased, and her fondness for rouge became proverbial; but she retained her vitality, her gay and voluble wit, and her passion for entertaining. In 1775, when she was Sardinian Ambassadress at Paris, she gave a spectacular series of *fêtes* to celebrate the marriage of Madame, the sister of

* Her conversion to Catholicism was described by Sir Joseph Yorke, British Minister at the Hague, to his brother Lord Hardwicke, 1st June 1764. (B.M. Add. MS. 35367, f. 96–7). 'She prest on all sides, enter'd into the Pale of the Romish Church, and as a reward for the little soul of her great body, the father was made Secretary of State for Foreign Affairs, and the son nominated to the Commission at the Hague.'

HENRIETTA JANE SPEED
From a painting by Peter Falconet, in the possession of Dr Brian Rhodes.

Louis XVI, to the Prince of Piedmont; and Walpole, who happened to be in Paris at the time, told his friends that she had completed the conquest of France. A year later, when sending her a copy of Mason's biography of Gray, he recalled the brilliance of those crowded weeks. 'Je me ressouviens à présent qu'au mois d'Août et de Septembre dernier, j'ai vu Madame de Viry fêter toute la France, répandant la gaieté au milieu des cérémonies, mettant la foule à son aise, et paraissant elle-même aussi gaie, aussi amusante et amusée que si (au lieu d'avoir imaginé des projets de pompe et de plaisirs pour tout Versailles et Paris) il y avait eu des légions de fées et de grâces occupées à l'amuser.'[60]

These *fêtes* were the crowning triumph of Madame de Viry's career, and also its turning-point. Flushed with success and ambition, she plunged deeply into political intrigues on her husband's behalf. In due course a secret correspondence was discovered, and brought to the notice of the King of Sardinia. They were recalled from Paris in disgrace, and banished to their country estate in Savoy. 'It is no small punishment I believe to my lady, who loved rolling in the great world (she is of an enormous size). But what do you think (they say) is her principal amusement? Why, milking 30 cows *all herself*. . . .' Such were the comments by English acquaintances less amicably disposed than Walpole—this particular specimen was from dear and charitable old Mrs Delany[61]—and it was no small punishment indeed. 'I do not think she will make quite a *Julie* in the country', Gray had once written; and poor Melissa found her compulsory exile in the Savoyard mountains, far from the courts where she had been accustomed to shine, a very different affair from those happy summers at Stoke Poges. In 1783 her friend Lord Shelburne persuaded King George III to ask a pardon for her and her husband from the King of Sardinia.[62] It was granted, and Madame de Viry made plans to set out for England; but in the excitement of the moment 'a fit of apoplexy occasioned by her excessive corpulency' brought about her death.

CHAPTER XI

THE COLLECTED POEMS:
THE PROFESSORSHIP OF MODERN
HISTORY: THE INSTALLATION ODE
1766-1769

I

G R A Y's summer tours had already made him familiar with many parts of England. He was acquainted with most of the northern and midland counties, with East Anglia, with much of the Thames valley, with Hampshire and the Isle of Wight. In 1766 he decided to explore the county of Kent, where his Cambridge friend William Robinson was now the rector of Denton, a few miles from Canterbury. He had looked forward for some years to renewing his old ties with 'the Reverend Billy', whom he confidently expected to find, since his marriage and his honeymoon, 'the travelled Mr Robinson with a thousand important airs and graces, so much *virtù*, so much *scavoir-vivre*! the husband, the father, the rich clergyman, warm, snug, and contented as a bishop'.[1]

He went to Denton towards the end of May, and stayed there with the cheerful and good-natured Robinsons until the beginning of July:

The country [he wrote to Nicholls] is all a garden, gay, rich, and fruitfull, and (from the rainy season) had preserved, till I left it, all that emerald verdure, which commonly one only sees for the first fort-night of the spring. In the west part of it from every eminence the eye catches some long winding reach of the Thames or Medway with all their navigation. In the east the sea breaks in upon you, and mixes its white transient sails and glittering blew expanse with the deeper and brighter greens of the woods and corn. This last sentence is so fine I am quite ashamed. But no matter! you must translate it into prose. . . .

He had ceased to be grateful for the rain long before his visit ended; but he took the advantage of a few fine days to look at the isle of Thanet, where he likened the town of Margate to 'Bartholomew Fair by the seaside', and to make a tour of the Cinque Ports.[2] The Robinsons accompanied him, and long afterwards described this tour to the eccentric Sir Egerton Brydges, who had married their daughter. At Ramsgate, 'the stone pier had just been built. Some one said, "For what did they make this pier?" Gray immediately said, "*For me to walk on*", and proceeded, with long strides, to claim possession of it.'[3]

In September he stayed with Palgrave in Suffolk, and also made a short excursion into Norfolk, mainly to see the great house of the Walpoles at Houghton. Under the rule of Walpole's erratic nephew, the third Earl of Orford, the house and estate had sadly fallen from the magnificence of Sir Robert's days; but the wonderful collection of pictures was still intact, and remained so until it was sold to the Empress Catherine of Russia in the next decade.

In the autumn Gray went to London, and for the first time made the acquaintance of Mason's wife, 'a pretty, modest, innocent, interesting figure, looking like eighteen, though she is near twenty eight'. Her health had always been frail, and a rapid consumption had now set in. The London doctors could do nothing for her, and a winter of exceptional severity 'nipt her', in Mason's words, 'as it would have done a flower half wither'd before'. His letters, usually so jaunty and self-satisfied, take on a tone of pathetic resignation. 'There are few Men in the world that can have a competent Idea of what I have of late felt, and still feel', he told Gray. 'Yet you are one of those few, and I am sure will give me a full share of your pity. Was I to advise Stonhewer to a Wife it should certainly be to a fine Lady. It should not be to one he could love to the same degree that I do this gentle this innocent creature.'[4]

In a last despairing attempt to restore her health, Mason took his wife to drink the waters of the spa at Bristol; but she died there at the end of March. Just at that moment her husband received from Gray a short letter which, as he said when he came to print it, 'breathed, and still seems to breathe, the very voice of Friendship in its tenderest and most pathetic note':

My dear Mason,

    I break in upon you at a moment, when we least of all are permitted to disturb our Friends, only to say, that you are daily and hourly present to my thoughts. If the *worst* be not yet past: you will neglect and pardon me. But if the last struggle be over: if the poor subject of your long anxieties be no longer sensible to your kindness, or to her own sufferings: allow me (at least in idea, for what could I do, were I present, more than this?) to sit by you in silence, and pity from my heart, not her, who is at rest; but you, who lose her. May He, who made us, the Master of our pleasures, and of our pains, preserve and support you! Adieu.

    I have long understood, how little you had to hope.[5]

    Mason placed a monument to his wife's memory in Bristol Cathedral, and wrote for it an epitaph in which the deepest sorrow contended in vain with his usual insipidity of expression:

> Take, holy earth! all that my soul holds dear:
>   Take that best gift which Heav'n so lately gave:
> To Bristol's fount I bore with trembling care
>   Her faded form: she bow'd to taste the wave,
> And died. Does Youth, does Beauty, read the line?
>   Does sympathetic fear their breasts alarm?
> Speak, dead MARIA! breathe a strain divine:
>   Ev'n from the grave thou shalt have power to charm.
> Bid them be chaste, be innocent, like thee;
>   Bid them in Duty's sphere as meekly move...

With a series of apostrophes of this kind the poem continued to its end. The four concluding lines were especially feeble, and Gray was moved to replace them with a quatrain of his own, which might without incongruity have found a place in the *Elegy*:

> Tell them, though 'tis an awful thing to die,
>   ('Twas ev'n to thee) yet the dread path once trod,
> Heav'n lifts its everlasting portals high,
>   And bids the pure in heart behold their God.

The touch of the master is unmistakable, and Mason's pathetically languid tribute is made to soar into unexpected beauty at its close.[6]

II

During the last five years of his life Gray's absences from Cambridge grew ever longer. He continued to spend the winter months at Pembroke; but in April he would go to London, in June he set out on a more distant excursion which sometimes lasted the whole summer, and in the autumn he usually returned to London and remained there until the beginning of December. Thus in 1765 he spent only five months at Cambridge; and now in 1767 he was again absent for the greater part of the year. He had in fact come to realise that travel and frequent change of scene were essential for his well-being, and that much of the illness and melancholy in earlier years had been due to the seclusion in which he then lived. 'Travel I must, or cease to exist', he wrote towards the end of his life; and the more he travelled, the more conspicuous was the improvement in his health and spirits.

His movements during 1767 can be followed in unusual detail, since his pocket-book for that year has been preserved at Netherhall, the Cumberland home of Humphrey Senhouse, one of the Fellows of Pembroke.[7] As always, he remained at Cambridge during the opening months of the year, which were among the coldest in living memory. He made a point of noting the indoor and outdoor temperatures, as was his custom, and on one occasion found it colder in his rooms than in the snow-covered garden outside. He was further depressed by 'a something growing in my throat, which nothing does any service to, and which will, I suppose, in due time stop up the passage',[8] a disquieting symptom which vanished with the coming of spring and did not reappear. In February and March the bulbs in his pots and water-glasses began to flower, and he recorded in his pocket-book the blooming of every hyacinth and narcissus. The hyacinths were a fine collection—Passe-tout, Morning-Star,

Empress, Rosy-Cross of Flora, Rubro-Caesar, Croon-Vogl, King of Great Britain, Barg-Vesuvius, Morinetta—and each was carefully described. Rubro-Caesar was a 'double Hyacinth, 16 bells, not large: bright rose with a crimson stripe in each petal. beautiful'; and King of Great Britain, another double hyacinth, displayed '11 very large bells, white, speckled with crimson within; the points of the outer petals and the centre within, of a pale green, very fine flower'. As the days advanced he noted also the gradual indications of spring—the first bee, the first crocus and primrose, the earliest song of the wren.

In April he went to London, and stayed at his accustomed lodgings in Jermyn Street until the middle of June. His pocketbook contains entries of expenses at operas and plays, coffeehouses and exhibitions. He went to Ranelagh, visited Walpole at Strawberry Hill, and gazed from Richmond Hill at the incomparable landscape below, where 'the face of the country looks an emerald'. Many friends were in London—Stonhewer, Palgrave, Hurd among the number; and he renewed an old acquaintance with Frederick Hervey, who will be remembered as the younger brother of that Lord Bristol who had offered to take him abroad as his secretary in earlier years. Frederick Hervey, hitherto an impoverished and somewhat erratic clergyman, had lately benefited from Lord Bristol's appointment as Lord Lieutenant of Ireland and had unexpectedly become Bishop of Cloyne. Next year he was advanced to the immensely rich see of Derry. He succeeded in due course to his brother's title and estates, and ended his days as the celebrated 'Earl-Bishop' in a whirl of luxurious travel and extravagant building. 'I have seen his lordship of Cloyne often', wrote Gray to Brown. 'He is very jolly, and we devoured four raspberry puffs together in Cranbourn-alley standing at a pastrycook's shop in the street.'[9]

In June he returned to Cambridge for a few days, and then set out with Brown to visit their friends in the north. They travelled in leisurely comfort by post-chaise to Mason's rectory at Aston, 'a wilderness of sweets, an Elysium among

the coal-pits, a terrestrial heaven'. Then all three went for a
tour of Dovedale and the wonders of the Peak, and thence to
Mason's prebendal house at York, after which Gray and
Brown journeyed on to stay with Wharton at Old Park. The
Whartons were a sociable family, and Gray grumbled a little
at the neighbourly visits in which he found himself involved;
but he was glad of the opportunity of seeing Lord Strathmore,
now married to Miss Bowes and in residence on one of her
Durham properties, and of making the acquaintance of the
bride herself. Presently Lord and Lady Strathmore carried
Brown off with them to Glamis, and Gray was at one time
half-tempted to accompany them and perhaps to spend a few
days with Beattie at Aberdeen. In the end, however, he decided
to remain at Old Park.

Much of the summer passed in further sightseeing expeditions in Wharton's company, visiting castles and monasteries,
the great houses of the north with their treasures of architecture and painting, the mountains and dales of Yorkshire and
Durham, and finally the Lakes. The golden age of the picturesque and antiquarian tour was approaching; but Gray,
with his intense love of natural beauty and his imagination
steeped in the history of England, had long since been one of its
pioneers. It is perhaps not too fanciful to see him and Wharton
as the figures in the delectable vignette upon the title-page
of Grose's *Antiquities*, gazing upon the knight's dilapidated
tomb in the abbey ruins, where the bushes have rooted in
the crumbling walls, the shattered columns litter the ground,
the sunlight streams through the broken tracery of the
windows. One of the figures is declaiming the famous passage
of Webster:

> I do love these ancient ruins;
> We never tread upon them but we set
> Our foot upon some reverend history...

and Gray, who knew such forgotten dramatists better than
most of his contemporaries, may on occasion have declaimed
it too.

These sightseeing tours sometimes induced in him an unwontedly gay and buoyant mood, as we have seen when he took formal possession of Ramsgate pier. This was especially so in the company of so old a friend as Wharton, who once jotted down a series of his impromptu verses which probably belong to this year. They included several derisive couplets about his former acquaintance Edmund Keene, once Master of Peterhouse and now Bishop of Chester, and a comment which he uttered as they were leaving after a visit to Raby Castle:

> Here lives Harry Vane,
> Very good claret and fine Champaign.

He also wrote during this tour an ingenious burlesque epitaph on the redoubtable Anne, Countess of Dorset, Pembroke and Montgomery, punning upon the names of four of her castles:

> Now clean, now hideous, mellow now, now gruff,
> She swept, she hiss'd, she ripen'd and grew rough,
> At Brougham, Pendragon, Appleby and Brough.[10]

The two friends started on their tour of Cumberland and the Lakes towards the end of August. They were unlucky in the weather; mountain and valley were shrouded in perpetual rain, and day after day they were tantalised with fleeting glimpses of the beauties they had come to see. Wharton was taken ill in the night with asthma; and although he struggled on bravely for a day or two, they were obliged to cut short their travels and return home. Despite these misfortunes Gray wrote to Mason that 'I am charm'd with my journey, and the Doctor dreams of nothing but Skiddaw, and both of us vow to go again the first opportunity'.[11] Then they settled down to enjoy the country pleasures of Old Park, the peaches and grapes from the garden and the cream and butter from the farm, until it was time for Gray to move southwards once more.

III

During Gray's visit to London in the spring his publisher, James Dodsley—the younger brother of the more famous

Robert, who was now dead—had asked his leave to prepare a collected edition of all his poems. Gray consented, subject to the omission of *A Long Story*—'which was never meant for the publick, and only suffer'd to appear in that pompous edition because of Mr Bentley's designs, which were not intelligible without it'—and sent Dodsley three of his translations from the Norse and Welsh to replace it, 'lest the bulk of so small a volume should be reduced to nothing at all'. He also decided to add the explanatory notes for which his friends and admirers had hitherto pleaded in vain.

Later in the year James Beattie, without knowing of Dodsley's project, had written to ask Gray if a volume of his collected poems could be undertaken by Robert and Andrew Foulis. These talented and enterprising brothers were the printers to the University of Glasgow, and for many years past had been issuing classical and other editions of outstanding typographical excellence and textual accuracy. Gray knew their work well, and considered their books, like those printed by Baskerville at Birmingham, to be at least equal in beauty to anything that contemporary Europe could produce.[12] He was much pleased by Beattie's suggestion, and was concerned lest it should be withdrawn when the Glasgow printers learnt of Dodsley's intentions. But it was finally decided that the two editions should go forward in friendly rivalry, and that Gray's notes should be available for both.[13]

Most of the notes were subjoined to the two Pindaric odes, providing a commentary which must have been welcomed even by the most intelligent of Gray's readers. He likewise explained the barbaric mythologies and legends which were the foundation of the newly printed poems, *The Fatal Sisters*, *The Descent of Odin* and *The Triumphs of Owen*. And throughout the book he drew attention to a surprisingly large number of passages and single lines which were imitated or directly borrowed from the writings of other poets—from Dante and Petrarch in the *Elegy*; from Virgil and Shakespeare, Milton and Matthew Green in the *Ode on the Spring*; from Dryden twice in the *Ode on a Distant Prospect of Eton College*; and in *The Progress of Poesy* and *The Bard* from a still wider range of sources both classical and modern. The Pindaric odes, as Lord David Cecil has said, 'especially are whispering galleries, murmurous with echoes of dead poets' voices', as much so as *The Waste Land* and the *Four Quartets* in our own day. Thus in *The Progress of Poesy* the phrase 'many-twinkling feet' had its origin in the *Odyssey*; that noble line 'He pass'd the flaming bounds of Place and Time' was an echo from the *flammantia moenia mundi* of Lucretius; 'with necks in thunder cloath'd' and 'the living Throne, the sapphire-blaze' could be traced, as devout readers may already have been aware, to the books of Job and Ezekiel; and Gray acknowledged other borrowings in the same ode from Phrynichus, Virgil, Petrarch, and twice from Cowley, as well as the direct reminiscences of Pindar throughout the poem. Of course there were unconscious echoes also, as when Gray used in the *Ode on the Spring* a thought which he eventually rediscovered in a poem, once read and later forgotten, by Matthew Green; and there were coincidences which must have been purely accidental. But more often than not these borrowings were deliberately introduced. Conscious as Gray was of the development of poetry in historic process, he wished—to quote Lord David Cecil again—'to enhance the effect of his own lines by setting astir in the mind memories of those great poets of whom he feels himself the heir'.[14]

The two editions of *Poems by Mr Gray* duly appeared in 1768. Dodsley's was the first in the field, a small and rather undistinguished octavo volume priced at half a crown, which was issued in March. The 1500 copies sold rapidly, and a further edition of 750 was printed before the end of the year. The Glasgow volume proved of much more interest to Gray. He had told Beattie that 'I rejoice to be in the hands of Mr Foulis, who has the laudable ambition of surpassing his Predecessors, the *Etiennes* and the *Elzevirs*, as well in literature, as in the proper art of his profession'; and the appearance of the volume fully came up to his expectations. The Foulis brothers wished it to be regarded as their masterpiece, and 'as an expression of their high esteem and gratitude' for Gray they spared no trouble or expense in its preparation. Special types were designed and cut by the well-known Alexander Wilson, professor of astronomy at Glasgow University, to whose mastery of type-founding their press had owed so much from its inception. 'This is the first work in the Roman character which we have printed with so large a type', they stated in their preface, and gratefully acknowledged the speed and care with which Professor Wilson had worked. The book was published in May, a quarto which could be bought for the very moderate sum of five shillings. It was in every way a beautiful volume, and Gray derived pleasure and pride from its sober perfection of design.[15]

Walpole saw a preliminary announcement of the Dodsley edition in a newspaper, and wrote a charming letter remonstrating with Gray for not having mentioned the project to him when they last met a few months before, especially as some unpublished material was to be included. 'Do you think I am indifferent, or not curious, about what you write? I have ceased to ask you, because you have so long refused to show me anything. You could not suppose I thought that you never write. No; but I concluded you did not intend, at least yet, to publish what you had written. As you did intend it, I might have expected a month's preference....' Gray replied at once that 'to your friendly accusation, I am glad I can plead not guilty with a safe conscience'. He assured Walpole that the unpublished material consisted of three short poems, two of which he had sent him long before, and of 'certain little notes, partly from justice (to acknowledge the debt, where I had borrowed any thing), partly from ill temper, just to tell the gentle reader, that Edward I was not Oliver Cromwell, nor Queen Elizabeth the witch of Endor'. Then he proceeded with one of the clearest statements he ever made of his own feelings upon that much-debated topic, the ebbing and flowing of his creative powers.

To what you say to me so civilly, that I ought to write more, I reply in your own words. . .'What has one to do, when *turned of fifty*, but really to think of finishing?' However, I will be candid (for you seem to be so with me) and avow to you, that till fourscore-and-ten, whenever the humour takes me, I will write, because I like it; and because I like myself better when I do so. If I do not write much, it is because I cannot.[16]

IV

Shortly before Gray sent Dodsley and Beattie his final instructions about the printing of his poems, he was once again subjected to an alarm of fire. In the small hours of a January morning he was aroused by his servant Stephen Hempstead with the words 'Don't be frighted, Sir! but the college is all of a fire', and he assured Nicholls that it was not at all an amusing experience. The whole north wing of the court, immediately opposite his own rooms, was ablaze, and would have been destroyed had not the alarm been given by two Methodists, 'who had been till very late at their nocturnal devotions'. Thanks to the timely warning of these enthusiasts, no lives were lost and comparatively little damage was done.[17]

Otherwise the winter of 1767 and the spring of 1768 passed without incident. Gray was troubled at intervals with the gout, pored over his Linnaeus, amused himself with his harpsichord and his microscope, discussed with Walpole his lately published *Historic Doubts on the Life and Reign of King Richard the Third*, and sympathised with him over the controversies provoked by that singular performance. He could not himself accept all the ingenious arguments by which Walpole maintained Richard's innocence of the manifold crimes laid to his charge, but he was in agreement with much of the book, and urged his friend to pay no attention to the critics. 'Pray do not be out of humour', he wrote. 'When you first commenced an author, you exposed yourself to pit, box and gallery. Any coxcomb in the world may come in and hiss, if he pleases; aye, and (what is almost as bad) clap too, and you cannot hinder him.'[18]

Gray went to London as usual in April, and spent much of the early summer in Kent. He stayed alone at Ramsgate in June, and then with the Robinsons at Denton once more. During that time he made an excursion to Kingsgate on the North Foreland, the seat of the politician Henry Fox, now Lord Holland. On his previous visit to Kent he had refused to see the place, on the explicit ground that it belonged to that detested nobleman;[19] and it is idle to speculate why he overcame his repugnance on this occasion.

In the course of his career Lord Holland had amassed an enormous fortune, broken violently with each of his political associates in turn, and incurred a degree of popular hatred that was almost without parallel. Gray held and expressed strong views upon the cynicism and ambition of many politicians— Sandwich, Charles Townshend, even Newcastle; but to him, as to most of his contemporaries, Holland was the most discreditable figure of all, self-seeking, rapacious, utterly indifferent to the public good. He would certainly have disputed Macaulay's verdict that this courageous and formidable man, whose private wit and charm of manner were soon to flower so abundantly in his younger son, was 'the most unpopular statesman of his age, not because he sinned more than most of them, but because he canted less'. Holland's political life was now over, his health was beginning to fail, and his domain at Kingsgate furnished the principal solace of his retirement. In that bleak situation on the windswept cliffs he had built himself a classical mansion, which he likened to Cicero's Formian villa, and was now engaged in surrounding it with an extraordinary assortment of follies and artificial ruins. A convent, with cells and cloisters, provided accommodation for his guests and servants; a tower gateway was the porter's lodge; the stables were arranged within a half-ruined castle; 'a chapel dedicated to Saint Peter' served as an inn for the throngs of curious visitors; and other towers, temples, monuments, gateways and castellations enhanced the strangeness of the scene.[20]

In the previous year, on his return from a sojourn in Italy, Holland had written and printed privately a set of verses attacking his former colleagues, 'white-liver'd Grenville and self-loving Gower', Shelburne and Rigby and Calcraft. These verses were known to Gray, and there are echoes of them in a poem which he composed shortly after this visit to Kingsgate. It was not a brilliant squib like the lines on Sandwich, but a weighty and impressive piece of satire which has no parallel amongst Gray's works.

> Old, and abandon'd by each venal friend,
>   Here Holland took the pious resolution
> To smuggle some few years, and strive to mend
>   A broken character and constitution.
>
> On this congenial spot he fix'd his choice,
>   Earl Goodwin trembled for his neighbouring sand;
> Here seagulls scream and cormorants rejoice,
>   And mariners, though shipwreck'd, dread to land.
>
> Here reign the blust'ring North and blighting East,
>   No tree is heard to whisper, bird to sing,
> Yet Nature cannot furnish out the feast,
>   Art he invokes new horrors still to bring.
>
> Now mould'ring fanes and battlements arise,
>   Arches and turrets nodding to their fall,
> Unpeopled palaces delude his eyes,
>   And mimick desolation covers all.
>
> 'Ah!' said the sighing peer, 'had Bute been true,
>   Nor Shelburne's, Rigby's, Calcraft's friendship vain,
> Far other scenes than these had blest our view,
>   And realis'd the ruins that we feign.
>
> Purg'd by the sword and beautifyed by fire,
>   Then had we seen proud London's hated walls;
> Owls might have hooted in St Peter's choir,
>   And foxes stunk and litter'd in St Paul's.'[21]

Gray had of course no thoughts of publishing the lines, but he could not keep them altogether to himself. According to Sir Egerton Brydges he left the original draft in the drawer of his dressing-room table at Denton Rectory, where it was found after he had gone and duly restored to him. But by the end of the year both Wharton and Mason were in possession of copies, and Mason had passed the secret on to Palgrave, somewhat to Gray's perturbation: 'Oh wicked Scroddles! there you have gone and told my *Arcanum Arcanorum* to that leaky mortal Palgrave.' Soon other copies were in circulation, and next year the poem was printed, fortunately without Gray's name, in a popular miscellany called *The New Foundling Hospital for Wit.* It is not known whether Holland was ever informed that Gray was the author. Walpole urged Mason not to print the lines in his biography of Gray, since their subject was then 'in so deplorable a state, that they would aggravate the misery of his last hours'; and although both Holland and his wife were dead several months before the book appeared, the kindly injunction was obeyed.[22]

V

Towards the end of July the Professor of Modern History at Cambridge, Laurence Brockett, was returning home drunk one evening after dining with Lord Sandwich at Hinchingbrooke, when he fell from his horse and received injuries from which he died soon afterwards. The young Duke of Grafton, who had risen rapidly to power during the administrations of Rockingham and Chatham, was now in effect Prime Minister, although Chatham, sunk in a melancholy stupor and living in complete retirement, was still nominally at the head of the Government. Stonhewer had remained Grafton's private secretary, and his intimate friend and adviser; and he lost no time in putting forward Gray's claims. The Duke was fully prepared to recognise them. Only three days after Brockett's death he wrote to Gray that he had the King's commands to offer him the vacant professorship, and 'that from private as well as publick considerations he must take the warmest part in approving so well judged a measure'.[23]

Gray was deeply gratified that his long-standing ambition should have been fulfilled in this way, as a tribute to his personal merits and without any solicitation on his own part. He had not seen Grafton since the days when they used to meet at the high table of Peterhouse; and there were other possible candidates, his friend Delaval among them, whose interest might have outweighed his own. He replied at once:

My Lord,

Your Grace has dealt nobly with me; and the same delicacy of mind that induced you to confer this favour on me, unsolicited and unexpected, may perhaps make you averse to receive my sincerest thanks and grateful acknowledgments. Yet your Grace must excuse me, they will have their way: they are indeed but words; yet I know and feel they come from my heart, and therefore are not wholly unworthy of your Grace's acceptance. I even flatter myself (such is my pride) that you have some little satisfaction in your own work. If I did not deceive myself in this, it would compleat the happiness of,

My Lord,

Your Grace's

Most obliged and devoted servant.[24]

It was intimated to him that the members of the Cabinet were united in their approval of his appointment, and that he should leave his name at their doors. A more formidable duty was his attendance at the next levee, when he kissed hands and was told that he owed his success to the King's particular knowledge of him, with many other gracious speeches—'though the day was so hot and the ceremony so embarrassing to me, that I hardly know what he said'.[25]

Chatham finally resigned in October, and Grafton became Prime Minister, the duties of which office he had in fact been carrying out, in an atmosphere of increasing difficulty and disunion, for the past eighteen months. In November the Duke of Newcastle died; and despite the unpopularity of Grafton and his ministry throughout the country, his influence at Cambridge was so powerful that he was elected Chancellor of the University, in succession to Newcastle, without opposition. One of his earliest duties as Chancellor was to receive from the newly appointed Professor of Modern History a memorandum suggesting how the functions of that chair might be more effectively carried out. With his Government drifting month by month into ever stormier waters, he is unlikely to have found much time to consider this matter. But it was to cause Gray a good deal of anxiety, and to cloud the happiness which his triumph had brought him.

There is no evidence that he regarded the professorship as anything but a sinecure. His predecessors had duly received their £400 a year, and had never delivered lectures, or supervised pupils, or done anything at all beyond paying two underlings to teach French and Italian. But in August, less than a month after Brockett's death, the holder of the same professorship at Oxford also died. This was Joseph Spence, who long ago had come to Walpole's rescue during his illness at Reggio after the quarrel with Gray. Spence was a good and kindly man, well known as a writer of pleasant trifles and the friend of literary men; but his neglect of his academic duties had been observed with displeasure at Oxford. The previous Cambridge professors, Turner and Brockett, had at least stayed in residence and taken some part in university and college life. Spence, throughout the twenty-six years during which he held the professorship, had lived in one or other of his comfortable parsonages or at his private house in Surrey, rarely setting foot in Oxford at all. So the heads of houses at Oxford now submitted to the king that 'it might be of signal service to the nation, if his Majesty would graciously be pleas'd to order that all his future Professors in Modern History' should be subjected to certain regulations. They suggested residence in full term, the delivering of fifty lectures a year, and more generous payments to the teachers of modern languages. The king thereupon signified his intention that the office should never again be held as a sinecure in either university. Before his appointment could be confirmed, Spence's successor at Oxford was required to submit to the Chancellor his comments upon the suggested regulations, and to make his own counterproposals. And although Gray had been appointed without conditions, and could not in fact be made liable to any new regulations, he too was invited to submit his views upon the matter to the Chancellor of his own university.

It was all very unexpected and disconcerting. Now that the question had been raised at Oxford, and was attracting a good deal of attention, he did begin to feel some conscientious scruples about doing nothing whatsoever in return for 'the best thing the Crown has to bestow upon a layman here'. He had no wish to become an absentee like Spence, and wrote to Beattie that 'as I lived here before from choice, I shall now continue to do so from obligation'.[26] But all his life he had been accustomed to work and to write just as he felt inclined, without any thought of publicity, and he dreaded the labour of preparing lectures and the ordeal of delivering them. Reluctantly he drew up his proposals and submitted them to the Chancellor. 'The Professor shall apply to the several Heads of Colleges, and desire them to recommend one or more young Gentlemen, who shall be instructed without expense in some of the modern languages, and shall attend such lectures as he shall give. The number (if each smaller College send one, and the larger two) will amount in the University of Cambridge to nineteen.' The professor should read a public lecture at least once a term to this chosen band, 'and any others that shall be present', and deliver private lectures to them and direct their studies. He should be careful to supervise the instruction given by the French and Italian preceptors whom he appointed and paid. He should reside in Cambridge for at least one-half of every term. And 'if he neglect those duties, he shall be subject to the same pecuniary mulcts, that other Professors are according to Statute'.

This scheme was a decided modification of the drastic suggestions made by the heads of houses at Oxford; but even so it was more than Gray, in the circumstances of his temperament and health, could have been expected to carry out. And in the end he did as little to adorn the professorship as the most casual of his predecessors. He resided more regularly in term than had been his custom during the past few years. But he never gave any lectures, either publicly or privately. He may have supervised the studies of an occasional promising young man, such as Nicholls had been; but he is not known to have done so. He was worried by this neglect, but could not bring himself to remedy it. He was always intending to prepare and read some lectures in the near future, and would even talk of resigning his chair if he could not justify his continuance in it; but the months and presently the years drifted by, and nothing was done. Even his inaugural lecture, of which he drew up an elaborate outline, and which he began to compose in a Latin which now came haltingly to his pen, was never delivered.[27]

VI

Nicholls had been ordained early in 1767, and before the end of that year had become the rector of Lound and Bradwell, on the Suffolk coast not far from Lowestoft. The next presentation of the living had been bought for him by an indulgent uncle; and as there was no parsonage attached, he and his mother were installed in a house in the adjoining parish of Blundeston. It was a charming place, with woods and a lake which tempted him at once into the pleasures of landscape gardening, and the sea breaking on the deserted shore two miles away. 'I bathe in it', he told Gray, 'you may admire it, and catch strange fishes, and call them by strange names, and tell me their history and adventures.' Gray did not fail to visit him at Blundeston that autumn, and was delighted to find his young friend so well and prosperously settled. Nicholls's devotion to him was increased, if possible, by a circumstance which he described many years afterwards:

I was extremely embarrassed because I had at that time with me an old relation and his wife, who were so entirely different from any thing that could give him pleasure that I thought it impossible he should reconcile himself to their conversation, or endure to stay with me. I think he perceived this, and determined to show me that I had mistaken him; for he made himself so agreeable to them that they both talked with pleasure of the time they passed with him as long as they lived.[28]

The great event of 1769 at Cambridge was to be the installation, with all the traditional pomp and ceremony, of the Duke of Grafton as Chancellor of the University. It was the custom at those functions for a special ode to be sung to music specially composed. Mason, although he did not care to be reminded of it, had written the ode for the Duke of Newcastle's installation twenty years before. Gray now reluctantly decided that he must express his gratitude to the new Chancellor for his professorship in a manner worthy of the occasion. One morning Nicholls, who was paying a return visit to Cambridge, knocked at the door of the poet's rooms, and was completely bewildered when he flung it open with a loud exclamation: *Hence! avaunt! 'tis holy ground.* It was the opening line of his Installation Ode, which he had long been pondering and was now beginning to compose.[29]

It was probably during the same visit that Nicholls one day found him absorbed in *The Public Advertiser*. 'Here is such writing', he said, 'as I never met with before in a newspaper.' He was reading the first of the letters of Junius, the mysterious figure who now began to assail Grafton and his fellow-ministers with unexampled fury.[30] All through the early months of 1769 the attack developed, exposing every aspect of Grafton's public conduct and private morals to scorn and ridicule, at the very time when Gray was striving to celebrate his virtues in exalted strains of poetry. The ministry and its supporters were under constant fire from a multitude of lesser writers; and Gray knew perfectly well that the sentiments of his ode would not pass unobserved. 'I know it will bring abuse enough on me', he confided to Wharton.[31] Edward Delaval, loud and vehement as ever, and a strong opponent of the Ministry, 'fell upon me tooth and nail (but in a very friendly manner)...told me of the obloquy that waits for me; and said everything to deter me from doing a thing that is already done'.[32] The ode was finished by April and duly presented to the Vice-Chancellor, after which Gray went off to London. 'The Spring is come in all its beauty', he wrote to Wharton, 'and for two or three days I am going to meet it at Windsor.'[33] It was probably the last time in his life that he visited those well-remembered scenes.

Before long there was trouble about the setting of the ode. The talented and pushing composer Charles Burney, who was seeking a Doctorate of Music at one or other of the universities, had approached Grafton and obtained this important commission. According to his daughter Fanny, writing in the richly bedizened manner of her old age, 'not a second did Mr Burney lose in forwarding every preparation for obviating any disgrace to his melodious muse, Terpsichore, when the poetry of the enchanting bard should come in contact with her lyre. He formed upon a large scale a well chosen band, vocal and instrumental, for the performance; and he engaged, as leader of the orchestra, the celebrated Giardini, who was the acknowledged first violinist of Europe.' At this stage the Duke asked how much it was all going to cost; and when Burney delivered his estimate, 'with the cheerfulest confidence that his selection fully deserved its appointed retribution, and was elegantly appropriated to the dignity of its purpose', he was told to reduce it by one-half, and promptly resigned.[34] The task was then entrusted to John Randall, the Professor of Music in the university. He arranged for its performance by a local orchestra and chorus, with a group of distinguished soloists, described by Gray as 'great names at Salisbury and Gloucester musick-meeting, and well-versed in Judas Maccabaeus'.* Gray's single cryptic comment upon the setting was that 'the musick is as good as the words: the former might be taken for mine, and the latter for Dr Randall's'.[35]

Gray had undertaken the ode with reluctance and from a sense of obligation. His gratitude towards Grafton was genuine, but no personal contact had been established between them over the professorship, and no warmth of human feeling could enter into the poem. Its form, too, was unfamiliar and probably

---

* Joseph Cradock claimed to have been present at one of the rehearsals, when Gray 'had so many directions to give, and such nice distinctions to make, it was well he had to do with the pliant Dr Randall' (Cradock, i, 107). There is no other evidence that Gray took part in the rehearsals.

uncongenial. In contrast to his other poems, so regular in their structure, it had necessarily to follow the lines of a cantata, with sections of varying length and metre, entitled 'Air', 'Recitative', 'Quartetto' and so forth, to suit the requirements of soloists and a chorus. In general the readers of his own day applauded it as a poem, while at the same time many of them condemned it as a venal and insincere tribute to a politician of whom they disapproved. Later critics have perceived in it all the defects of a poem written to order and not from the heart. And unquestionably it has its weaknesses. Unquestionably it was absurd of Gray to hymn 'the inborn royalty of mind' of a Prime Minister who had lately shocked an uncensorious age by appearing publicly at the opera with his mistress Nancy Parsons; and to discern 'a Tudor's fire, a Beaufort's grace' in the lowering young Fitzroy of whom Junius had lately said that 'sullen and severe without religion, profligate without gaiety, you live like Charles the Second, without being an amiable companion, and, for aught I know, may die as his father did, without the reputation of a martyr'.[36]

But with all these disadvantages the *Installation Ode* was a genuine rekindling of the fires of noble poetry which had been so long dormant in Gray. The flattery of Grafton may have been strained, the compliments over-elaborate; but a different note is sounded when he speaks of Cambridge itself, the university and its great figures of the past, the Lady Margaret, Burghley who was so long its Chancellor, Milton and Newton who had conferred such lustre upon it. It was as though the occasion had inspired him to offer a tribute of homage—and since he had little more than two years to live, it was also to prove a gesture of farewell—to the ancient home of learning in which, for all his outbursts of ridicule and complaint, 'I have pass'd so many easy, and (I may say) happy hours of my life'. In such a mood he wrote the splendid passage which portrayed the founders and benefactors of the university, advancing in procession to greet the latest of their line:

But hark! the portals sound, and pacing forth
With solemn steps and slow
High Potentates and Dames of royal birth
And mitred Fathers in long order go:
Great *Edward* with the lillies on his brow
From haughty *Gallia* torn,
And sad *Chatillon*, on her bridal morn
That wept her bleeding Love, and princely *Clare*,
And *Anjou's* Heroine, and the paler Rose,
The rival of her crown, and of her woes,
And either *Henry* there,
The murther'd Saint, and the majestic Lord,
That broke the bonds of *Rome*.
(Their tears, their little triumphs o'er,
Their human passions now no more,
Save Charity, that glows beyond the tomb)
All that on *Granta's* fruitful plain
Rich streams of regal bounty pour'd,
And bad these aweful fanes and turrets rise,
To hail their *Fitzroy's* festal morning come...

His own life at Cambridge was likewise suggested, remotely but unmistakably, in the lines which he put into the mouth of Milton, an exquisite echo of the *Ode on the Nativity*:

Ye brown o'er-arching Groves,
That Contemplation loves,
Where willowy *Camus* lingers with delight!
Oft at the blush of dawn
I trod your level lawn,
Oft woo'd the gleam of *Cynthia* silver-bright
In cloisters dim, far from the haunts of Folly,
With Freedom by my Side, and soft-ey'd Melancholy.

The installation of Grafton as Chancellor was a tremendous occasion, such as had not taken place for more than twenty years, and was not to take place again for thirty years to come. Cambridge was packed with important personages—ambassadors, politicians, most of the episcopal bench, all eager to compliment the Prime Minister by their presence; and when Gray had a letter from Nicholls, full of the delights of his

Suffolk garden and the weeping willows he had planted beside his lake, he could only long to be there too.

And so you have a garden of your own, and you plant and transplant and are dirty and amused! are not you ashamed of yourself? why, I have no such thing, you monster; nor ever shall be either dirty or amused as long as I live! my gardens are in the window, like those of a lodger up three pair of stairs in Petticoat-lane or Camomile Street, and they go to bed regularly under the same roof that I do. Dear, how charming it must be to walk out in one's own garding, and sit on a bench in the open air with a fountain, and a leaden statue, and a rolling-stone, and an arbour. . . .[37]

Such delights were not for him; and on Saturday, 1 July, he was duly present in the crowded Senate House when the installation ceremonies took place.

The proceedings began in confusion, with the waiting crowds rushing the building without regard to the tickets which had been issued, ladies losing their shoes and even their jewels, and the proctors vainly endeavouring to restore order. There were speeches by the Vice-Chancellor and the Public Orator, in which due attention was paid to 'the factious spirit of the times'. The newly created Chancellor forgot his prepared speech and replied *extempore*, and confessed afterwards that 'he never was so fluttered'. Then Dr Randall's strains were heard, and the *Ode* was performed to the satisfaction of the distinguished guests, who adjourned as soon as it was over to a banquet of turtle and venison in the hall of Trinity. The festivities of the evening included a performance of *Acis and Galatea* in the Senate House, and a disputation in Trinity Chapel on the question whether William the First came in by conquest or by the consent of the people.[38] In this debate, which hardly appears to provide scope for much argument, the part of an old English Baron was sustained by Lord John Cavendish's nephew Lord Richard, whom Gray had described on his first arrival in Cambridge as 'a sensible Boy, aukward and bashful beyond imagination, and eats a buttock of beef at a meal'.[39]

The Sunday was occupied with sermons and oratorios; the Monday with more speeches, the declaiming of verses and the conferment of degrees. Then Grafton left Cambridge, and a few days later Gray went to London and thence to his friends in the north. His *Ode* had been published at Cambridge by the university authorities, and promptly met with the abuse and ridicule which he had anticipated. Full-length parodies appeared in two newspapers:

> Hence! avaunt! 'tis *venal* ground:
> Wilkes and all his free-born crew...

began the *St James's Chronicle*, to be followed in due course by the *London Chronicle* with

> Hence! avaunt! 'tis sacred ground,
> Let pallid freedom ever fly...[40]

Neither of these contained any personal attack on Gray; but he was directly assailed in the *London Chronicle* in a parody of the epitaph at the close of the *Elegy*. The writer signed himself Marcus, and prefaced his effort by a note that 'as a certain Church-yard Poet has deviated from the principles he once profest, it is very fitting that the necessary alterations should be made in his epitaph':

> Here rests his head upon the lap of earth,
> One nor to fortune nor to fame unknown;
> Fair science frown'd not on his humble birth,
> And smooth-tongued flatt'ry mark'd him for her own.
>
> Large was his wish—in this he was sincere—
> Fate did a recompence as largely send,
> Gave the poor C...r four hundred pounds a year,
> And made a d...y Minister his friend.
>
> No further seek his deeds to bring to light,
> For ah! he offer'd at Corruption's shrine;
> And basely strove to wash an Ethiop white,
> While Truth and Honour bled in ev'ry line.[41]

Such things did not much disturb Gray's equanimity; but his friend Cole, that sturdy champion of the established order, was filled with indignation. He copied the offensive verses into one of his note-books, and added the following comment, with his usual lavish underlinings:

I have the *Unhappiness* to live in an *Age* when all *Decency*, both of *Behaviour* and *Language* is set at naught, and under a Notion of *Freedom* and *Liberty*, every man's private Character is made the object of *public* Censure, by means of a most *licencious Misuse* of the *Liberty of the Press*. Thus my *Friend Mr Gray*, a man void of all *ambitious views*, because his *Friend Mr Stonhewer* had pointed him out as a *most proper Person* to the *Duke of Grafton*, for the *Professorship* of *Modern History*, without the least *application* or *thought* of it *himself*, met with the most *illiberal Abuse* in the *public Papers*, for having, in a *grateful*, though *very slight manner* complimented his Patron in the *Ode* composed by him, and set to *Music* for his *Installation*. Such *bitter enemies* are these *bigotted Republicans and Wilkites* to all they suspect not to be *entire* with them![42]

The *Installation Ode* was not likely to escape the notice of Junius. In his next letter to the Prime Minister he made particular reference to the recent ceremonies at Cambridge, and concluded the passage with a single bitter sentence directed at Gray. The king, he said, must at last become convinced of Grafton's utter unsuitability to act as his chief adviser, and would discard him without hesitation:

You will then have reason to be thankful if you are permitted to retire to that seat of learning which, in contemplation of the system of your life, the comparative purity of your manners with those of their High Steward [Sandwich], and a thousand other recommending circumstances, has chosen you to encourage the growing virtue of their youth, and to preside over their education. Whenever the spirit of distributing prebends and bishopricks shall have departed from you, you will find that learned seminary perfectly recovered from the delirium of an installation, and, what in truth it ought to be, once more a peaceful scene of slumber and thoughtless meditation. The venerable tutors of the University will no longer distress your modesty by proposing you for a pattern to their pupils. The learned dullness of declamation will be silent; and even the venal muse, though happiest in fiction, will forget your virtues.[43]

VII

Gray travelled northwards in the middle of July, staying a few days with Mason at York, and then going on to spend the next two months with Wharton at Old Park. They hoped in the autumn to carry out the tour of the Lakes which had been interrupted by Wharton's illness two years before. On 29 September they set out full of expectation; but on the first night of their tour Wharton was once again seized with an attack of asthma in the inn at Brough, and returned home next morning. This time Gray went on alone. He kept a journal of his experiences during the next fortnight in his pocket note-books, and transcribed it in a series of letters to Wharton at intervals in the course of the winter.[44]

This journal was written without the least thought of pub-lication. Gray undertook it solely to give Wharton pleasure, to describe the scenes they might have viewed together, and to furnish him with a guide in case he should ever succeed in making the expedition himself. It was sprinkled with such asides as 'Oh Doctor! I never wish'd more for you. . .' and 'a picture which if I could transmit to you. . .', and even included at one point, for the benefit of Mrs Wharton, a local recipe for dressing perch. But it also contained some of his finest descriptive writing. Page after page the exquisite pictures unfold, sunlight on the mountains, lakesides at evening or in the morning mist, passing impressions of cloud or verdure, landscapes of a fresh and limpid beauty.

His first centres were Penrith and then Keswick, where he passed six days 'lap'd in Elysium'. Thence he had intended to move on to Ambleside; but finding that the best bed-chamber of the inn there was 'dark and damp as a cellar', he gave up his thoughts of exploring Windermere and sought refuge in a more comfortable establishment at Kendal. From all these places he saw everything that could be seen by a middle-aged gentleman of delicate constitution, who could not ride and was heard to express a strong preference for walking on reasonably dry and level ground. Fortunately the weather remained perfect throughout his tour. He carried with him everywhere his 'glass', a sort of camera obscura, described by Mason as 'a Plano-convex Mirror of about four inches diameter on a black foil, and bound up like a pocket-book', in which the scenes composed themselves into pictures in a manner which always delighted him. From Keswick he took some considerable walks, attended when necessary by the landlord of his inn bearing a cold tongue for refreshment, and although on one occasion he fell down in a dirty lane with his glass open in his hand, he sustained no harm beyond the grazing of his knuckles.

His most memorable day was perhaps 3 October. He rose at seven—it was a heavenly morning, he noted, with a south-east wind—and walked with his landlord towards Borrowdale, passing through 'the most delicious view, that my eyes ever beheld'. As they entered Borrowdale the rocks began to impend, so that he was reminded of the Alps; and the more so after they had viewed the waterfall of Lodore and were passing under the formidable bulk of Gowder Crag. At the village of Grange they met a young farmer who described how he had been lowered last year down a cliff to destroy an eagle's nest, and who took them to his house and regaled them on butter and oat-cakes. At Grange he felt almost at the end of the world, with the mountains forming their 'awful amphitheatre' all round, their height ever increasing and their summits of more fantastic forms. Then they walked slowly homeward, with the meridian sun altering the scenes through which they had passed in the morning. It was the only day on which it might have been possible for him to go up Skiddaw, but he had felt himself better employed; and at its close he had the most moving experience of all:

In the evening walk'd alone down to the Lake by the side of *Crow-Park* after sunset and saw the solemn colouring of night draw on, the last gleam of sunshine fading away on the hilltops, the deep serene of the waters, and the long shadows of the mountains thrown across them, till they nearly touch'd the hithermost shore. At distance heard the murmur of many waterfalls not audible in the day-time. Wish'd for the moon, but she was *dark to me and silent, hid in her vacant interlunar cave.*

Another unforgettable moment was his sight of Grasmere, on the road from Keswick to Ambleside. As his chaise entered Westmorland a second time, he began to see

Helm-Crag distinguish'd from its rugged neighbours not so much by its height, as by the strange broken outline of its top, like some gigantic building demolish'd, and the stones that composed it, flung cross each other in wild confusion. Just beyond it opens one of the sweetest landscapes, that art ever attempted to imitate. The bosom of the mountains spreading here into a broad bason discovers in the midst Grasmere-water. Its margin is hollow'd into small bays with bold eminences some of rock, some of soft turf, that half conceal, and vary the figure of the little lake they command; from the shore a low promontory pushes itself far into the water, and on it stands a white village with the parish-church rising in the midst of it; hanging enclosures, corn-fields, and meadows green as an emerald with their trees and hedges and cattle fill up the whole space from the edge of the water; and just opposite to you is a large farm-house at the bottom of a steep smooth lawn embosom'd in old woods, which climb half way up the mountain's side, and discover above them a broken line of crags, that crown the scene. Not a single red tile, no flaring gentleman's house, or garden-walls, break in upon the repose of this little unsuspected paradise, but all is peace, rusticity, and happy poverty in its neatest most becoming attire.

In general it was his fortune to view, during those golden October days, the calm and smiling aspects of the Picturesque; but he was also to achieve a glimpse of the Sublime. From Kendal he went for a couple of days to Lancaster, and thence, passing close to 'the foot of that huge creature of God, *Ingleborough*', and shivering a little in the keen Craven air, to Settle. Next morning he set out to visit Gordale Scar, his chaise struggling over fearful roads as far as the village of Malham:

From thence I was to walk a mile over very rough ground, a torrent rattling along on the left hand. On the cliffs above hung a

few goats: one of them danced and scratched an ear with its hind-
foot in a place where I would not have stood stock-still

for all beneath the moon.

As I advanced the crags seem'd to close in, but discover'd a narrow
entrance turning to the left between them. I followed my guide a
few paces, and lo, the hills open'd again into no large space, and then
all farther way is bar'd by a stream, that at the height of about 50
feet gushes from a hole in the rock, and spreading in large sheets
over its broken front dashes from steep to steep, and then rattles
away in a torrent down the valley. The rock on the left rises
perpendicular with stubbed yewtrees and shrubs, staring from its
side to the height of at least 300 feet. But these are not the thing!
it is that to the right, under which you stand to see the fall, that
forms the principal horror of the place. From its very base it begins
to slope forwards over you in one black and solid mass without any
crevice in its surface, and overshadows half the area below with its
dreadful canopy. When I stood at (I believe) full 4 yards distance
from its foot, the drops which perpetually distill from its brow, fell
on my head, and in one part of the top more exposed to the weather
there are loose stones that hang in air, and threaten visibly some
idle spectator with instant destruction. It is safer to shelter yourself
close to its bottom, and trust the mercy of that enormous mass, which
nothing but an earthquake can stir. The gloomy uncomfortable day
well suited the savage aspect of the place, and made it still more
formidable. I stay'd there (not without shuddering) a quarter of an
hour, and thought my trouble richly paid, for the impression will
last for life.

Gordale Scar was the culminating experience of his tour. It
provided the last of those descriptive passages which exerted,
from the time of their publication in the *Memoirs* six years
later, so great an influence upon the increasing throngs who
followed in his steps, and sketched and rhapsodised, and disputed on the true principles of the Beautiful and the Picturesque. The remainder of his journal, as he moved slowly on
through Yorkshire to Mason's parsonage at Aston, was little
more than a brief summary. He was sight-seeing still, but
nothing could compare with what he had already viewed. Then
he made his way gradually southwards, and was back at
Cambridge before the end of October.

CHAPTER XII

BONSTETTEN AND THE
FINAL YEARS
1769-1771

I

B A C K in his college rooms, Gray settled down to the accustomed quiet of the winter months. He wrote out the journal of his tour and sent the instalments to Wharton. He continued to reflect uneasily on his failure to carry out his professorial duties, and drew up synopses of the lectures which he knew he could never deliver. When Stonhewer's father died, he sent him one of those memorable letters with which he consoled his friends in their times of sorrow. 'May God preserve you my best Friend!' he concluded: 'and (long after my eyes are closed) give you that last satisfaction in the gratitude and affection of a Son, which you have given your Father.'[1]

So the November of 1769 wore uneventfully on, until one evening Norton Nicholls, who was concluding a rather protracted absence from his parish with a visit to Bath, happened to go to a ball at the Assembly Rooms. Light-hearted as ever, the youthful rector scrambled on to a table in order to have a better view of the dancing, and presently another young man did the same. They clutched one another for fear of falling, an unceremonious introduction which led to a lifelong friendship between them.[2]

The young man's name was Charles-Victor de Bonstetten, and he was the only son of a prominent member of the little group of patrician families which ruled the canton of Berne. He had studied at Geneva and Lausanne, cherished 'un amour très spirituel' for the future Madame Necker, paid his court to Voltaire, been intoxicated by Rousseau but disillusioned by his adversary Charles Bonnet, in short was tossed to and fro

by all the conflicting intellectual currents of the time. With
exceptional good looks and the most captivating personal
charm, he was enthusiastic, romantic, liable to fits of melancholy which would suddenly give way to long spells of radiant
happiness. In later years he recorded how one night in his
youth he was contemplating putting an end to all his woes,
the agony of his memories, the torments that life yet held in
store—'encore en chemise, étendu sur le sol entre deux pistolets
chargés, attendant le moment décisif'—when the moon shone
out and everything was changed on the instant.[3]

This charming and slightly absurd young gentleman caused
a good deal of perplexity in the canton of Berne. His father, the
Trésorier, disturbed by his 'ésprit ardent et inconstant', and
alarmed by the notions of liberty and equality which he had
developed, had allowed him to continue his studies in Holland,
and had then somewhat reluctantly sanctioned a visit to
England. And so, at the age of twenty-four, he went in the
summer of 1769 to learn English with a clergyman's family in
Berkshire. 'Oh! le bon pays que l'Angleterre! qu'il est doux
de vivre chez un peuple où les hommes sont généreux, bons,
humains, et les femmes belles et modestes....' He had
thoughts of marrying an attractive young heiress with forty
thousand pounds, but changed his mind and was filled with
immeasurable relief at having done so. 'O mon cher père, je
vais désormais être d'une gaieté admirable, et chanter et danser
tout le jour, comme un homme qui s'est réveillé d'un mauvais
songe.'[4] There are moments when the young Bonstetten bears
a surprising resemblance to the young Boswell.

Nicholls was delighted with his new friend. He himself
longed to travel and especially to visit Switzerland, and had
told Gray the year before that he 'would give a limb to be in
danger of breaking my neck among the Alps, or being buried
alive in everlasting snow'.[5] Bonstetten was just as enthusiastic
at the thought of meeting the greatest living English poet; so
Nicholls gave him a letter of introduction to Gray, and wrote
to warn Gray of the possibility of his arrival at Cambridge:

He seems to have read, and to be unwilling now to waste his time if he knew how to employ it; I think he is vastly better than any thing English (of the same age) I ever saw; and then, I have a partiality to him because he was born among mountains; and talks of them with enthusiasm—of the forests of pines which grow darker and darker as you ascend, till the *nemorum nox* is completed, and you are forced to grope your way; of the cries of eagles and other birds of prey adding to the horror; in short, of all the wonders of his country.[6]

Gray went to London early in December. He saw several of his friends—Stonhewer, Hurd, Lord Nuneham are mentioned in his letters—and it was in London, and not at Cambridge, that he first met Bonstetten. The young Swiss had now returned from Bath, armed with an introduction from Nicholls to Gray's acquaintance Thomas Pitt of Boconnoc. Pitt had at once taken charge of him, presented him at Court and shown him something of the world of London, where he much enjoyed himself and was instantly popular. But his meeting with Gray was far more important to him than the chance successes of social life. He listened reverentially to the conversation of the great poet, drinking in his words with all the enthusiasm of his eager nature. When Gray suggested that he should accompany him back to Cambridge, to spend a few weeks at the university and perhaps even do a little work under his supervision, he accepted with gratitude.

They went down to Cambridge together on 21 December. A few days before, as they were walking through the city, 'a large uncouth figure was rolling before them, upon seeing which Gray exclaimed, with some bitterness, "Look, look, Bonstetten!—the great bear!—There goes *Ursa Major*!"' Such, at least, was the account which Sir Egerton Brydges claimed to have received from Bonstetten many years afterwards.[7] The name of *Ursa Major* was independently bestowed upon Doctor Samuel Johnson four years afterwards by Lord Auchinleck, and duly recorded by his son in the *Journal of a Tour to the Hebrides*;[8] but it would be a pity to reject entirely the sole anecdote which brings together, even for a moment in a crowded street, these deeply antagonistic men. The two great literary figures of the day, both so influential, so admired, and within their private circles so beloved, were never to meet face to face. A gulf of incomprehension yawned between them. In all his correspondence Gray only once mentioned Johnson. He disliked him, wrote Nicholls, 'and declined his acquaintance; he disapproved his style, and thought it turgid, and vicious; but he respected his understanding, and still more his goodness of heart. I have heard him say that Johnson would go out in London with his pockets full of silver, and give it all away in the streets before he returned home.'[9] Johnson never achieved this note of charity in his references to Gray. Apart from the *Elegy*, he was contemptuous of his poetry, and down the ages will always echo the magisterial injustice of 'Sir, he was dull in company, dull in his closet, dull everywhere. He was dull in a new way, and that made many people think him GREAT.'[10]

II

Bonstetten was installed in lodgings at a coffee-house just across the road from Pembroke, no doubt the coffee-house habitually used by Gray and his circle.[11] Transported suddenly from the gaieties of London to the cloistered quiet of Cambridge, living amongst elderly scholars wedded to their books and studious young gentlemen in the medieval disguise of cap and gown, he felt himself in a completely different world. The atmosphere perplexed and at the same time amused him—the seclusion, the formality, the celibacy of a society in which no young or fashionable woman was ever seen. He described to his mother the extraordinary stiffness of a Cambridge evening party, with solemn elderly ladies and black-gowned professors seated in almost unbroken silence. His accustomed ease and grace of manner seemed out of place in such surroundings; terrified of being thought a coxcomb, he found it impossible 'croiser les jambes, adresser ce que nous appelons des honnêtetés aux hommes, relever un mouchoir tombé, prendre la tasse d'une femme', or lighten the gloom of the occasion in any way.[12] But he could always adapt himself cheerfully for a time to any new environment; and his veneration for Gray, the eagerness with which he was prepared to absorb instruction from so great a man, did away with any feeling of boredom in this strange community.

He was made welcome by Gray's friends at Cambridge, kindly James Brown and the rest. William Cole, now living close by at Milton, who was at this time keeping a laconic journal in French, dined on 29 December at Pembroke with Gray, and met Michael Tyson, a young Fellow of Corpus of antiquarian and artistic tastes, and 'Bonstaten Fils du Trésorier du Canton de Berne en Suisse, un jeune Homme d'une grande Beauté et beaucoup de mérite comme un Ecolier: il est venu à Cambridge il y a une semaine'. On New Year's Day he went with Tyson and Bonstetten, but apparently without Gray, to hear the organ in the chapel of Trinity, and then to the rooms of another antiquary, Michael Lort, the Regius Professor of Greek, a friend and correspondent of Walpole. Next month he arranged a party at Milton for Gray, Tyson, Bonstetten and a Mr Nasmith, which had to be put off as the house was freshly painted and not yet dry.[13] But Bonstetten had come to Cambridge in order to study; and study is the theme of the delightful letter which he addressed to Nicholls after a fortnight's experience of university life:

Hence vain deluding Joys is our motto hier, written on every feature, and ourly spoken by every solitary Chapel bel; So that decently you cant expect no other but a very grave letter. I realy beg your pardon to wrap up my thoughts in so smart a dress as an in quarto sheet. I know they should apear in a folio leave, but the Ideas themselves shall look so solemn as to belie their dress.—Tho' I wear not yet the black gown, and am only an inferior Priest in the temple of Meditation, yet my countenance is already consecrated. I never walk but with even steps and musing gate, and looks comercing with the skyes; and unfold my wrinkles only when I see Mr Gray, or think of you. Then notwithstanding all your learnings and knowledge, I feel in such occasions that I have a heart, which you know is as some others a quite prophane thing to carry under a black gown.

I am in a hurry from morning till evening. At 8 o'Clock I am roused by a young square Cap, with whom I follow Satan through Chaos and night. He explained me in Greek and Latin, the *sweet reluctant amorous Delays* of our Grandmother Eve. We finish our travels in a copious breakfast of muffins and tea. Then apears Shakespair and old Lineus strugling together as two ghost would do for a damned Soul. Sometimes the one get the better sometimes the other. Mr Gray, whose acquaintance is my greatest debt to you, is so good as to show me Macbeth, and all witches, Beldams, Ghost and Spirits, whose language I never could have understood without his Interpretation. I am now endeavouring to dress all those people in a french dress, which is a very hard labour.

I am afraid to take a room, which Mr Gray shall keep still much better. So I stop hier my everrambling pen. My respectful Compliments to M^d. Nichole. Only remember that you have no where a better or more grateful friend than your de Bonstetten.

Gray added a postscript:

I never saw such a boy: our breed is not made on this model. He is busy from morning to night, has no other amusement, than that of changing one study from another, likes nobody, that he sees here, and yet wishes to stay longer, tho' he has pass'd a whole fortnight with us already. His letter has had no correction whatever, and is prettier by half than English.[14]

At first Bonstetten worked most of the day in his lodgings. Mr Miller, the curator of the physic garden, gave private lectures to him upon the Linnaean system. The student whom he described as 'the young square cap', and whose identity remains unknown, continued to expound the dark places of Milton.* After they had gone he studied Johnson's *Dictionary* and the *Biographia Britannica*, which he had borrowed from the college library; and it was seldom before five o'clock that he felt his labours for the day were over, and he might now venture to intrude upon Mr Gray. But as the weeks went by, and his *protégé* still stayed on at Cambridge, Gray grew ever more fascinated by him. He insisted that he should visit him

* Leonard Whibley noted four quotations from Milton in Bonstetten's letter, and there may be others.

CHARLES-VICTOR DE BONSTETTEN
From a painting by an unknown artist, in the possession of
M. Wolfgang de Reding-Biberegg

at all times of the day, dine with him, work in his rooms. Together they read the English poets, went over the botanical lessons of Mr Miller, played on the new pianoforte—a present from Stonhewer—and talked on and on until the college gate was about to close.[15]

When he first met Bonstetten, a month or so before, Gray felt towards him much as he had felt towards Nicholls at the outset of their friendship. Here was another promising young man, with confused standards and uncertain ideals, eager to be guided by him into the true paths of learning and morality. Their relationship was once again to be that of master and disciple, with the older man instructing and the younger listening obediently to his precepts. But by now he realised that this newcomer was arousing in him emotions such as he had never experienced before, emotions obsessive and overwhelming. All his defences were swept away—the life so carefully organised, the formal and deliberate manner, the refuge which he had sought in books and antiquities and the interleaved Linnaeus. He was filled with disquiet, for he understood the secrets of his own nature; he knew the existence of temptations which could not for one moment be contemplated by one who had been, all his life long, a strict observer of the laws of God and the laws of man. At the same time the very presence of Bonstetten brought him unimagined happiness. For a few short weeks he enjoyed once more what he had never known since his childhood days, 'the sunshine of the breast'.

Bonstetten was perplexed by the change that had come over their relationship. He saw to his embarrassment that he had *comme subjugué* the poet whose fame had spread all over Europe. He lost nothing of his admiration for Gray; as he told his father, 'les Français raisonnent quelquefois bien et de Patrie et de Vertu, mais quand M. Gray m'en parlait je sentais des palpitations, j'étais ému comme si j'avais entendu la voix d'un dieu'.[16] But his veneration was now mingled with pity. He tried with boyish diffidence to show his sympathy, to talk to

Gray about his poetry and to learn something of his past life. On these topics Gray would say nothing. Bonstetten concluded, a little surprisingly in the circumstances which then prevailed, that he had never been in love.

More than sixty years afterwards, a very old man living in a world unbelievably changed, he set down his memories of those three months at Cambridge. English travellers, Lord Byron and Sir Egerton Brydges among the number, had sometimes asked him about Gray, and his answers were always non-committal. 'He was the most melancholy and gentlemanlike of poets', was the gist of what he told Byron;[17] and Brydges, besides the *Ursa Major* anecdote, carried away little more than an impression of Gray's unwillingness to talk about his own writings, and his apparent unawareness of the extent of his fame.[18] But in his *Souvenirs* of 1831 there is to be found a long account of this episode in his distant youth, and his own explanation of the riddle of Gray. It occurs in a chapter about his friend the poet Matthisson, and is introduced by a comparison between the serenity of Matthisson's temperament and the melancholy of Gray's. He mentions that he spent some months at Cambridge with Gray, who was thirty years older than himself, while Matthisson was sixteen years younger. Then he proceeds:

Ma gaieté, mon amour pour la poésie anglaise que je lisais avec Gray, l'avaient comme subjugué, de manière que la grande différence de nos âges n'était plus sentie par nous. J'étais logé à Cambridge dans un café, voisin de Pembrokhall; Gray y vivait enseveli dans une espèce de cloître, d'où le quinzième siècle n'avait pas encore déménagé. La ville de Cambridge avec ses colléges solitaires n'était qu'une réunion de couvens, où les mathématiques et quelques sciences ont pris la forme et le costume de la théologie du moyen âge. De beaux couvens, à longs et silencieux corridors, des solitaires en robes noires, de jeunes seigneurs travestis en moines à bonnets carrés, partout des souvenirs de moines à côté de la gloire de Newton. Aucune femme honnête ne venait égayer la vie de ces rats de livres à forme humain. Le savoir prospérait quelquefois dans ce désert du cœur. Tel j'ai vu Cambridge en 1769. Quel contraste de la vie de Gray à Cambridge avec celle de Matthisson à Nyon!

Gray, en se condamnant à vivre à Cambridge, oubliait que le génie du poète languit dans la sécheresse du cœur.

Le génie poétique de Gray était tellement éteint dans le sombre manoir de Cambridge, que le souvenir de ses poésies lui était odieux. Il ne se permit jamais de lui en parler. Quand je lui citais quelques vers de lui, il se taisait comme un enfant obstiné. Je lui disais quelquefois: *Voulez-vous bien me répondre?* Mais aucune parole ne sortait de sa bouche. Je le voyais tous les soirs de cinq heures à minuit. Nous lisions Shakespeare qu'il adorait, Dryden, Pope, Milton, etc., et nos conversations, comme celles de l'amitié, n'arrivaient jamais à la dernière pensée. Je racontais à Gray ma vie et mon pays, mais toute sa vie à lui était fermée pour moi; jamais il me ne parlait de lui. Il y avait chez Gray entre le présent et le passé un abîme infranchissable. Quand je voulais en approcher, de sombres nuées venaient le couvrir. Je crois que Gray n'avait jamais aimé, c'était le mot de l'enigme, il en était résulté une misère de cœur qui faisait contraste avec son imagination ardente et profonde qui, au lieu de faire le bonheur de sa vie, n'en était que le tourment. Gray avait de la gaieté dans l'ésprit et de la mélancholie dans le caractère. Mais cette mélancholie n'est qu'un besoin non-satisfait de la sensibilité. Chez Gray elle tenait au genre de vie de son âme ardente, reléguée sous le pôle arctique de Cambridge.[19]

III

For some while the Trésorier de Bonstetten had been insistent that his son should come home again that autumn, and should spend some months in France before he did so—'to improve his talents and morals', as Gray sardonically observed. Bonstetten protested in vain. He told his parents that Gray's friendship was procuring him attentions and honours from everyone at Cambridge, from the Vice-Chancellor downwards, and that he was the greatest writer, the first poet, the man of the first merit in England. Must he be parted from such a friend? 'Quand j'ai enfin trouvé un ami c'est pour le perdre et pour retomber dans cette sombre solitude où je reste la proie des vices et de toutes les misères humaines.'[20] But even this appeal could not soften his father's heart; and the end of March was fixed for his departure for France.

Gray was quite inconsolable. All the warmth, the contentment, the affection that had lately filled his life would be drained out of it once more, and nothing but loneliness and emptiness lay ahead. And apart from his desolating sense of personal loss, he was deeply anxious about Bonstetten's future. He had tried so hard to sober the volatile creature, to control the fantasies and aspirations that filled his brain. What dangers, what pitfalls of licentiousness and atheism now awaited him in France? What would happen to him when he returned to the domination of 'his cursed Father'? As the dreaded day of separation drew near he tried to confide in Nicholls, but despaired of conveying to him the extent of his distress. 'He gives me too much pleasure, and at least *an equal share* of inquietude. You do not understand him so well as I do, but I leave my meaning imperfect, till we meet. I have never met with so extraordinary a Person. God bless him! I am unable to talk to you about anything else, I think.'[21] He went to London with Bonstetten, and said farewell to him on 23 March at four o'clock in the morning, when the Dover coach rumbled away into the cold and darkness.

For ten days or so he stayed in London, then returned sadly to those rooms which would never seem quite the same again.

Here am I again [he told Nicholls] to pass my solitary evenings, which hung much lighter on my hands, before I knew him. This is your fault! Pray let the next you send me, be halt and blind, dull, unapprehensive and wrong-headed. For this (as Lady Constance says) *Was never such a gracious Creature born!* And yet—but no matter! burn my letter that I wrote you, for I am very much out of humour with myself and will not believe a word of it. You will think, I have caught madness from him (for he is certainly mad) and perhaps you will be right. Oh! what things are Fathers and Mothers! I thought they were to be found only in England, but you see....This place never appear'd so horrible to me, as it does now. Could not you come for a week or fortnight? It would be sunshine to me in a dark night![22]

Many letters were to pass between Gray and Bonstetten; but none of Bonstetten's have survived, and only three of

Gray's. These were printed in 1791 by Bonstetten's friend Matthisson, in the notes to a poem on the Lake of Geneva into which the figure of Gray was introduced. All three belong to the weeks immediately after their separation, when Gray's anguish was still most poignant, and his anxiety over the young man's safety amidst the temptations of Paris was at its height.

Never did I feel, my dear Bonstetten [he wrote in the first of these letters] to what a tedious length the few short moments of our life may be extended by impatience and expectation, till you had left me: nor ever knew before with so strong a conviction how much this frail body sympathizes with the inquietude of the mind. I am grown old in the compass of less than three weeks, like the Sultan in the Turkish Tales, that did but plunge his head into a vessel of water and take it out again (as the standers-by affirm'd) at the command of a Dervish, and found he had pass'd many years in captivity and begot a large family of children. The strength and spirits that now enable me to write to you, are only owing to your last letter, a temporary gleam of sunshine. Heaven knows, when it may shine again! I did not conceive till now (I own) what it was to lose you, nor felt the solitude and insipidity of my own condition, before I possess'd the happiness of your friendship.

But even at this time of grief he could not forget that he was Bonstetten's mentor as well as his friend. He turned to one of his Commonplace Books and copied, 'because it is very much to my purpose', some notes he had made many years before upon the sixth book of the *Republic*, wherein Plato describes 'the character of a Genius truly inclined to Philosophy'. Gentleness and magnanimity, fortitude and temperance, the love of truth and of justice—these and many other noble qualities formed 'the mind born to govern the rest of mankind'. But he went on to quote Plato's warning—and its application to Bonstetten was obvious—that 'those very endowments so necessary to a soul form'd for philosophy are often the ruin of it (especially when join'd to the external advantages of wealth, nobility, strength and beauty) that is, if it light on a bad soil; and want its proper nurture, which nothing but an excellent education can bestow'. Let him never forget that 'extraordinary vices and extraordinary virtues are alike the produce of a vigorous mind: little souls are alike incapable of the one or the other'.

If [his letter concluded] you have ever met with the portrait sketch'd out by Plato, you will know it again: for my part (to my sorrow) I have had that happiness: I see the principal features, and I foresee the dangers with a trembling anxiety. But enough of this, I return to your letter: it proves at least, that in the midst of your new gaieties, I still hold some place in your memory, and (what pleases me above all) it has an air of undissembled sincerity. Go on, my best and amiable Friend, to shew me your heart simply and without the shadow of disguise, and leave me to weep over it (as I do now) no matter whether from joy or sorrow.[23]

A week later he wrote to Bonstetten again:

Alas! how do I every moment feel the truth of what I have some-where read: *Ce n'est pas le voir que de s'en souvenir*, and yet that remembrance is the only satisfaction I have left. My life now is but a perpetual conversation with your shadow.—The known sound of your voice still rings in my ears.—There, on the corner of the fender you are standing, or tinkling on the pianoforte, or stretch'd at length on the sofa.—Do you reflect, my dearest Friend, that it is a week or eight days, before I can receive a letter from you, and as much more before you can have my answer, that all that time (with more than Herculean toil) I am employ'd in pushing the tedious hours along, and wishing to annihilate them; the more I strive, the heavier they move and the longer they grow. I can not bear this place, where I have spent many tedious years within less than a month, since you left me. I am going for a few days to see poor Nicholls. . . .

He then quoted from Nicholls's letter of invitation, which con-tained references to Bonstetten in the same tone of affectionate solicitude as his own. 'The miracle to me', Nicholls had written, 'is, how he comes to be so little spoil'd, and the miracle of miracles will be, if he continues so in the midst of every danger and seduction, and without any advantages, but from his own excellent nature and understanding. I own, I am very anxious for him on this account, and perhaps your inquietude may have proceeded from the same cause.' Nicholls had so far received

no letter from Bonstetten, and Gray reproached him for it.
'Sure you have wrote to him, my dear Bonstetten, or sure you
will! He has moved me with those gentle and sensible expressions of his kindness for you. Are you untouch'd by them?'

Further admonitions followed, urgent warnings against the
dangers to soul and body which now surrounded him:

You do me the credit (and false or true, it goes to my heart) of
ascribing to me your love for many virtues of the highest rank.
Would to heaven it were so; but they are indeed the fruits of your
own noble and generous understanding, that has hitherto struggled
against the stream of custom, passion, and ill company, even when
you were but a Child, and will you now give way to that stream,
when your strength is increased? Shall the Jargon of French
Sophists, the allurements of painted women *comme il faut*, or the vulgar
caresses of prostitute beauty, the property of all, that can afford to
purchase it, induce you to give up a mind and body by Nature distinguish'd from all others to folly, idleness, disease, and vain remorse?
Have a care, my ever-amiable Friend, *of loving, what you do not approve*, and know me for your most faithful and most humble Despote.[24]

Towards the end of April he went to stay with Nicholls,
stopping for a few days with Palgrave at Thrandeston on the
way. Nicholls was full of plans for a visit which they were both
to pay Bonstetten next year, when he would have finally
returned home to Switzerland. But Gray was still plunged in
sadness and foreboding. The peace of the garden at Blundeston,
in the soft spring weather with the sea murmuring beyond,
could not console him. If only fate had been a little kinder, and
the Trésorier's orders less peremptory, he might have been
sharing it with Bonstetten. On his return to Cambridge he
found another letter from Paris, to which he could only reply in
the same despondent strain:

I am return'd, my dear Bonstetten, from the little journey I had
made into Suffolk without answering the end proposed. The thought,
that you might have been with me there, has embitter'd all my
hours. Your letter has made me happy; as happy as so gloomy, so
solitary a Being as I am is capable of being. I know and have too
often felt the disadvantages I lay myself under, how much I hurt the

little interest I have in you, by this air of sadness so contrary to your nature and present enjoyments; but sure you will forgive, tho' you can not sympathize with me. It is impossible for me to dissemble with you. Such as I am, I expose my heart to your view, nor wish to conceal a single thought from your penetrating eyes.— All that you say to me, especially on the subject of Switzerland, is infinitely acceptable. It feels too pleasing ever to be fulfill'd, and as often as I read over your truly kind letter, written long since from London,* I stop at these words: *La mort qui peut glacer nos bras avant qu'ils soient entrelacés.*[25]

IV

Such intensity of emotion could not last for very long. It exhausted Gray's vitality at the time, and may well have had a permanent effect upon his health; but as the weeks went on he began to view the whole affair in a more reasonable light. He saw the absurdity of his relationship with Bonstetten as well as its sadness; and indeed the absurdity, for all his over-mastering charm, of Bonstetten himself. Even at this early stage he began to find the style of the letters from Paris 'un peu trop alembiqué', affected and over-refined. They were not to grow less so with the passage of time. Bonstetten made unconvincing excuses for not writing more often, and 'he seems at present to give into all the French nonsense and to be employ'd much like an English boy broke loose from his Governor'.[26] It was the natural reaction of a high-spirited young man after those sober months at Cambridge, months of serious reading and celibate living and an unequal friendship between youth and age; but it displeased Gray, and the pangs of separation began to torment him less.

And, after all, life had to go on. The world of literature and scholarship still held its interest for him. At the time of these fervent letters to Bonstetten he was also in correspondence with Beattie, who had sent *The Minstrel* to him for correction; and with Thomas Warton, now engaged on his *History of*

* The words 'written long since from London' are explained by the fact that Bonstetten went to London for a short time in February or early March, and then returned to Cambridge again (see *Corr.* 1113).

English Poetry, whom he furnished at Hurd's request with an outline of his own long-abandoned scheme for a similar work.[27] And he had lately made a new friend at Cambridge in Richard Farmer, Fellow and afterwards Master of Emmanuel. It was another instance of unexpected sympathy between two very different men, and was described by Cole in a characteristic note attached to a letter from Gray which Farmer had given him. The letter, he said, must have been written in 1770,

as the first time they ever met to be acquainted together, was about that time, when I met them at Mr Oldham's Chambers in Peter House to Dinner. Before, they had been shy of each other: and tho' Mr Farmer was then esteemed one of the most ingenious men in the University, yet Mr Gray's singular niceness in the Choice of his Acquaintance made him appear fastidious to a great Degree to all who was not acquainted with his manner. Indeed there did not seem to be any Probability of any great Intimacy, from the Style and Manner of each of them: the one a chearful, companionable, hearty, open, downright man, of no great Regard to Dress or common Forms of Behaviour: the other, of a most fastidious and recluse Distance of Carriage, rather averse to all Sociability, but of the graver Turn: nice and elegant in his Person, Dress and Behaviour, even to a Degree of Finicalness and Effeminacy. So that nothing but their extensive Learning and Abilities could ever have coalesced two such different men: and both of great value in their own Line and Walk. They were ever after great Friends, and Dr Farmer and all of his Acquaintance had soon after too much Reason to lament his loss, and the Shortness of their Acquaintance.[28]

Later in the spring Gray went to London again. Amongst other friends he saw Stonhewer as usual, and also Lord Strathmore and his brother Thomas Lyon, who had now resigned his fellowship at Pembroke. He received the homage of another enthusiastic young foreigner, the Marquis de la Villevieille, who was learning English and translating his poems into French. Then he went northwards to stay with Mason, and urged Nicholls to come too. 'You will meet me at Cambridge and we pursue our way together, trees blooming and nightingales singing all round us.'[29] Assuredly he was recovering his spirits once more; but he was worried about his neglected professorial duties, told Mason again of his intention to resign, and would scarcely listen to his arguments against such a course.[30] It is probable that Wharton came over to Aston during the fortnight that Gray was there, and thus the two old friends met for the last time.

In July he went for a tour, with Nicholls as his companion, through a part of England which he had never seen, 'five of the most beautiful counties in the kingdom'—Worcestershire, Shropshire, Herefordshire, Monmouthshire and Gloucestershire. On this occasion Nicholls kept the journal, which has not survived; and only a few sentences, in Gray's letters to Wharton and Mason, record the unclouded pleasure which he took in the last tour of his life. He saw the three cathedrals, the castles of Ludlow and Raglan, the park at Hagley, the little domain created by Shenstone at the Leasowes, the glorious views from the Malvern hills; but above all he delighted in the long descent of the Wye by boat from Ross to Chepstow, 'the chief grace and ornament of my journey', with Tintern Abbey and the famous woods at Percefield and the exquisite vale of Monmouth. On their way homewards he paid the only visit of his life to Oxford. Throughout the tour the weather was warm and serene, and his golden mood persisted even when the sociable Nicholls met some friends at Malvern, and persuaded him to stay there for a week in the mixed and uncongenial society of a fashionable watering-place.[31]

He had complained of headaches and threatenings of gout earlier in the year; and although his summer travels had their usual beneficial effect on his health, the improvement did not last for long. Soon after his return to Cambridge he was taken ill with a feverish disorder, which he overcame with copious draughts of sage tea. Then he was confined to his rooms for three weeks with a severe attack of gout. As soon as he could hobble about without assistance he went for a drive to the Gog Magog Hills, and caught a cold and cough which lingered depressingly for weeks. He exchanged condolences with Walpole on the subject of gout, their common affliction. It was usual to console people afflicted with the gout by describing it as an earnest of long life, and both Walpole and Gray had to suffer this platitude from well-intentioned friends.[32]

The new term brought to Cambridge two young men who were both destined to live far into the next century, longer even than Bonstetten, and are supposed to have been the last survivors of those who were personally acquainted with Gray. One was Lord George Cavendish, another nephew of Lord John's, who first entered at Trinity this autumn. The other was Alleyne Fitzherbert, the son of a Derbyshire gentleman, who came as a pensioner to St John's. Gray called upon him at the request of Mason, whom he told afterwards that 'the little Fitzherbert seems to have all his wits about him'.[33] Many years later Fitzherbert, now Lord St Helens and a well-known diplomatist, gave an account of this call to Samuel Rogers. Gray, he is alleged to have said, 'was accompanied by Dr Gisborne, Mr Stonhewer and Mr Palgrave, and they walked one after one, in Indian file. When they withdrew, every College man took off his cap as he passed, a considerable number having assembled in the quadrangle to see Mr Gray, who was seldom seen. I asked Mr Gray, to the great dismay of his companions, what he thought of Mr Garrick's *Jubilee Ode*, just published? He answered, "He was easily pleased".'[34] It makes an amusing story; but like the majority of Rogers's anecdotes about Gray and indeed about most other people, it must have been considerably embroidered by that incorrigible old gossip. There is no suggestion elsewhere that Gray moved about Cambridge in this ceremonial manner, or that his presence in any other college aroused the smallest curiosity. Of his three alleged attendants, Palgrave was a clergyman in Suffolk, Stonhewer deeply engaged in political life, and Gisborne, although a Fellow of St John's, a successful physician who spent more of his time in London than in Cambridge and was never an intimate friend of Gray. Garrick's *Jubilee Ode*, moreover, had appeared more than a year before, and was no longer a topic of conversation among intelligent undergraduates.

In December the Master of Pembroke, Roger Long, died at the age of ninety. For more than twenty years James Brown had been President, and latterly he had been the leading influence in all college affairs. He was now elected Master, to the great satisfaction of Gray and all his friends, on the night of Long's funeral. The late Master's eccentricities lent an unexpected touch of the macabre to the funeral itself. A leakage from the pool in his garden, round which in more active days he used to paddle on his velocipede, had trickled into the vault below the chapel; and the coffin, with verses composed by members of the college pinned to its pall, had to be lowered into a foot of water. Cole, who attended the funeral, was greatly shocked by this and other irregularities of procedure. Next day he wrote to Gray and commented on the 'unceremonious and indecent manner' in which the college had conducted the affair; to which Gray blithely replied—'How did we know, pray? No Body here remember'd another Burying of the kind: shall be proud of your Advice the next opportunity, which (we hope) will be some Forty years hence.'[35] It gave him great pleasure to watch the new Master's assumption of his dignities. 'The old Lodge', he wrote, 'has got rid of all its harpsichords and begins to brighten up: its inhabitant is lost like a Mouse in an old cheese.'[36]

V

By this time Bonstetten had returned home to Berne, and Nicholls was eagerly looking forward to the journey to Switzerland which he and Gray were to make later in the year. Gray was unwilling to disillusion him for the present, but it is improbable that at heart he ever supposed he could undertake it. A wet and stormy winter was followed by a cold late spring; he could not get rid of his cough, and never felt in full health or spirits. Moreover, the letters from Bonstetten, which he had once awaited with such eagerness, were growing so affected and capricious as to be downright tiresome; and when the much desired portrait, for which he had promised to sit in Paris, at last arrived, it proved a disappointment. It was 'no more like

than I to Hercules: you would think, it was intended for his
Father, so grave and so composed: doubtless he meant to look
like an Englishman or an owl'.[37]

The weeks passed, and Nicholls still awaited Gray's
decision. Bonstetten had written again, begging them to come
à deux genoux, promising that if they came he would revisit
England the summer after. 'Let us go then, my dear Mr Gray',
exclaimed Nicholls, 'and leave low thoughted care at the foot of
the mountains, for the air above is too pure for it.'[38] Gray still
hesitated, and his doubts were not removed by a particularly
exasperating letter which he received from Bonstetten at the
beginning of May:

I hardly know how to give you any account of it [he told
Nicholls] and desire you would not speak of it to any body. That
he has been *le plus malheureux des hommes*, that he is *decidé à quitter
son pays*, that is, to pass the next winter in England: that he cannot
bear *la morgue de l'aristocratie, et l'orgueil armé des loix*, in short,
strong expressions of uneasiness and confusion of mind, so much as
to talk of *un pistolet et du courage*, and all without the shadow of a
reason assign'd, and so he leaves me. He is either disorder'd in his
intellect (which is too possible) or has done some strange thing,
that has exasperated his whole family and friends at home, which
(I'm afraid) is at least equally possible. I am quite at a loss about
it. You will see and know more: but by all means curb these vagaries
and wandering imaginations, if there be any room for counsels.

Depression, ill-health, and now this flood of nonsense from
Bonstetten—it was almost too much; and when Nicholls wrote
to seek advice about his friend Temple, who was quarrelling in
Devonshire with his wife and his patron, Gray replied with unaccustomed petulance. Had he not enough troubles of his own?[39]

In the middle of May he went up to London, and soon afterwards wrote to Nicholls that he could not possibly accompany
him. 'My sense of my own duty, which I do not perform, my
own low spirits (to which this consideration not a little con-
tributes) and (added to these) a bodily indisposition make it
necessary for me to deny myself that pleasure, which perhaps
I have kept too long in view. I shall see however with your

eyes, and accompany you at least in idea.' The same day he wrote to Wharton that he hoped to spend the summer with him at Old Park, 'for travel I must, or cease to exist. Till this year I hardly knew what (mechanical) low-spirits were: but now I even tremble at an east wind.'[40]

Nicholls was naturally disappointed. 'For God's sake', he wrote, 'how can you neglect a duty which never existed but in your own imagination, which catches every alarm too quickly? It never yet was performed, nor I believe expected.'[41] But he finally realised that he would have to travel alone. When they met for the last time in London, just before his departure in June, Gray said: 'I have one thing to beg of you, which you must not refuse....Do not go to see Voltaire.' Nicholls promised not to do so, but asked what a visit from him could possibly signify. 'Every tribute to such a man signifies', answered Gray. Later in the year Nicholls found himself staying within easy reach of Ferney, and was greatly tempted to pay his compliments to a figure of such universal renown; but he kept his promise to Gray.[42]

During those weeks Gray's illness steadily gained upon him. There were feverish symptoms and threatenings of gout, and another unspecified complaint for which he thought the attention of a surgeon would be required. Dr Gisborne advised him to go to Kensington for a change of air, and he spent a fortnight in lodgings at that pleasant village. On his return to London he saw Walpole, who was just about to leave for Paris. He talked of the gout flying about him, and of sensations of it in his stomach. Walpole thought him altered in appearance, but had no idea that he could be in any danger.[43] The late Sir Humphry Rolleston, after considering all the available evidence, concluded that Gray suffered from chronic kidney disease, which was now about to terminate in uraemia.* The pains in his feet were unquestionably gout in its true form; but the other symptoms,

* The correspondence between Sir Humphry Rolleston and Leonard Whibley on this subject is now at Pembroke College. Sir Humphry, in advancing his own theory, did not reject M. Roger Martin's alternative theory that Gray died from arterio-sclerosis (*Essai sur Thomas Gray*, 12).

to which the name of gout was also given, probably resulted from this affection of the kidneys.[44]

Gray was anxious to get back to Cambridge, but did not feel well enough to do so until far into July. He often saw Stonhewer and others of his friends, and one day received a call from a lieutenant of marines named John Clarke, a friend of Nicholls and Temple. A letter from Clarke to Temple describing this call, written after Gray's death, reveals the impression that he could still make, despite his illness and despondency, upon a stranger. 'As much as I admired the man for his Genius, so much more did I adore him when I saw him for his benevolence and humanity which I never saw so strong in any body in my Life. It shined out in every word, look, and motion.'[45]

VI

Gray returned to Cambridge on 22 July. Two days later he was suddenly taken ill at dinner in the college hall, and was helped up to his rooms close by. The doctors thought he was suffering from gout in the stomach, and no one was at first greatly alarmed. But Gray thought differently. Several times he said to Mary Antrobus, who had come to help his servant Stephen Hempstead to nurse him, 'Molly, I shall die'. Before long everyone realised that he was gravely ill. As always in cases of uraemia, there were frequent convulsive fits and periods of delirium, in the intervals of which he was composed and firm. At these times he was sensible, Brown thought, of his approaching death, 'nor hath he expressed any Concern at the thoughts of leaving this world'. During his last hours he seemed to be past the sense of pain, and remained unconscious till he died at eleven o'clock on the night of 30 July. Four days later he was buried, as he had directed in his will, beside his mother in the vault beneath her tomb in the churchyard at Stoke Poges.[40]

CHAPTER XIII

CONCLUSION

I

THE news of Gray's illness and death came as a complete surprise to his friends. Stonhewer had hastened down from London and seen him before he died; but Mason was away from home, and could not reach Cambridge in time to accompany Brown, who had been appointed executor with him, on that last mournful journey to Stoke Poges. Walpole was in Paris, and learnt of his friend's death by chance from a newspaper. 'I started up from my chair when I read the paragraph—a cannon-ball would not have surprised me more!' He wrote at once to Cole, begging him to confirm or deny the news; and if, as he feared, it was true, to send him the fullest details. 'Our long, very long friendship and his genius must endear to me everything that relates to him.'[1]

Nicholls and Bonstetten were together in Switzerland, staying at a *château* near Lausanne; but at the moment when the news arrived, Bonstetten happened to be away for a day or two, and Nicholls had to bear his loss alone. He poured out his feelings in a heartbroken letter to his mother:

Afflicted you may be sure I am! you who know that I considered Mr Gray as a second parent, that I thought only of him, built all my happiness on him, talked of him for ever, wished him with me whenever I partook of any pleasure, and flew to him for refuge whenever I felt any uneasiness; to whom now shall I talk of all I have seen here? Who will teach me to read, to think, to feel? I protest to you, that whatever I did or thought had a reference to him. 'Mr Gray will be pleased with this when I tell him. I must ask Mr Gray what he thinks of such a person or thing. He would like such a person or dislike such another.' If I met with any chagrins, I comforted myself that I had a treasure at home; if all the world had despised and hated me, I should have thought myself perfectly recompensed in his friendship.[2]

Bonstetten's sorrow at the news must be imagined. 'I am the more alarmed for him', wrote Nicholls. 'His temper is lively and his passions violent.' Throughout his long and eventful life, as writer, philosopher, politician, traveller, he remembered those weeks at Cambridge and the long hours of talk in the quiet room at Pembroke. 'Qui occupe la chambre de Mr Gray?'[3] He was to live to the age of eighty-seven, active, intelligent, mercurial to the end. Byron in 1816 found him 'a fine and very lively old man'.[4] Sir Egerton Brydges, after his somewhat jaundiced fashion, recorded much the same impression:

He was a man of numerous accomplishments—brilliant, original, and enthusiastic—and of varied, though light, erudition. He was talkative and conceited; but amusing, and, in the common sense, amiable. An absolute model of gallantry, he always paid compliments to the youngest belle in the room, even to his last days. He was a lively little man, with smooth, round, blooming cheeks, who betrayed in conversation none of the enthusiasm he discovered in his writings, and also seemed to me to have the silly pride of wishing in company to appear a man of the world.[5]

No one ever had much success in pleasing Brydges; and his picture of Bonstetten's foibles may perhaps be discounted when it is remembered that in the year before his death this frivolous old creature set down those moving reminiscences of Gray which have already been quoted in full.

II

Gray had drawn up his last will with the care and thought which he bestowed upon all his private affairs, and had signed it just a year before his death. Stonhewer and Wharton, together with the two Antrobus sisters and some more distant relations on his father's side, received substantial bequests.*

* The specific money legacies amounted to nearly £4000. This was of course exclusive of the residue, which must have been fairly substantial, since £200 of it was to be applied to a private use of charity (see p. 148); and

The faithful Stephen Hempstead was not forgotten. He was now so established a figure at Pembroke that he entered the service of the college, and in due course succeeded the learned Richard Dunthorne as its butler. Mason and Brown, 'whose integrity and kindness I have so long experienced, and who can best judge of my true intention and meaning', were the executors and the residuary legatees; and to Mason were also left 'all my books, manuscripts, coins, musick printed or written, and papers of all kinds to preserve or destroy at his own discretion'.[6]

Mason's interpretation of this trust has been much criticised by later writers. He produced in 1775 his *Memoirs of Gray*, together with a new edition of the poems. The *Memoirs* were largely built up from Gray's letters, and liberties were taken with their text which would now be regarded as unpardonable. Mason thought fit to transpose, to garble and to paraphrase even the letters which had been lent to him by Wharton and Nicholls; and many of those which had passed under Gray's will into his own possession he subsequently destroyed, so that nothing now remains of them beyond the portions which he quoted in the *Memoirs*. It is exasperating to think that owing to Mason we shall never read Gray's letters to his mother from Eton and Cambridge, or more of those admirable descriptions of his travels which he sent to both his parents, or—saddest loss of all—his full correspondence with West.

Nevertheless, Mason was entitled by the terms of Gray's will do to as he thought best. He had been given absolute discretion in the use of his papers. The *Memoirs* were a carefully composed portrait, designed to show Gray as scholar and poet, as 'a virtuous, a friendly, and an amiable man'.[7] With all his shortcomings, Mason was a devoted and most trustworthy friend. He was not going to print, less than four years after Gray's death, the passages in his letters which reflected upon

exclusive also of the valuable house in Cornhill, which was left to Mary Antrobus. Gray had sold his other house properties, both in London and in Essex, some years earlier.

living people; nor, indeed, much of the badinage and nonsense which had been intended solely for private amusement. Still less did he propose to draw attention to the peculiarities which had brought ridicule upon the poet during his life, and which malicious gossip was only too ready to magnify after its close.[8] It was no part of his design to recall its less dignified passages—the precise circumstances, for example, of his flight from Peterhouse. 'I would be as wary as the Church of Rome is before they canonize a saint', Walpole had written.[9] Mason scarcely needed such advice. His judgement may in some respects be open to question; but no man is to be condemned for loyalty to the memory of his friend.

III

During the few days of Gray's last illness, and the weeks following his death, James Brown corresponded regularly with his more distant friends such as Wharton and Nicholls. These letters, in their combination of the deepest feeling with a punctilious and thoughtful attention to business details, bear out the impression derived from Gray's many grateful references to this admirable man.

Everything is now dark and melancholly at Mr Gray's Room [he had written sadly to Wharton]. Not a trace of him remains there, it looks as if it had been for some time uninhabited and the room bespoke for another inhabitant.... The thoughts I have of him will last, and will be useful to me the few years I can expect to live. He never spoke out, but I believe from some little expressions I now remember to have dropt from him that for some time past he thought himself nearer his end than those about him apprehended it.[10]

He never spoke out. Brown, of course, meant by this phrase exactly what he said—that Gray never told his friends that he believed his death was near. But the words were taken out of their context by Matthew Arnold, and used as the theme of his essay on the poet and his works.[11] 'Let us dwell upon them, and press into their meaning', wrote Arnold, 'for in following it we shall come to understand Gray.' Then the famous argument unfolds—that Gray fell upon an age of prose, when 'a sort of spiritual east wind was blowing', under whose influence his genius could not flower; that he would have been 'another man' if he had been born in the same year as Milton, when the spirit of the Elizabethan age still lived on, or in the same year as Burns, when he could have enjoyed the advantage of witnessing the French Revolution.

I hope it may have seemed to readers of this biography that in his earlier and more subjective poems, and still more in his letters, Gray spoke out both frequently and clearly. I have refrained throughout from introducing the terms or the conclusions of psycho-analysis, because I regard it as no part of a biographer's duty to carry speculation beyond the evidence; but I cannot feel there is likely to be wide agreement nowadays with Arnold's view that Gray would have been a different sort of man if he had lived in a different period of history. As he was aware from his early years, there were deep-seated differences of temperament between himself and the majority of other men. There was the further handicap of indifferent physical health; there was the lifelong melancholy whose workings he understood so well.

> To each his suff'rings: all are men,
> Condemn'd alike to groan....

There would have been no remedy for Gray's particular sufferings in the spiritual climate of any other age.

He was on the whole indifferent to fame; yet he once wrote that 'I love People, that leave some traces of their journey behind them'.[12] In this book I have followed him year by year along the course of his own journey. I have done my best to record it without exaggerating his merits or his frailties, and always remembering where 'in trembling hope' he had wished them to repose. A man is as he is made; and the contrast between the magnanimous eloquence of the *Elegy*, and the anxieties and affectations of 'delicate Mr Gray', is the range of our human condition.

THE COMPOSITION OF
THE 'ELEGY'

THERE have always been conflicting opinions as to the dates, and indeed the whole process of composition, of Gray's *Elegy*. We only know that he completed it in the early summer of 1750. He wrote to Walpole on 12 June of that year: 'Having put an end to a thing, whose beginning you have seen long ago, I immediately send it you.' But there is nothing to tell us the date of the 'beginning', or the date when he showed or sent that 'beginning' to his friend.

Mason wrote in his *Memoirs of Gray* when speaking of the summer of 1742: 'I am inclined to believe that the Elegy in a Country Church-yard was begun, if not concluded, at this time also.' At first Walpole had disagreed with this date. He wrote to Mason, when the *Memoirs* were in the course of preparation, that 'The *Churchyard* was, I am persuaded, posterior to West's death [in 1742] at least three or four years.... At least I am sure that I had the twelve or more first lines from himself above three years after that period, and it was long before he finished it' (Walpole to Mason, 1 December 1773). Mason replied in a letter which is now lost, and Walpole in his rejoinder wrote: 'Your account of the *Elegy* puts an end to my other criticism'—words which seem to imply that he accepted whatever else Mason may have said as to the date of the *Elegy* (Walpole to Mason, 14 December 1773).

If Gray had written the opening lines, or even the whole poem, in the summer of 1742, during the surge of creative activity which followed West's death, it is nevertheless perfectly understandable that nothing was shown to Walpole for 'above three years after that period'. The reconciliation between the two friends, who had quarrelled so violently in Italy in the spring of 1741, did not take place until November 1745. In any case Gray was a little chary of showing Walpole the poems which he had composed during the period of their estrangement. He seems to have allowed him to see the *Eton Ode* during the summer of 1764, and sent him the *Ode on the Spring* in October of that year; but the *Hymn to Adversity*, another composition of 1742, was not disclosed until 1751.

It was pointed out by Mason that Gray's original version of the *Elegy* was considerably shorter than the poem which he eventually printed. 'In the first manuscript copy of this exquisite Poem', he wrote, 'I find the conclusion different from that which he afterwards composed; and tho' his after-thought was unquestionably the best, yet there is a pathetic melancholy in the four rejected stanzas, which highly claims preservation.' The original version, in fact, consisted of the first eighteen stanzas and the four 'rejected stanzas', which I have given on pp. 99–100 from the Eton MS. 'And here', in Mason's words, 'the Poem was originally intended to conclude, before the happy idea of the hoary-headed Swain, &c. suggested itself to him.' Then, at some later date or dates, Gray added eleven more stanzas and the three stanzas of the Epitaph, incorporating certain lines and phrases from the four 'rejected stanzas', which otherwise disappeared.

In his *Note on the Composition of Gray's Elegy*, contributed to the *Essays on the Eighteenth Century presented to David Nichol Smith* (1945), Professor H.W. Garrod advanced a very interesting theory. Like other commentators he had been perplexed by the meagreness of the 'twelve or more first lines' which Walpole had received from Gray. Walpole's letter, like all his letters to Mason, is at present known only in a transcript by Mitford. Professor Garrod had observed that, exclusive of the four 'rejected stanzas', the earlier version of the *Elegy* consisted of eighteen stanzas or 72 lines. He suggested that if the original of Walpole's letter should ever come to light, we would find that he had written 'the 72 or more first lines', and that Mitford had misread '72'. as '12'. Thus, in his view, virtually the whole of the earlier version of the *Elegy*—72 or more lines—had been written between West's death in 1742 and the date, 'above three years after that period', when he first showed it to Walpole.

I differ with great hesitation from any view advanced by Professor Garrod; but I cannot help feeling that his theory is a little over-ingenious. I find it difficult to believe, in the first place, that when Gray wrote to Walpole about 'a thing whose beginning you have seen long ago', he was speaking of 72 or more lines as the 'beginning' of a poem which in its final form only extends to 128 lines.

Walpole, moreover, was not a modern textual critic. I feel confident that the idea of counting the lines of a long poem, the very conception of a poem as a thing consisting of a given number of lines, would never have occurred to him. 'Twelve or more', yes; he was accustomed to think in round numbers. But '72 or more'— that is surely very unlike the processes of his thought as recorded in the many thousands of his letters.

Finally, we know that when Walpole received the completed *Elegy* in 1750 he was quite unable to keep such a treasure to himself. He admired it so much that, against Gray's wishes, he gave copies to his friends; and these were copied in their turn, so that in two months the poem had reached Lady Cobham at Stoke, and in eight months it had got into the hands of the proprietors of a piratical magazine. If in 1746 or thereabouts he had received a version of the *Elegy* complete or almost complete in itself, its '72 or more lines' including many of the finest stanzas and most memorable lines in the poem, he could hardly have kept absolute silence about it for a few months, still less for four whole years.

To sum up—we may, I think, accept Mason's statement that the *Elegy* was begun in 1742, soon after West's death and as a direct result of it. But I think also that it was only a beginning, and that Walpole's recollection of being shown 'twelve or more first lines', soon after his reconciliation with Gray, is likely to have been correct. Professor Garrod's emendation to '72 or more first lines', implying that the earlier version of the *Elegy* was virtually completed by 1746, cannot be accepted without some contemporary evidence; and there is no such evidence, in Gray's own letters or elsewhere, that throws the smallest light upon the progress of the composition of the *Elegy*, until that day in the summer of 1750 when he despatched it to Walpole in its completed form.

NOTE. Since writing the above, I find that I am supported in my views by the editors of the Yale Edition of Horace Walpole's *Correspondence*, in their forthcoming volumes containing the letters between Walpole and Mason. Their note to the relevant passage in Walpole's letter of 1 December 1773 reads as follows: 'Professor Garrod...suggests that HW wrote '72' and that Mitford transcribed it '12' in error. We believe HW wrote 12: Mitford was not an impeccable transcriber, but HW's 1's and 7's are not at all similar, and it would have been unlike HW to count out the number of lines Gray sent him, or, if he had, to remember the total for a quarter of a century.'

A NOTE ON THE ILLUSTRATIONS

THE portrait of GRAY in boyhood (facing p. 8) has been discussed on pages 7–8, and the portrait in a Van Dyck dress by Eckhardt (facing p. 88) on pages 87–8. Gray did not sit to a painter again; and the only representations of him in later life, apart from certain amateur sketches and silhouettes of little value, are the portraits by Benjamin Wilson which were executed after his death.

Nevertheless I think Wilson's portraits may be accepted as reasonably good likenesses of Gray. They were based to some extent on sketches by Mason; but it seems probable that Wilson himself had seen Gray, if only when he was in Cambridge in 1770 painting the portrait of ROGER LONG, an engraving of which is reproduced in this book (facing p. 84). This view is supported by the wording of the inscription, *W. Mason & B. Wilson vivi memores delineavere*, on the engraving prefixed to Mason's *Memoirs of Gray* (1775). And Stonhewer, when bequeathing one of these portraits to Pembroke College, described it as 'the Picture of the late Thos. Gray Esqr. drawn from memory by Mr Benjamin Wilson'.

The portrait bequeathed to the college by Stonhewer shows Gray in profile, and bears a fairly close resemblance to the engraving in Mason's *Memoirs*. Two other versions of this profile portrait exist. The portrait belonging to Sir John Murray, which I have reproduced as the frontispiece to this book, shows him not in profile but almost in full face. The expression is more genial than that of the profile portraits, which have something of the 'blackness' and 'primness' to which some of his friends objected in the engraving. It depicts very clearly his physical characteristics in later life, the tendency to stoutness which was remarked by Cole and others, the brightness of the eyes upon which Nicholls often commented.

The pastel by Rosalba of HORACE WALPOLE (facing p. 44) was drawn during his stay in Venice in 1741, shortly after the quarrel with Gray. He is in masquerade dress; the nose and eyehole of the mask will be noticed just below his hat.

By an odd coincidence the only extant painting of BONSTETTEN as a young man (facing p. 250) also shows him in masquerade dress. This is not the painting which he sent to Gray from Paris (see p. 262), the whereabouts of which is unknown.

There is unfortunately no picture of HENRIETTA SPEED in her younger days. The portrait by Falconet (facing p. 214) suggests the corpulence of her later years. It must have been painted some years after her marriage, and presumably not earlier than 1766, when Falconet first came to England. It was painted for her friend the second Earl Harcourt (see p. 173), by whom the portrait of MASON (facing p. 188) was likewise commissioned from the same artist.

BIBLIOGRAPHY

[NOTE. The abbreviations in square brackets, at the end of certain items, are used to refer to those items in the notes. The place of publication is London, unless otherwise stated.]

I. CORRESPONDENCE

For the text of Gray's letters, and of letters addressed to him, I have in all cases used *The Correspondence of Thomas Gray*, edited by Paget Toynbee and Leonard Whibley (3 vols., Oxford, 1935) [*Corr.*]. I have preserved Gray's spelling, but have lengthened his contractions and abbreviations, and have ignored his habit of beginning sentences with a small letter. I have also made a few other minor adjustments for the reader's convenience.

When quoting from Walpole's letters, I have used as far as possible the Yale Edition of Horace Walpole's *Correspondence*, edited by W. S. Lewis, initiated in 1937 and still in progress [*Walpole* (Yale Edition)]. Where a particular letter has not yet appeared in that edition, I have used *The Letters of Horace Walpole*, edited by Mrs Paget Toynbee (16 vols., Oxford, 1903–5) and the supplements edited by Dr Paget Toynbee (3 vols., Oxford, 1918 and 1925) [*Walpole* (ed. Toynbee)].

A few references have also been made to:

The Correspondence of Gray, Walpole, West and Ashton, ed. Paget Toynbee (2 vols., Oxford, 1915) [*G.W.W.A.*].

The Correspondence of Horace Walpole and William Mason, ed. Rev. John Mitford (2 vols., 1851) [*Walpole-Mason*].

The Correspondence of Thomas Gray and William Mason, ed. Rev. John Mitford (1853) [*Gray-Mason*].

It would be ungrateful not to mention the edition of Gray's *Letters* by Duncan C. Tovey (3 vols., 1900–12). Although it is now superseded by the Toynbee-Whibley edition, its vigorous introductions and excellent footnotes may still be read with profit.

II. EDITIONS OF GRAY'S WORKS

Quotations from Gray's poems have in almost all cases been taken from the Oxford Standard Authors edition by Austin Lane Poole, revised by Leonard Whibley (1937). This edition reproduces the text of *Poems by Mr Gray* (1768), the last collection printed in Gray's lifetime and supervised by him; and it reproduces also his approved text of such poems as *A Long Story* and the *Installation Ode*, which did not appear in the 1768 edition. In certain cases of poems which were not printed until after Gray's death, there are variant texts. Here also I have usually followed the Poole-Whibley text; but I have preferred to quote the *Sonnet on the Death of Richard West* and the *Alliance of Education and Government* as they appear in Mason's *Memoirs of Gray*, and the lines on Lord Holland's house from the copy in Wharton's handwriting in the British Museum.

When discussing the *Elegy* I have found myself much indebted to the edition by F. G. Stokes (Oxford, 1929).

In my quotations from Gray's Latin poems I have adopted certain textual emendations suggested by Mr John Sparrow in his *Poems in Latin* (Oxford, 1941).

I have also made some use of the following editions of Gray's works:

The Works of Thomas Gray, ed. Thomas James Mathias (2 vols., 1814) [*Works* (ed. Mathias)].

The Works of Thomas Gray, ed. Rev. John Mitford (2 vols., 1816) [Mitford (1816)].

The Works of Thomas Gray, ed. Rev. John Mitford (4 vols., Pickering's Aldine Edition, 1835–6). A fifth volume, containing the correspondence between Gray and Nicholls, was added in 1843 [*Works* (ed. Mitford)].

Gray's Poetical Works...with...an original Life of Gray by the Rev. John Mitford (Eton, 1847) [Mitford (1847)].

The Works of Thomas Gray, ed. Edmund Gosse (rev. ed., 4 vols., 1902) [*Works* (ed. Gosse)].

III. BIOGRAPHIES

The authorised biography of Gray was Mason's *Memoirs of the Life and Writings of Mr Gray* (York, 1775), prefixed to a new edition of his *Poems* [Mason].

Mitford prefixed memoirs of Gray to the various editions of his *Works* enumerated in the preceding section. Occasional reference has been made to these in the notes.

Sir Edmund Gosse's volume on Gray in the English Men of Letters Series was first published in 1882.

Some new biographical material was printed by D. C. Tovey in *Gray and his Friends: Letters and Relics* (Cambridge, 1890) [Tovey].

Two important works by M. Roger Martin, *Essai sur Thomas Gray* and *Chronologie de la Vie et de l'Œuvre de Thomas Gray*, were published at Paris in 1934 [Martin, *Essai*; Martin, *Chronologie*].

The most recent biographical study of Gray is that by Lord David Cecil in *Two Quiet Lives* (1948).

On one particular aspect of Gray, his depth and range of scholarship, the volume *Thomas Gray, Scholar*, by Mr W. Powell Jones (Harvard, 1937) is of great value, and I gladly acknowledge my debt to it [Powell Jones].

IV. CRITICISM

No full-scale critical work on Gray's poetry has yet appeared. Matthew Arnold's chapter in *Essays in Criticism* (Second Series, 1888) will always arouse admiration and disagreement. Lord David Cecil's Warton Lecture for 1945, *The Poetry of Thomas Gray* (reprinted in *Poets and Story-Tellers*, 1949), is full of penetrating observations; and there is an interesting survey of Gray's poetry in the first chapter of Mr Graham Hough's *The Romantic Poets* (1953). Otherwise recent criticism seems to have been virtually confined to the *Elegy*. I would mention in particular the chapters on the *Elegy* in *The Well Wrought Urn*, by Cleanth Brooks (English edition 1949), and *English Poetry: a Critical Introduction*, by F. W. Bateson (1950), although I cannot agree with some of the views expressed by Mr Bateson. I must also record my dissent from several of the conclusions in the remarkable article by Mr F. H. Ellis, 'Gray's *Elegy*: the Biographical Problem in Literary Criticism', in the *Proceedings of the Modern Languages Association* for 1951.

I have discussed in Appendix A the *Note on the Composition of Gray's Elegy* by Professor H. W. Garrod in the *Essays on the Eighteenth Century presented to David Nichol Smith* (Oxford, 1945).

V. GENERAL

The following works are amongst those quoted or consulted:

Attwater, Aubrey, *Pembroke College, Cambridge: a Short History* (Cambridge, 1936) [Attwater].

Austen Leigh, R. A., *Eton College Lists, 1678–1790* (1907).

Bell, C. F., 'Thomas Gray and the Fine Arts', in *Essays and Studies by Members of the English Association*, vol. xxx (1945).

Bickham, George, *Deliciae Britannicae; or, The Curiosities of Hampton-Court and Windsor-Castle, delineated* (1742).

Bonstetten, Charles-Victor de, *Souvenirs, écrits en 1831* (2nd edition, Paris, 1833) [Bonstetten, *Souvenirs*].

Boswell, James, *Life of Johnson*, ed. George Birkbeck Hill, rev. L. F. Powell (6 vols., Oxford, 1934–50) [*Boswell's Life of Johnson*].

Boswell, James, *Boswell's London Journal, 1762–1763*, ed. Frederick A. Pottle (1950) [*Boswell's London Journal*].

Boswell, James, *Boswell in Holland, 1763–1764*, ed. Frederick A. Pottle (1952) [*Boswell in Holland*].

Brydges, Sir Samuel Egerton, *Autobiography* (4 vols., 1854) [Brydges].

Byron, *Letters and Journals* (ed. R. E. Prothero), 6 vols., 1898–9.

Campbell, Archibald, *The Sale of Authors, a Dialogue* (1767).

Carlyle, Alexander, *Autobiography*, ed. J. H. Burton (1910).

Chute, Chaloner W., *A History of The Vyne in Hampshire* (1888).

Clark, Kenneth, *The Gothic Revival* (1929).

Cole, William, *The Blecheley Diary*, ed. F. G. Stokes (1931).

Colman, George and Lloyd, Robert, *Two Odes* (1760).

Cradock, Joseph, *Literary and Miscellaneous Memoirs* (4 vols., 1828) [Cradock].

Cumberland, Richard, *Memoirs* (1807).

Bibliography

d'Arblay, Madame, *Memoirs of Doctor Burney* (3 vols., 1832).

Delany, Mrs, *Autobiography and Correspondence* (ed. Lady Llanover, 6 vols., 1861–2).

Dodsley, Robert (ed.), *A Collection of Poems* (6 vols., 1748–58).

Draper, John W., *William Mason: a Study in Eighteenth-Century Culture* (New York, 1924).

Evans, A. W., *Warburton and the Warburtonians* (1932).

Evans, Rev. Evan, *Some Specimens of the Poetry of the Antient Welsh Bards* (1764).

Facetiae Cantabrigienses (3rd ed., 1838).

Forbes, Sir William, *An Account of the Life and Writings of James Beattie* (2 vols., 1824) [Forbes].

Garrick, David, *Correspondence* (2 vols., 1831).

Gentleman's Magazine, The (various dates).

Green, Matthew, *The Spleen, and other Poems*, ed. J. Aikin (1796).

Gutch, Rev. John, *Collectanea Curiosa* (2 vols., Oxford, 1781).

Harcourt Papers, The, ed. Edward William Harcourt (14 vols., privately printed, n.d.).

Hazen, A. T., *Bibliography of the Strawberry Hill Press* (Yale, 1942).

Herking, Marie-L., *Charles-Victor de Bonstetten, sa vie, ses œuvres* (Lausanne, 1921) [Herking].

Hume, David, *Letters*, ed. J. Y. T. Greig (2 vols., Oxford, 1932).

Hurd, Richard and Mason, William, *Correspondence*, ed. Leonard Whibley (Cambridge, 1932).

Ilchester, Earl of, *Henry Fox, first Lord Holland* (2 vols., 1920).

Jenkinson Papers, The, ed. Ninetta S. Jucker (1949).

Johnson, Samuel, *Lives of the English Poets*, ed. George Birkbeck Hill (3 vols., Oxford, 1905).

Junius, The Letters of (2 vols., 1794).

Kilvert, Rev. Francis, *Memoirs of the Life and Writings of the Right Rev. Richard Hurd, D.D., Lord Bishop of Worcester* (1860).

Macpherson, James, *The Poems of Ossian* (new edition, 1806).

Mason, William, *Works* (4 vols., 1811).

Maxwell Lyte, H. C., *A History of Eton College* (1877).

Nichols, John, *Literary Anecdotes of the Eighteenth Century* (9 vols., 1812–15) [Nichols, *Anecdotes*].

Nichols, John, *Illustrations of the Literary History of the Eighteenth Century* (8 vols., 1817–58) [Nichols, *Illustrations*].

Northup, C. S., *Bibliography of Thomas Gray* (Yale, 1917).

Norton, Charles Eliot, *The Poet Gray as a Naturalist* (Boston, 1903).

Polwhele, Rev. Richard, *Traditions and Recollections* (2 vols., 1826).

Roberts, S. C., *Thomas Gray of Pembroke* (W. P. Ker Memorial Lecture, Glasgow, 1952).

Rogers, Samuel, *Table Talk* (1856).

Rogers, Samuel, *Recollections* (1859).

Bibliography

Sainte-Beuve, C.-A., *Causeries du Lundi*, vol. xiv, 'Charles-Victor de Bonstetten'.

Scholes, Percy A., *The Great Doctor Burney* (2 vols., Oxford, 1948).

Shenstone, William, *Works* (2 vols., 1764).

Smart, Christopher, *Rejoice in the Lamb. A Song from Bedlam*, ed. William Force Stead (1939).

Smart, Christopher, *Jubilate Agno*, ed. W. H. Bond (1954).

Snyder, Edward D., *The Celtic Revival in English Literature, 1760–1800* (Harvard, 1923).

Sutherland, James, *A Preface to Eighteenth Century Poetry* (Oxford, 1948).

Temperley, H. W. V., *Two Legends connected with Thomas Gray*. Contributed to *In Memoriam Adolphus William Ward, Master of Peterhouse* (Cambridge, 1924).

Temple, William Johnston, *Diaries*, ed. Lewis Bettany (Oxford, 1929).

Tillotson, Geoffrey, *Essays in Criticism and Research* (Cambridge, 1942).

Tillotson, Geoffrey, *The Manner of Proceeding in certain eighteenth- and early nineteenth-century Poems* (Warton Lecture for 1948).

Walker, T. A., *Peterhouse* (new ed., Cambridge, 1935). [Walker.]

Walker, T. A., 'Thomas Gray at Peterhouse', article in *The Athenaeum* (20 January 1906).

Walpole, Horace, *Works of Horatio Walpole, Earl of Orford* (5 vols., 1798) [Walpole, *Works*].

Walpoliana, ed. John Pinkerton (2 vols., 1799).

Winstanley, D. A., *The University of Cambridge in the Eighteenth Century* (Cambridge, 1922).

Winstanley, D. A., *Unreformed Cambridge* (Cambridge, 1935).

NOTES

CHAPTER I

1. *Corr.* 1286 (Walpole's *Memoir of Gray*); Cole, B.M. Add. MS. 5833, f. 12.

2. Mason, 120n.

3. *Corr.* 1195–6 (*The Case submitted to Dr Audley*).

4. *Corr.* 1306–8 (*Genealogies*). See also a valuable article, 'Ancestry of Thomas Gray the poet', by C. H. Crouch, in *The Genealogists' Magazine*, III (1927), pp. 74–8.

5. Mason, 119; *Corr.* 1195–6.

6. Mason, 2–3.

7. *Corr.* 741 (Gray to Wharton, 23 June 1761).

8. *Corr.* 1287 (Walpole's *Memoir of Gray*).

9. *Gentleman's Magazine* (1846), i, 140–3; Mitford (1847), lx-lxvi.

10. *Corr.* 1290 (Norton Nicholls's *Reminiscences of Gray*). Bryant quoted the lines to Nicholls, and also repeated them in his own reminiscences of Gray.

11. Cole, quoted in *Works* (ed. Mitford), I, cv.

12. Mason, 3–4. *Corr.* 191 (Gray to West, 8 April 1741). Jacob Bryant, in *Gentleman's Magazine* (1846), i, 141.

13. *Walpole* (Yale Edition), IX, 3–4 (Walpole to Montagu, 6 May 1736).

14. See pp. 16–18.

15. See a letter from R. W. Ketton-Cremer in *Times Literary Supplement*, 28 October 1949.

16. *G.W.W.A.* I, 101–2 (West to Walpole, August 1736). For other details in this chapter, see also L. Whibley, "Thomas Gray at Eton", *Blackwood's Magazine*, MCCCLXIII (1929), pp. 611–23; and R. A. Austen Leigh, *Eton College Lists*, 22, 27, 30.

CHAPTER II

1. L. Whibley, 'Thomas Gray, Undergraduate', *Blackwood's Magazine*, MCCCLXII (1930), pp 273–86.

2. *Corr.* 4 (Gray to Walpole, 31 October 1734).

3. *Corr.* 4, n. 6 (quoted from T. A. Walker, 'Thomas Gray at Peterhouse', *Athenaeum*, 20 January 1906).

4. *Corr.* 3 (Gray to Walpole, 31 October 1734).

5. *Corr.* 23–4 (Gray to Walpole, 4 February 1735).

6. Whibley, 'Thomas Gray, Undergraduate'. The set was identified with a cross by Walpole on a print of Peterhouse, inserted in his own copy of Mason's *Memoirs of Gray*, now in the Harvard College Library. The print is reproduced opposite p. 98 of vol. XIII of the Yale edition of Walpole's *Correspondence*.

7. *Corr.* 7 (Gray to Walpole, 17 November 1734).

8. *Corr.* 4, n.7 (quoting Walker, 'Thomas Gray at Peterhouse').

9. *Corr.* 9–12, 14–16 (Gray to Walpole, 8 December 1734; 29 December 1734; 6 January 1735).

10. *Corr.* 29–33 (Walpole to Gray, *c.* 15 October 1735).

11. *Corr.* 16 (Gray to Walpole, 12 January 1735).

12. *Corr.* 22 (Gray to Walpole, 27 January 1735).

13. *G.W.W.A.* I, 50 (Walpole to West, 9 November 1735).

14. *G.W.W.A.* I, 48 (West to Walpole, 29 October 1735).

15. *Corr.* 34 (Gray to West, *c.* 20 December 1735). The original of this letter is missing, and Mason in his *Memoirs of Gray* garbled it and combined it with part of another letter: but it probably does not differ substantially from what Gray wrote.

16. *G.W.W.A.* I, xxxiii.

17. *Corr.* 1095–7. The case was discovered early in the nineteenth century in a volume of manuscript law cases, and was dated 'February 9th 1735'. I have accepted Whibley's view that 'it is probable that Audley, as he was writing a legal document, followed the old style, and that the year may be taken to have been 1735/6'. It is, however, conceivable that 1735 may be the correct date.

18. *Corr.* 1307; Whibley, 'Thomas Gray, Undergraduate'.

19. *Corr.* 4, n. 7.

20. Whibley, 'Thomas Gray, Undergraduate'.

21. Cole, quoted in *Works* (ed. Mitford), I, cv. Cole calls the house Cant's Hall, but the name 'Cant's Hill' still survives in Burnham.

22. *Corr.* 46–8 (Gray to Walpole, August 1736).

23. *Corr.* 52–4 (Gray to Birkett, Birkett to Gray; October 1735); Whibley, 'Thomas Gray, Undergraduate'.

24. *Corr.* 56 (Gray to West, December 1736).

25. *Corr.* 55 (Gray to Walpole, 27 October 1736).

26. Whibley, 'Thomas Gray, Undergraduate'.

27. For an excellent treatment of Gray's studies at this time, and a list of his books up to the year 1742 or thereabouts, see Powell Jones, 31–6, 151–7.

28. *Corr.* 1198–9 (*Gray's Tripos Verses*).

29. *Corr.* 56 (Gray to West, December 1736).

30. *Corr.* 66 (Gray to West, 22 August 1737).

31. *Corr.* 115 (Gray to Ashton, 25 August 1739).

32. *Corr.* 57 (West to Gray, 22 December 1736).

33. *Corr.* 85–7 (Gray to West, June 1738).

34. *Corr.* 82 (Gray to Walpole, 20 March 1738).

35. *Corr.* 1204–5 (*Gray's Legal Studies*).

36. *G.W.W.A.* I, 157 (Ashton to West, September 1737).

37. *Walpole* (ed. Toynbee), VIII, 247 (Walpole to Mason, 2 March 1773).

38. Gutch, *Collectanea Curiosa* (1781), II, 347–51. See also a letter from R. W. Ketton-Cremer in *Times Literary Supplement*, 29 March 1947.

39. *Corr.* 120 (West to Gray, 28 September 1739).

40. *Corr.* 82 (Gray to Walpole, 20 March 1738).

41. *Corr.* 80 (Gray to Walpole, 23 February 1738).

42. *Walpole* (ed. Toynbee), VIII, 362 (Walpole to Mason, 27 November 1773).

43. Pope, *The Dunciad*, Book IV, 297–306.

CHAPTER III

1. *Corr.* 99 (Gray to Mrs Gray, 1 April 1739).

2. *G.W.W.A.* I, 273–4 (Walpole to West, 24 January 1740).

3. *Corr.* 139 (Gray to Wharton, 12 March 1740).

4. *Corr.* 101–4 (Gray to West, 12 April 1739).

5. *Corr.* 105 (Gray to Ashton, 21 April 1739); *G.W.W.A.* I, 207–11 (Walpole to West, 21 April 1739).

6. *Corr.* 106–8 (Gray to West, 22 May 1739).

7. Letter from Gray to West, 22 May 1737, owned by Mr W. S. Lewis and first printed in *Times Literary Supplement*, 22 October 1937.

8. *Corr.* 105–6, 109–10 (Gray to Ashton, 21 April, 29 May 1739).

9. *Corr.* 109 (Gray to Ashton, 29 May 1739).

10. *Walpole* (ed. Toynbee), VIII, 302 (Walpole to Mason, 5 July 1773). Whibley assumed, I think correctly, that Gray's letter to West was written from Rheims; and he also suggested that 'easily' in Walpole's letter to Mason might be a misprint for 'early'.

11. *Corr.* 113–14 (Gray to Mrs Gray, 21 June 1739). Cf. *Works* (ed. Gosse), I, 238‾9, an extract from his journal with names of his acquaintances at Rheims.

12. *Corr.* 907 (Gray to Walpole, 13 December 1765).

13. *G.W.W.A.* I, 225 (Walpole to West, 18 June 1739).

14. *G.W.W.A.* I, 246–7 (Walpole to West, 28 September 1739).

15. *Corr.* 128 (Gray to West, 16 November 1739). Cf. *Corr.*121–3 (Gray to Mrs Gray, 13 October 1739) and *Works* (ed. Gosse), I, 244.

16. *Corr.* 124 (Gray to Philip Gray, 25 October 1739).

17. *Corr.* 125–9 (Gray to Mrs Gray, 7 November; to West, 16 November 1739); *G.W.W.A.* I, 254–6 (Walpole to West, 11 November 1739).

18. *Corr.* 129–31 (Gray to West, 21 November 1739).

19. Gray's notes on the paintings in the Pitti are printed in Tovey, 216–22. His notes on the sculpture in the Uffizi are contained in a notebook belonging to Sir John Murray, K.C.V.O., D.S.O., and are at present unpublished. An elaborate "Chronological List of Painters", with comments on their styles and details of their history, which he compiled when in Italy, was printed by Mason at the end of his translation of du Fresnoy's *Art of Painting* (1783). His views on Italian painting are admirably discussed by Mr C. F. Bell in 'Thomas Gray and the Fine Arts', *Essays and Studies by Members of the English Association*, xxx (1945), and it is with pleasure that I refer the reader to that masterly essay.

20. *Works* (ed. Mitford), IV, 231.

21. *G.W.W.A.* I, 273–4 (Walpole to West, 24 January 1740).

22. *G.W.W.A.* I, 266 (Walpole to West, from Bologna, 14 December 1739).

23. *G.W.W.A.* I, 277–9 (Walpole to West, 27 February 1740).

24. *G.W.W.A.* I, 276 (Walpole to West, 27 February 1740).

25. *Corr.* 146 (Gray to Mrs Gray, 2 April 1740).

26. Gray's notes taken in Rome were printed in *Works* (ed. Mitford), IV, 225–305.

27. *Corr.* 150, 155–8, 159–61 (Gray to West, 16 April, 20 May, –May 1740).

28. *G.W.W.A.* I, 283 (Walpole to West, 16 April 1740).

29. *G.W.W.A.*, I, 308 (Walpole to Ashton, 28 May 1740).

30. Tovey, 223–60.

31. *Corr.* 162–4 (Gray to Mrs Gray, 14 June 1740).

32. The researches of Dr George L. Lam have lately identified

the houses at Florence which were owned and occupied at various times by Mann. I am greatly indebted to Dr Lam for his help in this matter, especially as I have erroneously stated elsewhere, in common with all other writers on Gray and Walpole, that they stayed at Casa Manetti.

33. *Corr.* I, 172 (Gray to West, 31 July 1740).

34. *G.W.W.A.* i. 326 (Walpole to West, 31 July 1740).

35. *Walpole* (ed. Toynbee), I, 84–5 (Walpole to Conway, 25 September 1740).

36. *Walpole* (ed. Toynbee), VIII, 245 (Walpole to Mason, 2 March 1773).

37. *G.W.W.A.* I, 341 (Walpole to West, 2 October 1740).

38. *Corr.* 181–2 (Gray to West, 21 April 1741).

39. *Works* (ed. Mitford), II, 174.

40. See p. 74; and Tovey, 9.

41. Mann to Walpole, 23 May 1741 (MS. in the possession of Mr W. S. Lewis).

42. Mann to Walpole, undated: end of May 1741 (MS. in the possession of Mr W. S. Lewis).

43. Mann to Walpole, 10 June 1741 (MS. in the possession of Mr W. S. Lewis).

44. Mann to Walpole, 1 July 1741 (MS. in the possession of Mr W. S. Lewis).

45. Mason, 116–17.

CHAPTER IV

1. *Corr.* 186–7 (Gray to Chute, 7 September 1741).

2. Mason, 119.

3. *Corr.* 230 (Gray to Walpole, 3 February 1746).

4. See in particular West's letter of 5 June 1740, and Gray's reply of 16 July (*Corr.* 164–5, 167–70).

5. *Corr.* 1300 (Norton Nicholls's *Reminiscences of Gray*).

6. *Corr.* 192, 195 (Gray to West, 8 April 1742; West to Gray, 12 April 1742).

7. *Corr.* 190 (West to Gray, 4 April 1742).

8. *Corr.* 200–3 (West to Gray, 5 May; Gray to West, 8 May; West to Gray, 11 May 1742).

9. *Corr.* 213–14 (Gray to Ashton, 17 June 1742).

10. This endorsement appears upon Gray's transcript of the poem in his Commonplace Book (Pembroke MSS.).

Notes

11. *Corr.* 1300 (Norton Nicholls's *Reminiscences of Gray*).

12. It is not known how far Gray proceeded with *De Principiis Cogitandi*. The only portions which now survive are some two hundred lines of the First Book, and the passage quoted here, intended as the preface to the Fourth Book. The date of the latter passage is recorded in Gray's Commonplace Book at Pembroke.

13. This scene has not reached us in the form intended by Gray. It consisted mainly of a single speech by Agrippina, which Mason 'improved' in his *Memoirs of Gray* by breaking it up and giving portions to the confidante (Mason, 136 n.).

14. *Corr.* 299–301 (Gray to Walpole, January or February 1748). Gray has omitted one couplet in his quotation from Green's poem.

15. *Corr.* 209 (Gray to West, 27 May 1742).

16. *Corr.* 215–18 (Gray to Chute and Mann, July 1742).

17. *Corr.* 188 (Gray to West, *c.* 1 April 1742).

18. Cole, B.M. Add. MS. 5833, f. 13.

19. F. W. Bateson, *English Poetry: a Critical Introduction* (1950), 186, 188.

20. *Corr.* 215–16 (Gray to Chute, July 1742).

21. Mason, 120, 171; *Corr.* 1204–6 (*Gray's Legal Studies*).

CHAPTER V

1. Walker, 75–7.

2. *Corr.* 220 (Gray to Wharton, 27 December 1743), 1206–8 (*Gray's Legal Studies*).

3. *Corr.* 138–43 (Gray to Wharton, 12 March 1740).

4. *Corr.* 223 (Gray to Wharton, 26 April 1744).

5. *Corr.* 352 (Gray to Wharton, 10 October 1751).

6. *Corr.* 287 (Gray to Wharton, August 1747), 328 (Gray to Wharton, 9 August 1750); *Walpole* (Yale Edition), xv, 291–315 (*Anecdotes of Middleton* by Walpole and Cole).

7. *Corr.* 638, 648, 955 (Gray to Mary Antrobus, *c.* 12 September and 24 November 1759, May 1767); pocket-book of 1760.

8. Walker, 14.

9. Mason, 41 n. (quoting Walpole's letter of 2 March 1773). I am indebted to Mr W. S. Lewis for the information about Mrs Kerr.

10. *Corr.* 226–7 (Gray to Wharton, 14 November 1745).

11. *Corr.* 236–7 (Gray to Wharton, 10 August 1746).

12. *Corr.* 248 (Gray to Chute, 12 October 1746).

13. *Corr.* 237 (Gray to Wharton, 10 August 1746).

14. *Walpole* (ed. Toynbee), III, 2–3 (Walpole to Mann, 25 July 1750).

15. *Corr.* 250–2 (Gray to Walpole, 20 October 1746).

16. *Corr.* 238, 241 (Gray to Wharton, 10 August and 11 September 1746).

17. *Corr.* 326 (Gray to Walpole, 12 June 1750).

18. See p. 103.

19. *Corr.* 245–8 (Gray to Chute, 6 and 12 October 1746); 255 (Gray to Wharton, 11 December 1746).

20. *Corr.* 266 (Gray to Walpole, 8 February 1747).

21. *Corr.* 261 (Gray to Wharton, 27 December 1746).

22. *Corr.* 294–303 (Gray to Walpole, January or February 1748).

23. *Corr.* 307 (Gray to Wharton, 5 June 1748).

24. *Corr.* 323 (Gray to Wharton, 8 August 1749).

25. *Corr.* 302–3 (Gray to Walpole, January or February 1748).

26. *Corr.* 355 (Gray to Walpole, 26 November 1751).

27. B.M. Add. MS. 5868 f. 48.

28. *Gentleman's Magazine* (1786), I, 25. There are also references to Etough on pp. 96, 190 and 281 of this volume, the last being defence and vindication of him by a friend who signed himself 'D.M.'

29. The poem was first printed, with the omission of the third and fourth lines, in *Gentleman's Magazine* (1785), II, 759.

30. Attwater, 92.

31. Roberts, *Thomas Gray of Pembroke*, 12–15.

32. Mason, 172.

33. *Corr.* 315 (Gray to Wharton, 9 March 1749).

34. Attwater, 94–7. *Corr.* 1210–13 (*The Controversy between the Master of Pembroke Hall and his Fellows*).

35. *Corr.* 275–6 and notes (Gray to Wharton, 17 March 1747).

36. *Corr.* 806 (Gray to Wharton, 5 August 1763).

37. *Corr.* 274–5, 291–2 (Gray to Wharton, 17 March, 30 November 1747).

38. In his fable *The Brocaded Gown and Linen Rag*, first published in *Gentleman's Magazine* (1754), 89–90. The original version read 'all-accomplish'd Gray', for which 'great Augustan' was a later substitution.

39. *Facetiae Cantabrigienses* (1836), 90.

40. *Corr.* 303–6, 321 (Gray to Wharton, 5 June 1748, 25 April 1749).

41. *Corr.* 303–4 (Gray to Wharton, 5 June 1748).

42. Walpole, *Works* (1798), II, 436 (*Description of Strawberry Hill*).

43. *Walpole* (Yale Edition), IX, 72 (Walpole to Montagu, 11 August 1748).

44. *Walpole* (Yale Edition), IX, 76 (Walpole to Montagu, 3 September 1748).

45. Mason, 157.

46. *Corr.* 310 (Gray to Wharton, 19 August 1748).

47. Mason, 192.

48. *Corr.* 317 (Gray to Wharton, 9 March 1749).

49. *Corr.* 1291 (Norton Nicholls's *Reminiscences of Gray*).

50. Gibbon, *Decline and Fall* (ed. J. B. Bury), III, 332.

51. Rogers, *Recollections* (1859), 38.

52. *Corr.* 210 (Gray to West, 27 May 1742).

53. Substantial extracts from the Commonplace Books were printed in the second volume of Mathias's edition of his *Works* (1814), but otherwise they remain largely unpublished. There is an analytical table of their contents in Martin's *Chronologie de Thomas Gray* (134–47). Mr W. Powell Jones has based his book *Thomas Gray, Scholar* upon a close study of the Commonplace Books, with admirable results.

54. Powell Jones, 56–8; *Corr.* 276–7 (Gray to Wharton, 17 March 1747).

55. Mason, 335.

56. *Corr.* 259–60 (Gray to Wharton, 27 December 1746).

57. Mason, 205 n.; Powell Jones, 44, 55.

58. *Corr.* 520, 666, 677 (Gray to Hurd, 25 August 1757: to Wharton, 22 April and 20 June 1760).

59. *Corr.* 317–18 (Gray to Wharton, 25 April 1749).

CHAPTER VI

1. *Corr.* 326–7 (Gray to Walpole, 12 June 1750).

2. West's *Monody on the Death of Queen Caroline* (Dodsley's *Collection of Poems*, vol. II).

3. Johnson, *Lives of the Poets* (ed. Birkbeck Hill), III, 441.

4. The phrase is Tennyson's: see Johnson, *Lives of the Poets* (ed. Birkbeck Hill), III, 445. I owe this reference to Professor Geoffrey Tillotson.

5. The lines occur only in the Eton MS., and are quoted exactly as they appear in that text. They were also given, with punctuation

added and a single verbal alteration, by Mason in his 1775 edition of the *Poems*, p. 109.

6. In the first edition this line read:

'Awake, and faithful to her wonted Fires.'

The alteration was made in the eighth edition, printed in 1753, and in the edition with Bentley's illustrations in the same year.

7. Landor, in an undated letter to John Forster, spoke of 'the tin-kettle of an epitaph tied to the tail' of the *Elegy*. (Forster, *Life of Landor* (1876), 426.)

8. *Corr.* 355 (Gray to Wharton, 18 December 1750).

9. From a photostat of the original, now in the John Work Garrett Library at The Johns Hopkins University, Baltimore.

10. *Walpole* (ed. Toynbee), IX, 188 (Walpole to Mason, 25 April 1775).

11. From a photostat of the original, now in the John Work Garrett Library at The Johns Hopkins University, Baltimore.

12. *Corr.* 334–5 (Gray to Wharton, 18 December 1750).

13. *Corr.* 335 (Gray to Wharton, 18 December 1750).

14. *Corr.* 341 (Gray to Walpole, 11 February 1751).

15. *Corr.* 335 (Gray to Wharton, 18 December 1750).

16. *Corr.* 341–2 (Gray to Walpole, 11 February 1751).

17. *Walpole* (Yale edition), XV, 58 (Walpole to Dalrymple, 15 October 1759).

18. In the foregoing pages I have reproduced a few sentences from a broadcast talk of my own, 'How Gray's Elegy Came to be Published', printed in *The Listener*, 12 July 1951. I would like to repeat here my debt to the edition of the *Elegy* by the late F. G. Stokes (1929), with its most valuable bibliographical and historical introduction.

19. *Corr.* 342–3 (Gray to Walpole, 20 February 1751).

20. *Walpole* (ed. Toynbee), III, 166–8 (Walpole to Mann, 12 June 1753).

21. Walpole, *Works* (1798), II, 398 (*Description of Strawberry Hill*).

22. *Walpole* (Yale Edition, IX, 105 (Walpole to Montagu, 23 June 1750).

23. *Walpole* (Yale Edition), IX, 116 (Walpole to Montagu, 13 June 1751).

24. *Corr.* 347–8 (Gray to Walpole, 8 September 1751).

25. *Corr.* 362–3 (Gray to Walpole, 8 July 1752).
26. *Corr.* 371 (Gray to Dodsley, 12 February 1753).
27. *Corr.* 372 (Gray to Walpole, 13 February 1753).
28. *Corr.* 374 (Walpole to Gray, 20 February 1753).
29. Clark, *The Gothic Revival* (1929), 67.
30. *Thomas Gray and the Fine Arts*, 80.
31. *Memoirs of Richard Cumberland* (1807), I, 23.

CHAPTER VII

1. *The World*, nos. 22, 36.
2. Shenstone, *Works* (1764), II, 289.
3. The 1754 pocket-book is now in the Huntington Library, and was described by H. T. Swedenberg Jr. in the *Huntington Library Quarterly*, III (October 1939). The 1755 pocket-book is at Pembroke College. Its contents were printed in full in *Gentleman's Magazine* (1845), II, 229–33; and the Latin entries relating to Gray's health were reprinted in Martin, *Chronologie*, 151–5.
4. *Corr.* 430–1, 433–4 (Gray to Chute, 14 August; to Wharton, 21 August 1755).
5. See pp. 264–5.
6. *Corr.* 385–7 (Gray to Wharton, 18 October 1753).
7. *Walpole* (ed. Toynbee), III, 138 (Walpole to Mann, 11 December 1752). See also *Walpole* (Yale Edition, II, 370–2).
8. *Corr.* 316, 329 (Gray to Wharton, 9 March 1749, 9 August 1750).
9. *Corr.* 324 and n. 8 (Gray to Wharton, 8 August 1749).
10. Mason, *To a Young Nobleman leaving the University* (*Works*, I, 93–6).
11. *Corr.* 1302 (Norton Nicholls's *Reminiscences of Gray*).
12. *Corr.* 355–7 (Gray to Walpole, 26 November and 31 December 1751).
13. *Corr.* 379–80 (Gray to Brown, 24 July 1753).
14. *Corr.* 381 (Gray to Mason, 21 September 1753).
15. *Corr.* 385 (Gray to Wharton, 18 October 1753).
16. *Corr.* 385–6 (Gray to Wharton, 18 October 1753).
17. *Corr.* 446–7, 456 (Gray to Bedingfield, 25 December 1755; to Wharton, 9 January 1756).
18. Pocket-book of 1754.
19. *Corr.* 408–10 (Gray to Wharton, 18 September 1754).
20. *Corr.* 406–7 (Gray to Wharton, 18 September 1754).

21. *Corr.* 1287–8 (Walpole's *Memoir of Gray*).

22. *Corr.* 428 (Gray to Wharton, 6 August 1755).

23. *Corr.* 442 (Gray to Wharton, 18 October 1755).

24. *Corr.* 364 (Gray to Walpole, July 1752).

25. *Walpoliana* (1799), I, 27.

26. *Corr.* 364 (Gray to Wharton, July 1752).

27. *Corr.* 462 (Gray to Bedingfield, 29 April 1756).

28. *Corr.* 412–16 (Gray to Wharton, 26 December 1754).

29. Gray made some interesting technical comments on the writing of this ode in his letter to Wharton of 9 March 1755 (*Corr.* 420–1), which should be read in conjunction with the footnote (quoted there) from Mason, 233.

30. See p. 93.

31. Powell Jones, 64–5.

32. *Corr.* 1290 (Norton Nicholls's *Reminiscences of Gray*).

33. Johnson, *Lives of the Poets* (ed. Birkbeck Hill), III, 436–40.

34. *Corr.* 420 (Gray to Wharton, 9 March 1755).

35. Mason, 238.

36. Mason, 235. The 'memorandum-book of 1754', from which Mason copied the outline of this poem, has disappeared. It was different from the 1754 pocket-book mentioned on pp. 118–19.

37. *Corr.* 391–400 (Gray to Walpole, 3 March 1754).

38. The article *Cambri* is reproduced in full in Martin, *Chronologie*, 169–181; see also Powell Jones, 90–9.

39. Mason (*Notes on the Poems*), 91.

40. Mason, 233. *Corr.* 432–4 (Gray to Wharton and to Stonhewer, 21 August 1755).

41. Mason (*Notes on the Poems*), 91–2.

42. *Corr.* 501–3 (Gray to Mason, 24 or 31 May 1757).

43. Johnson, *Lives of the Poets* (ed. Birkbeck Hill), III, 438.

44. *Corr.* 457 (Gray to Wharton, 9 January 1756).

45. First printed in Nichols's *Illustrations*, VI, 805 (Rev. John Sharp to Rev. John Denne, 12 March 1756).

46. See the references to Gray in Sharp's letters to Garrick in 1769 (*Correspondence of David Garrick*, I, 334, 337, 339, 349).

47. See *Two Legends Connected with Thomas Gray* by H. W. V. Temperley in the Memorial Volume to Adolphus William Ward, Master of Peterhouse (Cambridge University Press, 1924), 104–11; and *Corr.* 1216–20 (*Gray's Removal from Peterhouse to Pembroke*).

48. *Corr.* 458 (Gray to Wharton, 25 March 1756).

Notes

CHAPTER VIII

1. *Corr.* 314 (Gray to Wharton, 9 March 1749).
2. *Corr.* 467–74 (Gray to Walpole, 30 July; to Mason, 30 July; to Walpole, 4 August 1756).
3. *Corr.* 468 (Gray to Walpole, 30 July 1756).
4. *Corr.* 260 (Gray to Wharton, 27 December 1746).
5. Roberts, *Thomas Gray of Pembroke*, 22.
6. *Corr.* 318, n. 3A.
7. *Corr.* 323–4 (Gray to Wharton, 8 August 1749).
8. Roberts, *Thomas Gray of Pembroke*, 21.
9. *Corr.* 421 (Gray to Wharton, 9 March 1755).
10. *Corr.* 716 (Gray to Mason, 10 December 1760).
11. Attwater, 100–1; Roberts, *Thomas Gray of Pembroke*, 13, 14; *D.N.B. sub* 'Richard Dunthorne'.
12. *Corr.* 466 (Gray to Mason, 23 July 1756).
13. *Corr.* 479 (Gray to Walpole, 8 September 1756).
14. *Corr.* 525, 576 (Gray to Wharton, 7 September 1757; to Walpole, 22 July 1758).
15. *Corr.* 495–500 (Gray to Wharton, 17 February, 3 March, 17 April; to Walpole, 11 March; to Mason, 23 April 1757); and 1206–10 (*Henry Tuthill*).
16. *Corr.* 499 (Gray to Mason, 23 April 1757). It was pointed out by Tovey that Gray probably meant to write 'the Evangelist and the Baptist'.
17. *Corr.* 500–1 (Hurd to Gray, *c*. April 1757).
18. *Corr.* 499 (Gray to Mason, 23 April 1757).
19. *Corr.* 497 (Gray to Wharton, 17 April 1757).
20. See p. 135.
21. *Corr.* 508–9, 512 (Gray to Brown, 25 July; to Mason, 1 August 1757).
22. *Walpole* (ed. Toynbee), IV, 78–9 (Walpole to Mann, 4 August 1757).
23. *Corr.* 508 (Gray to Walpole, 11 July 1757).
24. *Walpole* (ed. Toynbee), IV, 73 (Walpole to Chute, 12 July 1757).
25. Hazen, *Bibliography of the Strawberry Hill Press*, 23–31. In these pages Mr Hazen also discusses the 'thick-paper' copies of the *Odes* which were long a puzzle to bibliographers, and proves that they were forgeries made by Walpole's last printer, Thomas Kirgate, some time after 1790.

26. *Corr.* 508–10 (Gray to Brown, 25 July 1757).

27. *Corr.* 514 (Gray to Bedingfield, 10 August 1757).

28. *Corr.* 1002, 1012 (Gray to Beattie, 1 February 1768; Beattie to Gray, 16 February 1768).

29. *Corr.* 797 (Gray to Brown, February 1763).

30. *Corr.* 461 (Gray to Bedingfield, 29 April 1756).

31. *Corr.* 513–16 (Gray to Walpole, 10 August; to Bedingfield, 10 August; to Brown, 14 August 1757).

32. *Corr.* 518–20 (Gray to Wharton, 17 August; to Hurd, 25 August 1757).

33. *Corr.* 517, 521 (Hurd to Gray, 16 and 28 August, 1757).

34. *Walpole* (ed. Toynbee), Supplement II, 100–1 (Lyttelton to Walpole, 31 August 1757).

35. *Corr.* 518, 523–6 (Gray to Wharton, 17 August; to Mason, 7 September; to Wharton, 7 September 1757).

36. Benjamin Stillingfleet to William Windham, 20 December 1757 (MS. letter in the author's possession).

37. *Corr.* 519–20 (Gray to Hurd, 25 August 1757).

38. *Walpole* (ed. Toynbee), IV, 84–5 (Walpole to Lyttelton, 25 August 1757).

39. *Corr.* 525 (Gray to Wharton, 7 September 1757).

40. *Boswell's London Journal*, 105–6.

41. *Corr.* 532–3 (Gray to Wharton, 7 October 1757).

42. *Corr.* 523 and n. (Gray to Mason, 7 September 1757).

43. See the article by W. Powell Jones, 'The contemporary reception of Gray's Odes', in *Modern Philology*, XXVIII (1930–31), 61–82. Mr Jones was the first scholar to disinter and discuss the review in the *Literary Magazine*, which is not mentioned by Gray in his extant letters.

44. *Corr.* 532 (Gray to Wharton, 7 October 1757).

45. *Corr.* 532 (Gray to Wharton, 7 October 1757); and 538 (Gray to Bedingfield, 31 October 1757).

CHAPTER IX

1. *Corr.* 543–5 (Gray to Mason, 19 December 1757).

2. *Corr.* 517 n. 4; Mason, 237. Walpole was still writing of the collaboration between Gray and Mason as late as 1761.

3. *Corr.* 517 (Hurd to Gray, 16 August 1757).

4. These articles are admirably analysed in Powell Jones, 84–107. See also Martin, *Essai sur Thomas Gray*, 220 ff.

5. *Works* (ed. Mathias), ii, 55–80 (see especially 71–3).

6. *Corr.* 564 (Gray to Wharton, 21 February 1758). These notes were printed by Mason in 1773, in a small volume called *The Traveller's Companion, in a Tour through England and Wales. By the late Mr Gray.* They were nothing more than bare lists, with scarcely any comments or illustrative matter.

7. *Corr.* 565–6 (Gray to Wharton, 8 March 1758).

8. *Corr.* 571 (Gray to Wharton, 18 June 1758).

9. *Corr.* 569–71 (Gray to Wharton, 9 April and 18 June 1758).

10. *Corr.* 561 (Gray to Mason, 3 February 1758). See also the letter which Gray wrote this summer to Stonhewer, discussing the views of an acquaintance who had 'harped on the subject of materialism' (*Corr.* 582–3, 18 August 1758); and his paper refuting certain opinions of Bolingbroke, printed in Mason, 264–8.

11. *Corr.* 578 (Gray to Wharton, 9 August 1758).

12. *Corr.* 584 (Gray to Wharton, 31 August 1758).

13. *Corr.* 592 (Gray to Wharton, 9 November 1758).

14. *Corr.* 631 (Gray to Palgrave, 24 July 1759).

15. *Corr.* 629–33 (Gray to Mason, 23 July; to Palgrave, 24 July; to Brown, 8 August 1759).

16. *Corr.* 642–3 (Gray to Wharton, 18 September 1759).

17. *Corr.* 625–6, 641–2 (Gray to Wharton, 21 July to 18 September 1759).

18. *Walpole* (Yale Edition), ix, 251 (Walpole to Montagu, 21 October 1759).

19. There are valuable discussions of this episode by Professor H. W. V. Temperley in the Memorial Volume to Adolphus William Ward, Master of Peterhouse (Cambridge University Press, 1924), pp. 113–23, and by F. G. Stokes in his edition of Gray's *Elegy* (Oxford University Press, 1929), pp. 83–8.

20. *Corr.* 638–40 (Gray to Mary Antrobus, *c.* 12 September, but corrected in the addendum on p. xxxv to *c.* 5 September 1759).

21. *Corr.* 651 (Gray to Wharton, 28 November 1759).

22. *Corr.* 636–8 (Miss Speed to Gray, 25 August 1759).

23. *Corr.* 704 (Gray to Wharton, 21 October 1760).

24. *Corr.* 677 (Gray to Wharton, 20 June 1760).

25. *Corr.* 704 (Gray to Wharton, 21 October 1760).

26. *Corr.* 677 (Gray to Wharton, 20 June 1760).

27. *Corr.* 647–8 (Gray to Mrs Jennings, 27 October 1759).

28. *Harcourt Papers*, VIII, 1–3. The greater part of the 'Portrait' was also printed in *Corr.* 332, n. 1.

29. *Corr.* 692–3 (Gray to Clerke, 12 August 1760). This is the only one of Gray's letters to Clerke that has survived.

30. *Walpole* (Yale Edition), IX, 285–6 (Walpole to Montagu, 4 July 1760).

31. *Corr.* 689–91, 693 (Gray to Mason, 7 August; to Clerke, 12 August 1760).

32. *Corr.* 670–1, 681, 722 (Gray to Wharton, 22 April and 20 June 1760; to Mason, 22 January 1761).

33. *Corr.* 673–5, 681 (Gray to Mason, 7 June; to Wharton, c. 20 June 1760).

34. *Corr.* 664–5, 679–80 (Gray to Walpole, c. April; to Wharton, c. 20 June 1760).

35. *Letters of David Hume*, ed. J. Y. T. Greig (1932), I, 328–30 (Hume to Sir David Dalrymple (?), 16 August 1760).

36. *Corr.* 685–6 (Gray to Stonhewer, 29 June 1760). The dialogue, supposed to be 'a thousand years later than Ossian', is given in a note to the Ossianic poem called *Croma*.

37. *Cath-Loda: a Poem* (Duan Third).

38. *Corr.* 1223–9 (*Gray and James Macpherson*); *D.N.B. sub* 'James Macpherson'.

39. *Corr.* 1229–31 (*Gray's Studies of Welsh Poetry*); *D.N.B. sub*. 'Evan Evans'. In 1764 Evans published his *Specimens of the Poetry of the Antient Welsh Bards*, which included many new translations into English in addition to his Latin treatise *De Bardis Dissertatio*.

40. *Poems* (1768), 'Advertisement' on p. 75.

41. Powell Jones, 99–104.

42. *Walpole* (Yale Edition), IX, 364 (Walpole to Montagu, 5 May 1761).

43. Powell Jones, 101–2.

44. *Walpole* (Yale Edition), IX, 364 (Walpole to Montagu, 5 May 1761).

45. Scc p. 154.

46. *Corr.* 725 (Gray to Wharton, 31 January 1761).

47. *Corr.* 1231–4 (*Gray and Thomas Percy*); Powell Jones, 103–4.

48. *Corr.* 706–7, 746 (Gray to Brown, 23 October 1760; to Mason, August 1761).

49. *Corr.* 752–8 (Gray to Brown, 24 September 1761); *Walpole* (Yale Edition), ıx, 386–9 (Walpole to Montagu, 24 September 1761).

50. *Corr.* 770–1 (Gray to Wharton, 11 January 1762).

51. *Publications of Catholic Record Society*, xı, 367–8, quoted in *Corr.* 770–1, n. 12.

CHAPTER X

1. *Corr.* 766 (Gray to Mason, 8 December 1761).

2. *Corr.* 677 (Gray to Wharton, *c.* 20 June 1760).

3. *Corr.* 770 (Gray to Wharton, 11 January 1762).

4. *Essays presented to D. Nichol Smith* (1945), 116.

5. *Corr.* 714, 782–3, 967 (Gray to Mason, 10 December 1760, September 1762, 19 July 1767).

6. See pp. 268–9.

7. Mason, *Ode to a Friend* (sometimes known as *Ode to Melancholy*), *Works*, ı, 44.

8. *Corr.* 641 (Gray to Wharton, 18 September 1759).

9. Cole, *Blecheley Diary*, 95.

10. *Corr.* 1303–4. (Norton Nicholls to William Johnson Temple, 13 June 1762). This letter was printed from the original in the possession of Mr W. S. Lewis, to whom I am indebted for permission to reprint it here.

11. *Corr.* 1297 (Norton Nicholls's *Reminiscences of Gray*).

12. *Boswell's London Journal*, 257 (13 May 1763).

13. *Corr.* 1175 (Gray to Walpole, 17 March 1771).

14. *Corr.* 1289 (Norton Nicholls's *Reminiscences of Gray*).

15. *Corr.* 781–2 (Gray to Brown, 19 July 1762).

16. *Corr.* 784–7 (Gray to Wharton, 4 December 1762).

17. *Corr.* 787–8 (Gray to Wharton, 4 December 1762); 1253–4 (*Gray and the Professorship of Modern History*). A letter from yet another candidate, the Rev. Gregory Sharpe—'unsuccessful in my profession, and infirm, and lame, I am compelled to sollicit for some addition to my present income'—is printed in *The Jenkinson Papers, 1760–1766* (ed. Ninetta S. Jucker, 1949), 68–9.

18. Mason, 264 n.

19. *Corr.* 799 (Algarotti to Gray, 24 April 1763).

20. *Corr.* 813 (Gray to Algarotti, 10 September 1763).

21. *Corr.* 801–4 (Mason to Gray, 28 June: Gray to Mason, July 1763

Notes

22. *Jubilate Agno* (ed. W. H. Bond, 1954), 150–2.

23. *Jubilate Agno*, 109. The suggestion that Smart's line contained a reference to the *Elegy* was first made by Mr W. Force Stead in his edition of *Jubilate Agno* (1939).

24. *Walpole* (Yale Edition), x, 130 (Walpole to Montagu, 16 July 1764).

25. *Corr.* 805 (Gray to Wharton, 5 August 1763).

26. A portion of Gray's letter was copied by Cole into one of his notebooks, now in the British Museum (Add. MS. 5825, ff. 283 *b*, 284 *b*). It was identified by Mr H. W. Starr of Temple University, Philadelphia, in an article in *Times Literary Supplement*, 30 March 1951.

27. Cole, *Blecheley Diary*, 125, 127.

28. The jottings by Cole are mainly in B.M. Add. MSS. 5833 and 5870. Mitford quotes others which I have not traced to their sources in the volumes of Cole's manuscripts. The extracts from the annotated copy of Mason's *Life* are printed in *Works* (ed. Mitford), i, civ–x. At that time the volume was in the possession of Samuel Rogers. See also Mason, 342–3.

29. *Corr.* 377, 573, 677 (Gray to Wharton, 28 June 1753; to Mason, 20 June 1758; to Wharton, *c.* 20 June 1760).

30. *Corr.* 832 (Gray to Wharton, 21 February 1764).

31. *Walpole-Mason*, 159, 163 (Walpole to Mason, 16 September; Mason to Walpole, 2 October 1774). The poem was first printed, under the title of *The Candidate*, on the inside pages of a folded sheet. The sheet bears no date or imprint; but it is extremely probable that the printing was done at the Strawberry Hill Press shortly after Walpole rediscovered the manuscript of the lines, which he had mislaid, in September 1774 (see Hazen, *Bibliography of the Strawberry Hill Press*, 212–14).

32. *Walpole-Mason*, 66, 156 (Mason to Walpole, 20 March 1773; Walpole to Mason, 23 August 1774).

33. *Corr.* 1236–42 (*The Contest for the High Stewardship and Gray's Verses on Lord Sandwich*). The contest for the High Stewardship is treated in fascinating detail in D. A. Winstanley's *The University of Cambridge in the Eighteenth Century* (1922), 55–139.

34. *Corr.* 836–7, 842 (Gray to Wharton, 10 July; to Mary Antrobus, 24 September or 1 October 1764).

35. From the original letter in the possession of Mr W. S. Lewis.

It is undated, but there are references to the contest over the High Stewardship which prove it to belong to 1764. It was printed in the *Annual Gazette* of the Pembroke College Society in June 1938, but is otherwise unpublished.

36. Nicholls to Temple, 17 September 1763 (unpublished letter in the possession of Mr W. S. Lewis).

37. *Boswell in Holland*, 14 (Temple to Boswell, 23 August 1763).

38. *Boswell in Holland*, 32, 242.

39. *Corr*. 852–3 (Gray to Nicholls, 19 November 1764).

40. *Corr*. 888 (Gray to Wharton, 30 September 1765).

41. *Autobiography of Alexander Carlyle of Inveresk, 1722–1805*, ed. J. H. Burton (1910), 485.

42. Forbes, I, 73 (Gregory to Beattie, 1 January 1766).

43. Nicholls to Temple, 3 November 1779, quoted in *Corr*. 888 n. 8.

44. *Corr*. 889–94, 899 (Gray to Wharton, *c*. 30 September; to Mason, 8 November, 1765).

45. *Corr*. 885 (Beattie to Gray, 30 August 1765).

46. Forbes, I, 65 (Beattie to Forbes, 7 December 1765).

47. *Corr*. 895–6 (Gray to Beattie, 2 October 1765).

48. *Corr*. 895 (Gray to Beattie, 2 October 1765).

49. *Corr*. 1246 (*Advice to a Friend travelling in Scotland*).

50. Information of Samuel Rogers to John Mitford, quoted in Tovey, 19.

51. *Corr*. 900–8, 911–19 (Gray to Walpole, *c*. 10 November, 13 December 1765; Walpole to Gray, 19 November 1765, 25 January 1766).

52. *Corr*. 919 (Gray to Wharton, 5 March 1766).

53. *Walpole* (ed. Toynbee), xv, 54 (Walpole to Lady Ossory, 8 September 1791).

54. Powell Jones, 134.

55. *Corr*. 575 (Gray to Mason, 20 June 1758).

56. *Works* (ed. Mathias), II, 570.

57. See *The Poet Gray as a Naturalist*, by Charles Eliot Norton (Boston, 1903). Gray's interleaved Linnaeus passed after various vicissitudes to Ruskin, after whose death it was given by Ruskin's heir Mrs Arthur Severn to Mr Norton. The pocket-books in the possession of Sir John Murray contain lists of 'Plants observed about Glamis Castle', 'Insects caught by the family at Old-Park near Durham', and similar rough material for the interleaved Linnaeus.

58. In the summer of 1768 Lady Mary Coke was staying in the same house as Mason, and they discussed Gray. 'Mr Mason tells me he has been very unfortunate', she wrote to her sister. 'His melancholy turn of mind is, I think, very discernible in his writings. He has lately taken to the study of Nature, it carries him abroad, which he finds good for his health, and the contemplation of the wonderful works of nature has dissipated a part of his melancholy, and made him, he thinks, a happier Man.' (*Letters and Journals of Lady Mary Coke* (privately printed, 1889–96), II, 292.) I owe this reference to Mr C. F. Bell.

59. *Corr.* 923 (Gray to Wharton, 5 March 1766).

60. *Walpole* (ed. Toynbee), IX, 250, 453 (Walpole to Conway, 8 September 1775; to Madame de Viry, April 1776).

61. *Autobiography and Correspondence of Mrs Delany* (ed. Lady Llanover), 2nd series, II, 455 (Mrs Delany to Mrs Port of Ilam, 9 August 1779).

62. *Walpole*, (ed. Toynbee), X, 112 (Walpole's footnote to his letter to Mason of 18 September 1777).

CHAPTER XI

1. *Corr.* 824 (Gray to Robinson, 10 October 1763). This is Gray's only letter to Robinson that has survived. Robinson did not consider Mason equal to the task of writing the life of Gray, and refused to lend him the letters in his possession or to help him in any way.

2. *Corr.* 926–30 (Gray to Nicholls and Wharton, 26 August 1766). Pocket-book in the possession of Sir John Murray.

3. This anecdote does not occur in Brydges's numerous works, but was told by him to Mitford.

4. *Corr.* 945, 950 (Gray to Brown, 18 November 1766; Mason to Gray, 2 February 1767).

5. Mason, 324 and n.; *Corr.* 953 (Gray to Mason, 28 March 1767).

6. Mason, *Works*, I, 137; *Corr.* 957 (Gray to Mason, 23 May 1767), 1294 (Norton Nicholls's *Reminiscences of Gray*).

7. The entries contained in it were first published in 1950 by its present owner, Mr Roger Senhouse, in an edition of 107 copies issued by the Mill House Press at Stanford Dingley. For Humphrey Senhouse, see p. 143.

8. *Corr.* 949 (Gray to Mason, 27 January 1767).

9. *Corr.* 958–60 (Gray to Brown, *c.* 28 May 1767).

10. B.M. Egerton MS. 2400, ff. 181, 233, 234.

11. *Corr.* 976–7 (Gray to Wharton, 11 September 1767); *Pocket-book of 1767* (ed. Senhouse). The latter shows that Gray and Wharton started on their tour on the 22nd and not the 29th of August as stated (presumably by a slip of the pen) by Gray in his letter to Mason quoted above.

12. *Corr.* 827 (Gray to How, November 1763).

13. *Corr.* 982–3 (Gray to Beattie, 24 December 1767). Forbes, I, 103–5.

14. Lord David Cecil, *Thomas Gray* (the Warton Lecture on English Poetry, 1945) reprinted in *Poets and Story-Tellers* (1949), p. 62.

15. *Corr.* 999–1004, 1048 (Gray to Dodsley, *c.* 1 February; to Beattie, 1 February and 31 October 1768); *D.N.B. sub* 'Robert Foulis' and 'Alexander Wilson'.

16. *Corr.* 1013–18 (Walpole to Gray, 18 February; Gray to Walpole, 25 February 1768).

17. *Corr.* 998 (Gray to Nicholls, 28 January 1768).

18. *Corr.* 1006–9 (Gray to Walpole, 14 February 1768).

19. *Corr.* 927 (Gray to Nicholls, 26 August 1766).

20. *Henry Fox, first Lord Holland,* by the Earl of Ilchester, II, (1920), 279–82. See also 'An Epic of Ruin-Building' by Mr Hugh Honour in *Country Life,* 10 December 1953.

21. There are variations in the existing versions of this poem, none of which is in Gray's own hand. I have followed the copy in Wharton's handwriting (B.M. Egerton MS. 2400 f. 232), but have punctuated it rather more generously and printed it with intervals between the stanzas.

22. *Corr.* 1259–62 (*Gray's Verses on Lord Holland's Villa at Kingsgate*).

23. *Corr.* 1033–4. Grafton's letter has not survived. Gray quoted a few sentences from it in letters to his friends, but withheld the many compliments and 'expressions of kindness' which it contained.

24. *Corr.* 1034 (Gray to the Duke of Grafton, 27 or 28 July 1768).

25. *Corr.* 1034–40, 1048 (Gray to Mary Antrobus, 29 July; to Wharton and Mason, 1 August; to Nicholls, 3 August; to Beattie, 31 October 1768).

26. *Corr.* 1048–9 (Gray to Beattie, 31 October 1768).

27. Mason, 395–8; *Corr.* 1253–9 (*Gray and the Professorship of Modern History*). Gray's original memorandum is now in B.M. Add. MS. 38334, ff. 149 et sqq.

28. *Corr.* 1042 (Nicholls to Gray, 6 August 1768), 1300 (Norton Nicholls's *Reminiscences of Gray*).

29. *Corr.* 1300–1.

30. *Corr.* 1301. The first letter of the continuous series appeared on 21 January 1769, and Nicholls did not come to Cambridge until some little while after that date; but I have thought it best to accept his anecdote as it stands.

31. *Corr.* 1057 (Gray to Wharton, 20 April 1769).

32. *Corr.* 1058 (Gray to Brown, *c.* 20 April 1769).

33. *Corr.* 1058 (Gray to Wharton, 20 April 1769).

34. Madame d'Arblay, *Memoirs of Doctor Burney* (1832), I, 210–12. Percy A. Scholes, *The Great Doctor Burney* (1948), I, 140–2. There is no mention of this episode in Gray's letters, or, so far as I know, in any contemporary document; but I hesitate to reject an account so detailed as that given by Madame d'Arblay, in spite of certain improbabilities in her story.

35. *Corr.* 1065 (Gray to Nicholls, 24 June 1769).

36. *Junius to the Duke of Grafton*, 30 May 1769.

37. *Corr.* 1065 (Gray to Nicholls, 24 June 1769).

38. Nichols, *Illustrations* v, 315–17 (Richard Gough to Rev. Benjamin Forster, 6 July 1769).

39. *Corr.* 1050 (Gray to Nicholls, 8 November 1768).

40. Both parodies were reprinted in *The Foundling Hospital for Wit*, part IV, (1771), 8–22, together with the original *Ode*.

41. *Corr.* 1071, n. 5.

42. B.M. Add. MS. 5833 f. 12.

43. *Junius to the Duke of Grafton*, 8 July 1769.

44. They are printed in *Corr.* 1074–80, 1087–91, 1094–1110, 1125–7 (Gray to Wharton, 18 and 29 October, November 1769; 3 January and 18 April 1770).

CHAPTER XII

1. *Corr.* 1081 (Gray to Stonhewer, 2 November 1769).

2. The account of their first meeting is that given by de Bonstetten in a letter to his friend Heinrich Zschokke after Nicholls's death, quoted in Marie-L. Herking, *Charles-Victor de Bonstetten, sa vie, ses œuvres*, 64–5.

3. Herking, 56.

4. Herking, 64.

5. *Corr.* 1042 (Nicholls to Gray, 6 August 1768).

6. *Corr.* 1086 (Nicholls to Gray, 27 November 1769). *Nemorum nox* is a quotation from the *Alcaic Ode*, which Gray had evidently shown him in manuscript.

7. Brydges, II, 111.

8. *Boswell's Life of Johnson*, V, 384.

9. *Corr.* 1290 (Norton Nicholls's *Reminiscences of Gray*).

10. *Boswell's Life of Johnson*, II, 327.

11. See p. 205.

12. *Corr.* 1265–6 (Bonstetten to his mother, 6 February 1770).

13. B.M. Add. MS. 5835, ff. 216, 218.

14. *Corr.* 1110–2 (Bonstetten and Gray to Nicholls, 6 January 1770).

15. Bonstetten, *Souvenirs*, 118; *Corr.* 1267 (Bonstetten to his mother, 6 February 1770).

16. Herking, 68 (Bonstetten to his father; date uncertain).

17. Byron, *Letters and Journals* (ed. R. E. Prothero), III, 340–1.

18. Brydges, I, 116, 330.

19. Bonstetten, *Souvenirs*, 116–19.

20. *Corr.* 1267–9 (Bonstetten to his mother, 6 February 1770).

21. *Corr.* 1114 (Gray to Nicholls, 20 March 1770).

22. *Corr.* 1115–16 (Gray to Nicholls, 4 April 1770).

23. *Corr.* 1117–19 (Gray to Bonstetten, 12 April 1770). The extracts from Plato in the Commonplace Book are printed in *Works* (ed. Mathias), II, 441–4.

24. *Corr.* 1127–8 (Gray to Bonstetten, 19 April 1770).

25. *Corr.* 1132 (Gray to Bonstetten, 9 May 1770).

26. *Corr.* 1133 (Gray to Nicholls, 22 May 1770).

27. *Corr.* 1122–5, 1128–30 (Gray to Warton, 15 April; Warton to Gray, 20 April 1770); 1130–2, 1140–1 (Beattie to Gray, 1 May; Gray to Beattie, 2 July 1770).

28. *Corr.* 1119–20 (Gray to Farmer, 12 April 1770), with Cole's note (B.M. Add. MS. 5860, f. 57) quoted in footnote.

29. *Corr.* 1133–6 (Gray to Nicholls and Brown, 22 May 1770).

30. Mason, 398–9.

31. *Corr.* 1141–4 (Gray to Wharton, 24 August; to Mason, 7 September 1770); 1299 (Norton Nicholls's *Reminiscences of Gray*).

32. *Corr.* 1148 (Gray to Walpole, 17 September 1770).

33. *Corr.* 1149–50 (Gray to Mason, 24 October 1770).

34. *Gray-Mason*, 443 n. Rogers passed the account on to Mitford.

35. *Corr.* 1155 (Gray to Cole, 22 December 1770). B.M. Add. MS. 5875, ff. 65–6.

36. *Corr.* 1164 (Gray to Wharton, 2 February 1771).

37. *Corr.* 1157 (Gray to Nicholls, 26 January 1771).

38. *Corr.* 1172 (Nicholls to Gray, 16 March 1771).

39. *Corr.* 1184–5 (Gray to Nicholls, 3 May 1771).

40. *Corr.* 1188–9 (Gray to Nicholls and to Wharton, 24 May 1771).

41. *Corr.* 1190 (Nicholls to Gray, 27 May 1771).

42. *Corr.* 1289 (Norton Nicholls's *Reminiscences of Gray*).

43. *Walpole* (Yale Edition), ii, (Walpole to Cole, 12 August 1771).

44. *Corr.* 1272 (*Gray's Last Illness and Death*).

45. *Corr.* 1191–2 (Clarke to Temple, 23 July 1772). Letter owned by Professor C. B. Tinker.

46. *Corr.* 1269–82 (*Gray's Last Illness and Death*).

CHAPTER XIII

1. *Walpole* (Yale Edition), i, 228–9 (Walpole to Cole, 12 August 1771).

2. *Works* (ed. Mitford), v, 147–9 (Nicholls to his mother, 15 August 1771).

3. *Works* (ed. Mitford), v, 151 (Bonstetten to Nicholls, quoted in Nicholls to Barrett, 31 May 1773).

4. Byron, *Letters and Journals* (ed. R. E. Prothero), iii, 340–1.

5. Brydges, ii, 378–99.

6. *Corr.* 1283–6 (*Gray's Will*).

7. Mason, 2.

8. A typical instance of this is the long review by John Langhorne of Mason's *Memoirs of Gray* in the *Monthly Review* for 1775 (i, 377–87; ii, 1–11, 97–104).

9. *Walpole* (ed. Toynbee), viii, 444 (Walpole to Mason, 17 April 1774).

10. *Corr.* 1275 (Brown to Wharton, 17 August 1771).

11. First published to introduce the selection from Gray's poems made by Arnold in vol. iv of T. H. Ward's *English Poets* (1880); republished in *Essays in Criticism*, Second Series (1888).

12. *Corr.* 579 (Gray to Mason, 11 August 1758).

INDEX

Index

Gray, Thomas—Life (*cont.*)
  relations with Miss Speed, 103–7, 163–4, 170–5, 184–5, 214
  spends two years in London, 165–85
  projected *History of English Poetry*, 160–1, 179–81, 183, 258–9
  journey to Scotland, 207–11
  visits to Lakes, 221, 222, 241–4
  publication of *Collected Poems*, 223–5
  appointed Professor of Modern History, 229–32
  writes *Installation Ode*, 234–40
  relations with Bonstetten, 247–58, 262–3
  illness and death, 262–5

Characteristics
  attitude towards Cambridge, 10–12, 20, 24–5, 68, 70–1, 210, 236–7
  character and temperament, 27–8, 46–7, 89–90, 163–4, 174, 251, 270
  financial position, 18, 67, 87, 165, 267–8
  health, 2, 4, 66, 118, 126, 132, 205, 207, 260, 264–5
  interest in nature and natural history, 19, 118–19, 167, 182, 212–13
  mannerisms and affectations, 12, 89–90, 116–17, 200, 259
  melancholy, 15, 23, 56, 65–6, 94, 118, 146, 161, 163, 219, 252–3
  personal appearance, 13, 14, 27–8, 88–9, 116–17, 191, 199–200, 274
  poetic impulse, 4, 59, 91, 126, 212, 226
  religious views, 35, 50–1, 101–2, 162–3, 193, 251
  studies, 4, 21–2, 38–40, 44, 92–4, 132–3, 160–1, 166–7, 178–81, 212–13

Poems
Adversity, Hymn to, 59, 63–4, 112
Agrippina, 55–6, 90
Alcaic Ode, 50–1
Alliance of Education and Government, 90–2
Barbaras aedes, 24
Bard, The, 130, 132–6, 146, 150–7, 224
Candidate, The, 202–4, 228

Cat, Ode on a, 79, 80, 92, 114–15
Collected Poems (1768), 127–8, 223–5
Death of Richard West, Sonnet on the, 59, 64–5
De Principiis Cogitandi, 44, 57–9, 90
Descent of Odin, The, 180, 223
Elegy written in a Country Churchyard, 19, 59, 64, 67, 76, 96–102 *passim*, 107–10, 114, 117, 167–70, 193, 239, 270; note on its composition, 271–3
Epitaph on a Child, 162, 193
Epitaph on Mrs Clerke, 162, 193
Epitaph on Sir William Williams, 183
Eton College, Ode on a Distant Prospect of, 8, 9, 59, 62–6, 76, 79–81, 86, 88, 114, 224, 270
Fatal Sisters, The, 180, 223
Ignorance, Hymn to, 68
Installation of the Duke of Grafton, Ode on the, 234–40
Long Story, A, 104–6, 112, 114–15, 133, 164, 223
Lord Holland's Villa, Lines on, 227–9
Luna est Habitabilis, 22
O lachrymarum fons, 24
Pleasure arising from Vicissitude, Ode on the, 131–2, 146
Progress of Poesy, The, 127–30, 150–7, 224
Six Poems (with illustrations by Bentley), 111–15, 223
Sketch of his own Character, 196
Spring, Ode on the, 19, 57, 59–61, 64–5, 76, 80, 86, 96, 115, 131, 223–4
Stanzas to Richard Bentley, 112
Tophet, 82–3
Triumphs of Owen, The, 181, 223
William Shakespeare to Mistress Anne, 207

Green, Matthew, 60–1, 80–1, 223
Gregory, Dr John, 208
Grifoni, Marchesa, 43, 46
Grignion, Charles, 112
Grose, Francis, his *Antiquities*, 221

Hardwicke, Philip Yorke, 1st Earl of, 201–2

Index

Oliffe, Mrs (*née* Jane Antrobus), 2, 112, 165
Onslow, Arthur, 156
Orford, George Walpole, 3rd Earl of, 121, 217
Ossian, 177–9, 209

Palgrave, Rev. William, 145, 182, 189, 217, 220, 229, 257, 261
Parry, John, 134–6, 149–50
Pelham, Right Hon. Henry, 57, 75
Pembroke College
  Gray's interest in, 22–3, 70, 83–4
  removal to, 139
  life and activities there, 140–5, 186, 200, 219–20
Perceval, Viscount (later 3rd Earl of Egmont), 137–8
Percy, Rev. Thomas, 182–3
Peterhouse
  Gray's undergraduate life at, 10–13, 18, 21, 22
  life as fellow-commoner, 69–70, 72, 82, 119–20
  departure from, 137–9
Peyrière, Baron de la (*see under* Henrietta Jane Speed)
Piazza, Hieronimo Bartolommeo, 20, 21, 195
Pitt, Thomas (later 1st Lord Camelford), 190, 247
Pitt, William, *see* Chatham, 1st Earl of
Plumptre, Dr Russell, 205
Pond, Arthur, 8
Pope, Alexander, 14, 29, 74, 81, 102, 160
  Gray's meeting with, 54
Powell Jones, Mr W., 128, 183
Prévost d'Exiles, Abbé, 31
Prior, Matthew, 104
Purt, Rev. Robert, 102, 114

Randall, Dr John, 235 and n., 238
Reynolds, Sir Joshua, 76
Richardson, Jonathan, 7, 38 n.
Richardson, Jonathan the Younger, 38 and n.
Roberts, S. C., Master of Pembroke, 51 n., 144
Robertson, William, 208
Robinson, Rev. William, 190, 216–17, 227

Robison, Professor John, 168–70
Rockingham, Charles, 2nd Marquess of, 189, 229
Rogers, Jonathan, 2, 19, 55, 66–7
Rogers, Mrs Jonathan (*née* Anne Antrobus), 2, 19, 55, 103–5, 156, 165
Rogers, Samuel, 211, 261
Rolleston, Sir Humphry, 264 and n.
Royston, Viscount, *see* Hardwicke, 2nd Earl of

Sackville, Lord George, 171
Sandwich, John Montagu, 4th Earl of, 201–5, 227, 229, 240
Schaub, Sir Luke, 103
Schaub, Lady, 103–5, 114
Selwyn, George, 34, 120, 151 n.
Senhouse, Humphrey, 143, 219
Shakespeare, William, 129, 134, 136, 153, 223, 253
Sharp, Rev. John, 137–8
Shenstone, William, 117, 153, 158, 260
Smart, Christopher, 85–6, 143, 197–8
Southwell, Edward, 145, 148
Sparrow, John, 24
Speed, Henrietta Jane, 103–7, 114–15, 126, 146, 155, 163–4, 170–5, 181
  Lord Harcourt's *Character* of her, 173
  as Baronne de la Peyrière and Comtesse de Viry, 184–5, 214–15, 275
Spence, Joseph, 48, 231
Spenser, Edmund, 112, 136
Spenser, Richard, 143
Squire, Rev. Samuel, 196
Stephen, Sir Leslie, 138
Sterne, Rev. Laurence, 176
Stevenson, John Hall, 176
Stillingfleet, Benjamin, 154, 182, 190
Stoke Poges, 55–6, 67, 75, 95–107 *passim*, 122, 146, 156, 164–5, 171–2, 186, 265
Stonhewer, Richard, 85–6, 120, 122, 134, 144, 188–9, 200, 217, 220, 229, 240, 245, 251, 261, 265, 274
Strathmore, John Lyon, 9th Earl of, 144, 148, 189–90, 207–10, 221, 259

309